550

P9-DNC-908

Adele H. Lewis
450 Elm Avenue
Haddonfield, N.J.

NEW JERSEY:
PAST AND PRESENT
A Record of Achievement

NEW JERSEY:
PAST AND PRESENT
A Record of Achievement

STANLEY N. WORTON ★ WILBUR E. APGAR
DANIEL JACOBSON ★ ABRAHAM RESNICK

HAYDEN BOOK COMPANY, INC., NEW YORK
a division of HAYDEN PUBLISHING COMPANY, INC.

Copyright © 1964

HAYDEN BOOK COMPANY, INC.

All rights reserved. This book
or any parts thereof may not be
reproduced in any form or in any
language without permission.

Library of Congress Catalog Card Number 64-20175

Printed in the United States of America

Preface

New Jersey: Past and Present is a totally new and up-to-date book written for use as a basic text in secondary schools and colleges. The teacher, researcher or casual reader will find it equally useful, for it is comprehensive in scope and high in interest.

The text is divided into four major segments covering vital information about the geography, history, government and sociology of New Jersey. In each section the authors deal with the changes which vitally affect institutional patterns. Cause and result relationships are stressed throughout, affording the student an opportunity to understand significant events, practices and trends that may directly affect his life.

Inherent in the contents are valuable lessons for the student about the essential requirements for a working democracy. Underlying the account of New Jersey's rich heritage, present-day problems, and contributions to the nation is an affirmation of the need for responsibility and participation on the part of its citizens. The concepts and understandings in *New Jersey: Past and Present* are enhanced by provocative "Do/Discuss" activities—questions and assignments which follow key topical areas. A number of specially prepared maps, charts and other visual materials are offered for synoptic use by reader and teacher.

The authors are indebted to each of the divisions of government of the State of New Jersey which cooperated in the preparation of the book. Special assistance was given by the Departments of Education, Institutions and Agencies, Health, Agriculture, Treasury, and Conservation and Economic Development. Among the numerous officials who lent valuable assistance, particular thanks should be given to Mr. B. Budd Chavooshian, Director of the Division of State and Regional Planning; and to Mr. Eugene J. Schneider, Chief of the Bureau of Regional Planning. The authors are also most grateful to the many others who have contributed so generously to the completion of the book. Permission to use the special materials employed was graciously granted by Sister Mary Veronica, O.S.F., St. Anthony's Motherhouse, Syracuse, New York; Mr. Frank O'Malley, State Promotion Section, Department of Conservation and Economic Development, Trenton; and Mr. Richard Cross of the Public Service Electric and Gas Company, Newark.

The authors wish to give special thanks to Miss Miriam V. Studley, Principal Librarian, New Jersey Section, Free Public Library, Newark, for her authoritative and constructive critique of the manuscript.

Stanley N. Worton
Wilbur E. Apgar
Daniel Jacobson
Abraham Resnick

Climate

Contents

vii

SECTION I
Geography

New Jersey's products travel "piggyback" from Port Newark to market.

CHAPTER 1

The Geography of New Jersey

The Changing Landscape

New Jersey's three centuries of history (1664-1964) have been marked by dynamic changes. Agriculture, manufacturing, the professions, the service industries, the life of the housewife — all phases of New Jersey life have been profoundly altered through time. And so, too, has the face of the land itself been greatly changed.

In 1664 the Lenni-Lenape — or Delaware Indians — still held most of New Jersey. They took trees from the forest, built villages near the rivers, and made small clearings in the woods for their primitive agriculture. They hunted and fished. They moved over well-defined paths and trails to the ocean to obtain fish and shells. But their numbers were few (2,000 to 10,000, according to the best estimates) and their impact on the landscape, though important, was relatively slight. When the Dutch, English, and Swedish settlers moved into New Jersey, therefore, they did not find a virgin landscape. But it was nearly so.

The Europeans occupied stretches of land on New Jersey's principal waterways. The Dutch centered their control on the Hudson River, the English between the Navesink and Passaic rivers, the Swedes on the lower Delaware. And despite changing national affiliations, the settlements were permanent.

Newark, founded in 1666, illustrates well the pattern and permanence of English settlement. The founders, Robert Treat among

1

them, brought with them the idea of the compact agricultural village. Newark, they hoped, would have its village green, its town lots dispersed about the green, and the common fields beyond. But every settlement must take local topography into account. The town's founders were compelled to consider the position of the neighboring marshlands, the ponds and brooks, the Lenni-Lenape trails, the small hillocks just beyond the marsh, and, perhaps most important of all, the river.

A line was drawn from the bend in the Passaic River in the north to the encroaching marshland in the far south. Near the northern end of the line a small area triangular in shape was set aside for a market place; immediately to the southeast a larger triangle was planned for a training ground; less than a mile south of the training ground, along the same line, a large common was planned. Present-day Newarkers will recognize the market place as Washington Park, the training ground as Military Park, and the common in the south as Lincoln Park—all important features in today's city.

A broad road—eight rods wide—linked the common and training ground. Roads less wide were planned to parallel the main road on either side. A fourth road—six rods wide—was to cut the other three at right angles. It was along these four roads that the earliest settlers of Newark established their town lots. Broad Street is still the city's main artery and that point where Market Street cuts Broad Street at right angles is still the center, the heart of the city.

Before long, homes of oak and cedar were going up along the broad road. Fences were constructed to keep cattle and pigs from the marsh. A meetinghouse was begun in 1668 and a cattle pound the following year. The English had come to the Passaic River to stay.

1664—1764. In the century that followed, the settlers opened up New Jersey's hinterland. They pushed south into the Pine Barrens, where they cut down the trees and built sawmills. They moved into the river valleys of western and southern New Jersey, where they put the land to the plow and made beginnings in animal husbandry and the growing of fruit. They turned north, where they discovered the rich magnetic ores of Bergen, Passaic, and Morris counties.

By 1764 New Jersey's farmers had virtually tamed the wilderness. Lush farmland had already replaced much of the forest. Flour and lumber mills dotted the landscape. Commerce was flourishing. And roads, poor and stump-infested though they were, provided links between farm, mill, and river.

Changes on the New Jersey landscape during the century between 1664 and 1764 can be inferred from the activity at Raritan Landing.

The river port stood at the head of sloop navigation on the Raritan River. In 1764 its wharves and warehouses were beehives of activity. Grain, chiefly wheat and corn, flour, hardtack, lumber, barrels and casks, beef, mutton, and pork all found their way to the wharves at Raritan Landing. The farmers of the upper Raritan filled the river with flatboats and scows. At Raritan Landing the goods were transferred to sloops for the passage to New York, to New England, or to the West Indies. The port's warehouses were piled high with return cargoes of every description. Cornelius Low, Raritan Landing's leading merchant, prized especially the cargoes of sugar, molasses, rum, and madeira.

The prosperity of Raritan Landing would not be crushed until the coming of the Revolutionary War, when British troops occupied the port and the neighboring community of New Brunswick.

1764—1864. Between 1764 and 1864 many remarkable changes took place on New Jersey's landscape. After the Revolution the young American nation, eager to launch domestic manufacturing, began the search for its finest industrial site. At least a half-dozen locations were considered. But none had the imposing credentials of the site at the Great Falls of the Passaic River: the easily accessible iron ores, the forest in the nearby hills, the nearness of the great market in New York, the clear, soft water of the river, and, most important, the power of the waterfall itself.

Paterson grew up at the site of the Great Falls. In 1791 only ten dwellings and one church occupied the site. By 1832 Paterson could boast of over 6,000 inhabitants, seven churches, fifteen cotton factories, four turning and bobbin factories, machine shops, iron works, a sawmill, and a flax factory.

Meanwhile, Newark, with the advantages of an earlier start, was growing even faster. In 1832 it had nearly 15,000 people. Its construction progress was phenomenal. One hundred nine new dwellings went up in 1832 alone! Shoe factories, hat factories, carriage plants, tanneries, soap and candle plants, iron and brass foundries, breweries, and dyeing establishments dominated the skyline.

Newark and Paterson both were flexing New Jersey's bulging industrial muscles.

In South Jersey the furnaces were blazing. Charles Read was creating an "Empire in Iron."

Prior to the boom years many roads had been pushed into New Jersey's back-country. Turnpikes of crushed stone, gravel, and earth — often of very poor quality — were built to tap the farming areas and the mineral-producing districts. Conestoga wagons and mules moved over the Morris Turnpike (between Elizabeth and Phillipsburg), for example, very early in the 19th century. Traffic was also brisk on the turnpike between Trenton and New Brunswick, the main road between New York and Philadelphia. Turnpikes helped to spark the beginning of Newark's importance as a market center; Paterson profited in the same way.

But all was not well in northern New Jersey. Soil depletion and the still inadequate roads had contributed to the inflation of food prices. Farmers found it increasingly difficult to get their produce to market. It was the same for the ironmongers, whose problems were aggravated by a growing lack of fuel. The forests, source of vital charcoal, were being systematically destroyed. These factors raised the cry for the building of a canal from the Delaware River to tidewater at Newark. Farmers' produce could then be brought to market easily, and the dying iron furnaces would be restored to health by Pennsylvania coal.

Construction on the Morris Canal was begun in 1825. On November 1, 1830, a trial run was made between the heights near Dover to Newark. Five boats loaded with iron ore passed the inclined planes with ease. Two years later the *Walk-in-the-Water* made the entire passage from the Delaware River to tidewater. While the total haul on the Morris Canal amounted to less than 60,000 tons in 1845, by 1860 it was well over 700,000 tons. Boonton, Paterson, and Newark were booming. The future looked bright.

Meanwhile, the Delaware and Raritan Canal was officially opened on June 25, 1834. Its terminal cities, Trenton, at the head of navigation on the Delaware River, and New Brunswick, also experienced a great spurt in their industrial output.

But the seeds of the canals' doom had already been planted. The railroad had come to New Jersey.

In 1833 the Camden and Amboy Railroad tracks were completed between Bordentown and South Amboy. Tracks were pushed into Camden the following year. Other lines also were built to connect the Hudson and Delaware rivers. By 1840 Jersey City and Philadelphia were linked by the magic rails. By 1864 the state was crossed by numerous rail lines.

The "civilizing rails" helped to spur New Jersey's manufacturing. Towns and cities began to grow up along the railroad lines. And the population mounted accordingly. By 1860 New Jersey already could boast over 670,000 people. The new immigrants were moving to the cities. Newark, the state's largest city, had nearly 72,000 people; Jersey City, nearly 30,000; Paterson, nearly 20,000.

The new transportation also permitted the beginnings of specialization in agriculture, and helped New Jersey's farmers to bring their wares to market quickly and with less chance of waste. Fewer fields were planted in wheat. Much more attention was paid to dairying, poultry raising, and the growing of fruits and vegetables.

Although New Jersey businessmen had important interests in the South prior to the Civil War, New Jersey fought loyally for the Union. Residents of New Jersey were also active in bringing Negro slaves to the state via the "underground railroad."

1864 — 1964. The century between 1864 and 1964 witnessed changes on New Jersey's landscape that far outpaced those of the preceding 200 years. New patterns developed in industry, in transportation, in agriculture — in every facet of New Jersey life.

The changes were sparked in part by the inventions in the 1880's and 1890's of an Ohio-born Jerseyman, Thomas Alva Edison. Equally significant was the development of the motor car early in the twentieth century.

Edison's inventions — the incandescent lamp, the dynamo, the motor, and others — helped to create the electrical revolution. Light was brought to New Jersey's homes, factories, and city streets. Electric railroads began slowly to replace the huffing-puffing steam engines. New Jersey's cities were covered with a network of trolley car lines. And factories, no longer confined to the large population centers, began to move to the fringes and beyond.

Meanwhile, the motor car was creating its own revolution. The number of roads in the state began to multiply soon after the establishment of the State Highway Department in 1917. Roads and highways were built east and west and north and south. The late twenties saw the completion of the Delaware River Bridge from Camden to Philadelphia, the Tacony-Palmyra and Burlington-Bristol bridges, the Outerbridge Crossing and Goethals bridges to Staten Island, and the Holland Tunnel. The Bayonne Bridge, the George Washington Bridge, and the Lincoln Tunnel were completed in the thirties. Motor cars, highways, bridges, and tunnels had all helped to change the face of the land. In 1915 81,000 motor car registrations were issued in New Jersey. By 1935 there were nearly 900,000 such registrations.

The world depression and World War II put dampers on road construction. But after the war the roadbuilders went to work once more. An act creating the New Jersey Turnpike Authority was passed in 1948. By early 1952 the 118-mile swath of the New Jersey Turnpike was completed between Deepwater and Ridgefield Park. Thirty-one streams had been crossed; 194 highway and railroad crossings had been made. The road had been linked at intervals with twenty-one interchanges and fourteen service areas. In May, 1956 the link between the New Jersey and Pennsylvania turnpikes was put into operation. The face of the land would never be the same again.

To meet ever-mounting needs other roads were constructed. The most significant, perhaps, was the Garden State Parkway, one of America's safest highways, linking the northern part of the state with points along the Jersey shore.

Cars, trucks, and busses crowded the highways. In 1957 more than 2,250,000 motor car registrations were issued in New Jersey. On June 30, 1961 over 200,000 vehicles travelled over the New Jersey Turnpike alone. The state's highways were the busiest in the nation.

Significant changes on New Jersey's landscape were also due to the growth and development of the state's manufacturing industries. During World War II old plants were enlarged and new plants built. New Jersey became the second largest shipbuilding state in the nation; she ranked fourth in the manufacture of airplanes. She turned out iron and steel products, electrical machinery, chemicals, drugs, radios, textiles, parachutes, rubber goods, and many miscellaneous items in a remarkable war effort.

The impetus given to manufacturing by the war was keenly felt in later years. Between 1954 and 1956, for example, about 1,800 new manufacturing plants began operations in New Jersey. Most of these were small plants employing fewer than fifty persons. They were to produce apparel, fabricated metals, electrical and nonelectrical machinery, furniture, textiles, and many other items. Adequate space, excellent transportation facilities, a large labor pool, and a growing market had attracted the plants to New Jersey. But all did not locate in the old manufacturing centers (Newark, Paterson, Jersey City, Elizabeth, Trenton, Camden). Numbers of new plants began to dot the landscape in Monmouth, Burlington, and Atlantic counties, and the impact was felt in Cumberland, Gloucester, and Salem counties, as well as in Hunterdon and Somerset.

Industrial growth helped to stimulate growth in basic research. Hundreds of research plants, including the James Forrestal Research Center in Princeton and the David Sarnoff Research Center in West Windsor Township, were built in a fifty-mile swath across the central part of the state. In the early 1960's New Jersey ranked first in the nation in actual dollars devoted to research.

Meanwhile, New Jersey's farmers were far from idle. The fine pastures of northern New Jersey continued to be well used for dairy farming. The level acres of central and southern New Jersey were given over to raising poultry, eggs, fruits, and vegetables. Monmouth County, in particular, was pockmarked with coops for laying birds. Farther south the fields were ripe with grains, hay, potatoes, asparagus, and tomatoes. Everywhere New Jersey was in the forefront in scientific farming. The herds were growing larger, the livestock breeds were improving, farmers were making richer applications of fertilizers to the soils, much more control was exercised over insects and pests, and irrigation was becoming a symbol of the new agriculture.

1964. New Jersey's population was 6,066,782 in 1960, an increase of 1,231,000 over the 1950 figure. The state's population had increased by more than 25 per cent. If the population increases at a similar rate during the coming decades, New Jersey will have over 7,500,000 people in 1970, and well over 12,000,000 people by the year 2000. Signs of growth can already be seen on the landscape in 1964, and plans for even further growth are constantly being made.

Modern factories, surrounded by bands of green grass, are going up along newly paved highways. New roads, freeways, bridges, and clover-leaf patterns are being built where empty or abandoned land once stood. Where necessary, buildings are being torn down to make way for the new roadways. Bright new industrial parks and shopping centers continue to impress countless Sunday drivers. In the cities and suburbs tall apartment houses are raising their heads to the sky. One-family dwellings are being built in what once was described by Jersey people as the "country." The building of new schools and additions being made to old ones are common in the New Jersey of 1964. The people of Newark are particularly proud that a "new" Newark is rising to replace the old city. Other cities are also clearing the slums and engaging in urban renewal. The Round Valley reservoir is fast nearing completion. Large ocean-going vessels will soon be docking at the growing ports of Elizabeth and Trenton. There is talk of clearing the Hackensack Meadow and putting the new land to industrial use. There is talk of a "jetport" to serve better the transportation needs of the metropolitan area. There is talk of growth and progress.

The Face of the Land

The drama of New Jersey's 300-year history has taken place on a remarkably diverse landscape. The 8,224 square miles of land and water that encompass the state show the effects of long periods of geological time, of the work of water, of volcanoes, of wind, sun, and ice.

RELATIVE RELIEF OF NEW JERSEY

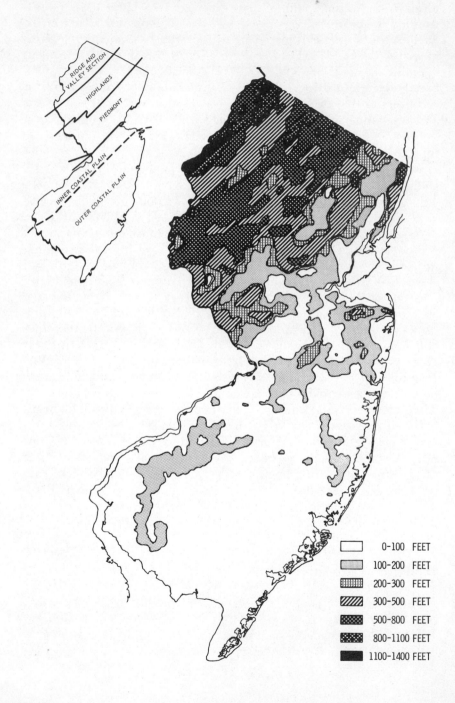

0-100 FEET

100-200 FEET

200-300 FEET

300-500 FEET

500-800 FEET

800-1100 FEET

1100-1400 FEET

Some of the oldest rocks in North America can be found in northern New Jersey; some of the youngest can be seen near the seashore. Water has helped to chisel the Delaware Water Gap through the Kittatinny Mountains; charged with sea salt it has formed the salt marshes of the lower Hackensack and Passaic rivers; it is even now carrying many New Jersey acres to the sea.

Volcanic materials erupting on the land surface long ago threw a long line of hills—the Watchung Mountains—across the face of the land. Other volcanic materials meanwhile lay embedded in the earth. It was left for the forces of erosion to uncover them. The embedded rock—the Palisades of the Hudson—can be seen today from the New York side of the Hudson River. Winds, driving the ocean currents, have slashed against the New Jersey coast. They have helped to create the barrier beaches; they often take part in their destruction. Glaciers, or moving sheets of ice charged with rock, helped to scour the land. They helped to fashion many of the lakes in the northern part of the state. One large glacial lake—called Lake Passaic by geologists—was once situated north and west of the Watchung Mountains. The lake was formed when the retreating ice sheet ponded the waters of the Passaic River. The old lake's remnants can be seen today in the Great Swamp, now an important national wildlife refuge. Glaciers also provided the materials from which the northern farmers produced their stone fences. They heaped up piles of rock in a line stretching north and west from Perth Amboy through Dover, Morristown, and Belvidere—the terminal moraine of the geologists. South Jersey did not feel the impact of the moving ice.

Moving ice and volcanic tremors no longer disturb the New Jersey earth. But the work carried on by wind, sun, and water goes on. The landscape continues to change, albeit the changes rarely can be seen by the naked eye. But despite the daily changes, one factor at least has remained constant throughout New Jersey's history—the state's topographic regions. New Jersey can be divided—as it could have been divided 300 years ago—into four topographic regions: the Ridge and Valley, the Highlands, the Piedmont, and the Coastal Plain. (See map on page 8.) Each will be described in turn.

The Ridge and Valley. The Ridge and Valley region of New Jersey is part of the Great Appalachian Valley that extends from New York State to central Alabama. The Lehigh, Susquehanna, Cumberland, Shenandoah, and Coosa valleys are all parts of the Great Valley. The Delaware and Kittatinny valleys, oriented northeast-southwest, form parts of the Great Valley in New Jersey. Their floors, composed of sedimentary rock layers, chiefly limestone, have been greatly folded and compressed. They stand between 300 and 600 feet above sea level. Like other sections of the Great Valley, they have provided ease of movement both north and south.

Between the Delaware and Kittatinny valleys rises the bold ridge of Kittatinny Mountain (Shawangunk Mountain in New York and Blue Mountain in Pennsylvania). The mountain, like the valleys, is oriented northeast-southwest. Its heights average between 1,600 and 1,800 feet in elevation. From High Point, Sussex County, the highest point in the state (1,804 feet), one has a clear view west across the Delaware into Pennsylvania, east over the broad Kittatinny Valley to the Highlands, and north into New York State.

The accompanying topographical cross section of New Jersey points out how Kittatinny Mountain towers over the surrounding

CROSS SECTION OF NEW JERSEY

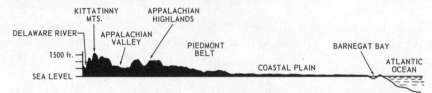

areas. The cross section also points out the height of the Delaware River, which falls from a height of over 500 feet near the New York State line to 287 feet at Delaware Water Gap. There the river cut through Kittatinny Mountain as the land was uplifted and produced one of the great natural wonders of America. The gap is a prime tourist attraction. The river itself may become even more important. It may help to solve one of New Jersey's growing problems—the problem of a fine potable water supply.

The Highlands. The Highlands are located south and east of the Ridge and Valley in the north central part of New Jersey. Their trend, like the Ridge and Valley, is northeast-southwest. They are part of the long Appalachian Mountain chain.

A number of broad, rounded, or flat-topped ridges that rise be-between 400 and 600 feet above the neighboring low areas make up the Highlands. The rocks are basically metamorphic, the oldest and hardest rocks in the state. But streams have managed through geological time to cut deep valleys through them.

Among the familiar rivers in the Highlands are the Delaware (for a portion of its course), the Musconetcong, the Rockaway, and the Pequannock. Lake Musconetcong, Budd Lake, Lake Hopatcong, and many other lakes are scattered through the Highlands. All are important summer resorts. Many are products of the continental glaciation, although most of them have been altered since by man. Lake Hopatcong, 913 feet above the sea, was the highest elevation on the Morris Canal. The highest elevation in the Highlands, 1,496 feet, is near Vernon.

The Piedmont. The low or rolling land that makes up the Piedmont slopes gently south and east from the Highlands. The area north of Paterson and Hackensack lies at elevations of only 300 feet. The flats of the upper Passaic River and the plains of the Raritan are even lower.

The highest elevations in the Piedmont are found in the knobs and ridges that stand above the general level of the topography. Among the ridges, produced by upwelling lava from below the earth's surface, are the Watchung Mountains, which swing south and east from Paterson to Millburn, Watchung, and Martinsville, and then north toward Pluckemin. But even in the Watchungs the highest elevation is but 879 feet, at High Mountain north of Paterson.

Overlooking the Hudson River is the rim of the Palisades. The Palisades decrease in height from over 547 feet near Closter to forty feet near Bayonne. The early Dutch settlements were located on the Palisades Ridge.

Cushetunk Mountain and Sourland Mountain also rise above the nearby low country. It is in the horseshoe hollow of Cushetunk Mountain — Round Valley — that New Jersey is now completing a vast reservoir site.

The Coastal Plain. The Coastal Plain of New Jersey is located south of the Piedmont. It consists of young sedimentary rocks that dip gently to the east. The surface is level and low. No elevations exceed 500 feet; more than half of the Coastal Plain lies below 100 feet. In several places, isolated hills, between 100 and 200 feet high, stand above the surrounding countryside. Among the examples are Spring Hill, Mount Holly, and Apple Pie Hill. A divide of less than 100 feet separates west-flowing Rancocas Creek from east-flowing Mullica River.

Conspicuous features of the ocean fringes of the Coastal Plain are tide marshes, drowned river valleys, and barrier beaches. The sand of the barrier beaches, the ocean water itself, and the cool breezes are welcome sights to summer travellers. The Jersey Shore is the state's prime recreational area.

Locked in the sedimentary layers beneath the Coastal Plain are excellent ground water resources. They may one day help to lure numerous industries to South Jersey.

A portion of the Coastal Plain extends for 100 miles out under the Atlantic Ocean. This is the so-called *continental shelf*. It is in the waters above the continental shelf that many New Jersey fishermen try their "deep sea" luck in summer.

Climate

Significant climatic differences can be expected between the Ridge and Valley and Highland areas and New Jersey's southeastern coast. The northern areas are influenced by the frequent storms that cross the Great Lakes; only rarely do such storms strike the Cape May littoral. Elevation also plays a major role in the differences. The heights in the Ridge and Valley and Highlands help to produce low winter temperatures and much snowfall. January average temperature at Newton, Sussex County, is just above 27°; at Cape May it is just below 35°. Differences in summer average temperatures are not nearly as great. Snowfall averages 150 inches in the Highlands, only fourteen inches at Cape May.

Mountain heights also have an effect upon the rainfall. While New Jersey ranks high among the states in total precipitation, there are notable differences within the state itself. Newton records nearly forty-five inches of precipitation each year, Dover nearly fifty inches. Atlantic City receives forty inches, Cape May less than thirty-eight inches.

Unlike many other areas in the United States where precipitation is quite variable from year to year, New Jersey's precipitation is remarkably dependable. Individual years of extreme variability are not uncommon, however. In the "dry" years local communities often restrict the use of their water supplies.

Of particular significance to the farmer is the length of the growing season. In the Ridge and Valley the time between the last killing frost in spring and the first killing frost in autumn averages 220 days. The average for Cape May is 255 days. (See map on page 13.)

Precipitation looms as a critical factor in New Jersey's future. Water is needed for the growing population, the growing commercial and industrial bases, and for agricultural use. The requirement for 1975 has been estimated at over 700 million gallons per day. Water development programs in the Hackensack, Passaic, Delaware, Raritan, and Mullica-Wading river basins have long been urged.

DURATION OF VEGETATIVE GROWING SEASON
IN NEW JERSEY (DAYS)

REPRESENTATIVE CLIMAGRAPH

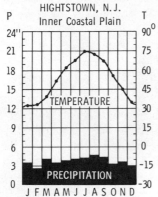

HIGHTSTOWN, N.J.
Inner Coastal Plain

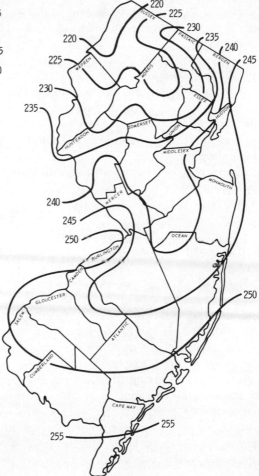

Water Development

On November 4, 1958 the voters of New Jersey decided that the state should issue $45,850,000 in bonds to finance a long-range water development program. Studies of ground water supplies in South Jersey and engineering studies of the Raritan Basin were to be made; and new reservoir sites at Spruce Run and Round Valley, in Hunterdon County, were to be built.

Round Valley is a fine reservoir site. It lies between 300 and 400 feet below the horseshoe-shaped frame of Cushetunk Mountain. The open end of the horseshoe, the western end, has slopes that rise over 200 feet above the valley floor. But to enclose the horseshoe completely, dams are being built in the northwest corner across the South Branch of Rockaway Creek, and in the southwest corner across Prescott Brook. A dike is also being built at another low spot in the northwest.

The reservoir, supplied largely from the South Branch of the Raritan River, is expected to hold fifty-five billion gallons of water. Seventy million gallons will be sent each day to potential subscribers. At least eighteen communities—among them Elizabeth, Bernardsville, Bound Brook, Kearny, Cedar Grove, and Verona—have already applied for Round Valley water. Demands are certain to exceed available gallons.

The removal of homes in the valley was begun in 1959. In April, 1961, dam construction was started. The Round Valley Project should be completed in 1965.

Other Natural Resources

Minerals. New Jersey is not endowed with an extremely wealthy natural resource base. The New Jersey earth does not contain vast quantities of coal, iron ore, petroleum, and natural gas—resources that ordinarily help to power giant industrial complexes.

The mineral base does include, however, quantities of sand and gravel, greensand marl, crushed stone, serpentine, ilmenite, clay, iron, and zinc. During the Colonial Period New Jersey's bog iron resources—from the Pine Barrens in South Jersey—served well the vigorous iron furnaces. So, too, were the magnetites of Morris and adjacent counties turned into fine iron products. But the development of the iron ores of the Lake Superior District led to the eventual demise of New Jersey's iron industry.

Zinc, taken from mines at Franklin and Ogdensburg, was for many years New Jersey's most valuable mineral. The Franklin mine is now closed, but the new shaft recently completed at Ogdensburg is in production once more. This Franklin-Ogdensburg mineral assemblage, one of the most varied in the world, was and is a favorite haunt of the "rock hound."

Soils. The soils of New Jersey are part of the Great Soil Group called the *Podzols,* which extend across the northeastern part of the United States from the Great Lakes to New England, and south into the Middle Atlantic states. Podzols form in humid climates under forest vegetation. They are not inherently fertile. To make full use of their agricultural capacity they must be heavily fertilized.

Individual soil series vary considerably. The Hermon-Colton series of the Ridge and Valley, for example, were formed largely from glacial materials. They are moderately acid. Farmers use them for dairying and general farming. Many acres have simply been left idle.

The Penn series of the Piedmont includes shallow soils composed of red shale; the Lansdale series is made up of gray and yellow sandstone. Some of the soils are well drained, others poorly drained. Dairying and general farming are the chief uses to which the soils are put. Near the Watchung Mountains the soils are formed from gray shale or argillite. They are often heavy with trap rock materials. Little agriculture is practiced on them.

The Sassafras, or Aura, soils, of southwestern New Jersey, on the other hand, produce fine fields of vegetables, corn, and hay. They are brownish-gray on the surface, but have a reddish tinge in the subsoil. They overlie deep deposits of gravel and sand. The soils must be well cared for to maintain their productivity.

Natural Vegetation. The forests of New Jersey had already been modified by the Lenni-Lenape at the time of European settlement. The settlers used forest resources for fuel, fencing, and building materials. While the hill lands of northern New Jersey remained largely in forest, highly settled areas in the Piedmont and portions of the Coastal Plain early lost their forest cover. These areas were early transformed into farmsteads and cleared fields. Poor soils often precluded settlement in other parts of the Coastal Plain.

During the nineteenth century excessive cutting and uncontrolled fires led to the deterioration of the quality of much New Jersey forest land. Since 1900, however, conservation and scientific forestry have endeavored to save New Jersey's trees.

Forty-six per cent of New Jersey is still in forest. The northern hills (Northern Deciduous Forest) are covered with oak, hickory, ash, maple, and hemlock trees. Shortleaf, pitch, and scrub pines (Southern Coniferous Forest) are the dominant trees of South Jersey. The oak is also common in the Pine Barrens. Merchantable timber is used for railroad ties, cordwood, baskets, and boxes.

Location. Location is not, strictly speaking, a natural resource, but it is and has been of the utmost significance in New Jersey's development. The state grew up between the throbbing urban centers of New York and Philadelphia. It fronts on the Atlantic Ocean. As such it has had access to one of the largest urban markets in the world — and to wide overseas markets. A circle with a radius of 250 miles centered on Newark, New Brunswick, or Trenton intersects twelve states with a population of over fifty-four million. Market-oriented industries have long located in New Jersey. And New Jersey's poor soils have been urged to yield fine crops to serve the large urban centers. Problems of transportation, port development, water supply, and urban renewal all can be traced in part to New Jersey's superior location. Location, as much as any other single factor, has contributed much to New Jersey's relative prosperity and population growth. And it has always been so.

The Industrial Scene

Much of New Jersey's growth and development has been based upon a thriving industrial machine. New Jersey ranks seventh among the states in the United States in value added after manufacture, and produces a variety of goods second to none in the nation. Over 14,000 factories in the state produce chemicals, electrical instruments and machinery, apparel, stone, clay, and glass products, foods, fabricated metals, textiles, pulp and paper products, transportation equipment, petroleum and coal products, leather and leather goods, and numerous miscellaneous items. Newark alone boasts of producing over 300 types of manufactured products.

Leading Industries. Manufacturers have been attracted to New Jersey for numerous reasons: the ease of assembling raw materials, excellent transportation and port facilities, adequate supplies of water, the presence of capital, one of the world's largest markets, and a general belief in industrial growth and progress that permeates the population. New Jersey's largest industry, the chemical industry (it is also the largest chemical industry in the country), may well have developed in New Jersey for these and at least one other good reason: good fortune.

William Colgate moved his small chemical plant from New York City to Jersey City in 1847. He began at once to produce soap and soap products, glycerin, cosmetics, and organic chemicals. Meanwhile, in Newark, James J. Mapes turned his attention to the production of synthetic fertilizers. Both ventures were crowned with almost immediate success. Colgate and Mapes had helped to lay the foundations for New Jersey's chemical industry.

The location of the great oil refineries at Bayonne in the 1870's continued to spur the industry's growth. So did the coming of World War I. When local manufacturers were cut off from their German sources of supply, they turned to manufacturing their own products. The du Ponts, for example, established their plant at Deepwater to make dyestuffs. Other manufacturers followed the du Ponts' lead.

Today, over 800 chemical plants dot the New Jersey landscape. While individual plants can be found in each of the state's counties, most are located in the great industrial arc between New York City and Philadelphia. Middlesex, Essex, Union, and Hudson counties lead the state in the number of people employed by the chemical industry.

The manufacture of electrical machinery, New Jersey's second leading industry, also shows marked concentration in the New York-Philadelphia industrial arc. Communications equipment and electrical apparatus manufacturing are particularly concentrated in and around the Newark area. The nonelectrical machinery and foods and kindred products industries follow similar patterns.

Chemicals, electrical machinery, nonelectrical machinery, and food and kindred products are New Jersey's leading industries. Together they produce nearly half of the total value added by manufacture to goods in the state. If transportation equipment, fabricated metals, apparel, and primary metals are included, the figure for value added by manufacture goes to 75 per cent. Many small industries help to make up the remainder.

To see how New Jersey's leading industries rank nationally, consult the diagram on page 18.

Research

Research and development are in large measure responsible for maintaining New Jersey's high national rank in manufacturing, science, and technology. More than 10 per cent of all the research undertaken in the United States is performed in New Jersey labora-

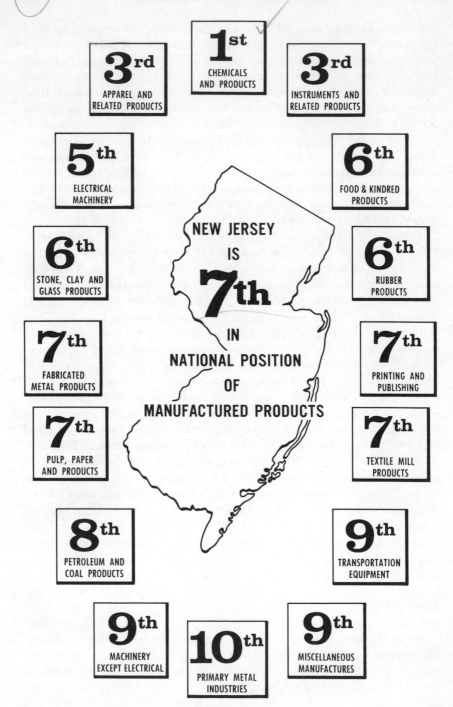

3rd APPAREL AND RELATED PRODUCTS

1st CHEMICALS AND PRODUCTS

3rd INSTRUMENTS AND RELATED PRODUCTS

5th ELECTRICAL MACHINERY

6th FOOD & KINDRED PRODUCTS

6th STONE, CLAY AND GLASS PRODUCTS

6th RUBBER PRODUCTS

NEW JERSEY IS **7th** IN NATIONAL POSITION OF MANUFACTURED PRODUCTS

7th FABRICATED METAL PRODUCTS

7th PRINTING AND PUBLISHING

7th PULP, PAPER AND PRODUCTS

7th TEXTILE MILL PRODUCTS

8th PETROLEUM AND COAL PRODUCTS

9th TRANSPORTATION EQUIPMENT

9th MACHINERY EXCEPT ELECTRICAL

10th PRIMARY METAL INDUSTRIES

9th MISCELLANEOUS MANUFACTURES

tories. Many notable contributions have already been made. The transistor, for example, was developed by Bell Telephone at Murray Hill. Bell Telephone also developed Nike's electric brain. Color television was perfected by the Radio Corporation of America in Princeton. The James Forrestal Research Center did pioneer work on interplanetary rockets. At Esso, in Linden, the development of better fuels and lubricants is a cardinal research theme. At Western Electric new and more sensitive electric instruments are being studied and prepared.

Over 600 research laboratories, most of them allied to either the chemical or electrical industries, can be found in the state. Some are devoted to improving old products; some to developing new ones. Others perform "basic research." They are helping New Jersey and the nation to peer into the future.

Agriculture

New Jersey's agricultural acres lie both north and south of the New York City-Philadelphia industrial arc. They are the most intensively farmed acres in the United States. Bulging populations, high costs and prices, and scientific farming have all been responsible for the state's mounting agricultural production.

Farmers point out that they are planting finer crop varieties, breeding better livestock, and using more fertilizers than ever before. They have learned to control the insects and many of the plant diseases. Many farmers no longer rely exclusively upon available precipitation. They supplement normal water supplies with irrigation water. The results have been phenomenal. Production has risen sharply. New Jersey farmers' cash receipts from marketings per acre exceed those from any other state.

Less than half of the state's farmland, however, is used for crops. Much of it remains in pasture or forest, or is allowed to stay idle. More than 60 per cent of the cropped land itself is devoted to grains and hay. Nearly 25 per cent is used to raise vegetables, fruits, and berries. The remainder is used for many miscellaneous but important items.

Many types of garden vegetables, fruits, and berries are grown. Asparagus, sweet corn, lettuce, snap beans, white potatoes, onions, and tomatoes are all valuable crops. So too are apples, peaches, cranberries, blueberries, and strawberries. The state is a large producer of eggs and dairy products.

MAJOR AGRICULTURAL AREAS

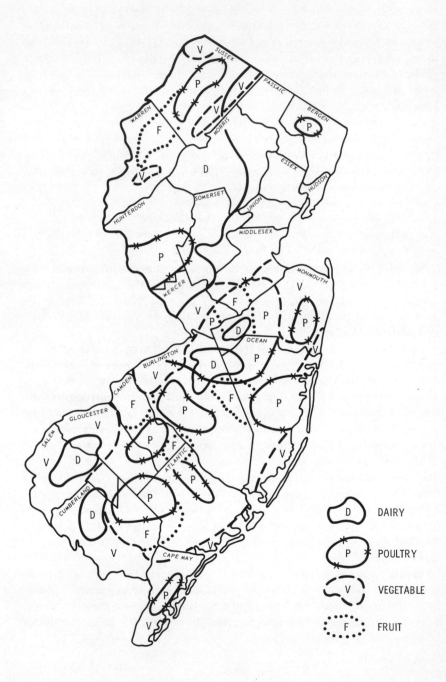

Many of the fresh vegetables and fruits are sold at supermarkets, vegetable stores, and roadside stands. But nearly 50 per cent go into processing. There are over fifty vegetable- and fruit-processing plants in New Jersey — most of them south of the New York City-Philadelphia industrial arc. The largest is Seabrook Farms, in Cumberland County, probably the largest vegetable-processing plant in the United States.

Eggs and milk, however, both normally outstrip vegetables and fruits as dollar earners in the state, although vegetables did lead in 1963. The egg belt centers in Monmouth, Ocean, Atlantic, and Cumberland counties. New Jersey's best eggs are sold at auctions in Flemington, Vineland, Hightstown, Mount Holly, Hackettstown, and Paterson. The milk belt is confined largely to Sussex, Warren, Hunterdon, Morris, and Somerset counties. New Jersey's 120,000 milk cows help to supply the bulging metropolitan area milk sheds. The Walker-Gordon farm at Plainsboro alone has over 1,500 cows. And few milk producers can compete with Ideal Farms' Senator's Marie, a fine Guernsey, which holds four records with production over 20,000 pounds.

For these reasons, little appreciated by outsiders or urban New Jerseyites, the state well deserves to be called the "Garden State."

The Urban Scene

New Jersey men and women are urban dwellers. A map of population distribution focuses sharply on the heavily populated sections of the northeastern part of the state. Bergen, Hudson, Union, and Essex counties are decidedly urban. Portions of Passaic, Middlesex, Somerset, and Morris counties are becoming increasingly so. There are large urban conglomerations in Camden and Atlantic counties.

The Essex County complex points out the teeming intensity of the urban centers. A long bus ride on Bloomfield Avenue from Newark, through Bloomfield, Glen Ridge, Montclair, Verona, and Caldwell leads through a continuous "city." People unfamiliar with the area never know they have left one community for another. The urban impingement is complete. And the "city" is pushing west into West Caldwell and Pine Brook, and will undoubtedly stretch further west on Route 46 in years to come.

At the moment, four of New Jersey's largest cities are located in the northeastern part of the state. Camden makes up most of the Camden County urban complex; Trenton is the largest urban center in Mercer County.

New Jersey's six largest cities are:

Newark (population 405,220*). Newark is the largest city in New Jersey. It has long been one of America's largest manufacturing, commercial, and financial centers. It is a prime shopping center.

The city is served by many rail lines, fine highways, by bus, truck, ship, and airplane. Newark Airport, a part of the dynamic New York Port Authority, is one of the busiest airports in the country. Port Newark has a thirty-five-foot channel where numerous ocean-going vessels can dock easily. The port is the leading importer of lumber and foreign-made automobiles on the East Coast.

A major urban redevelopment program is springing a "new" Newark to life. Large slum areas are being cleared. The city literally is having its face lifted. The YMCA building, the Mutual Benefit Life, Prudential, and Fidelity Union buildings, and the underground parking lot at Military Park are all evidences of the new beauty of the "new" Newark.

Jersey City (population 276,101). Jersey City's significance is derived largely from its position on the Hudson River opposite the City of New York. Railroad terminals and deep-water port facilities line the river. Fine highways lead deep into the metropolitan hinterland. All help to carry the city's manufactured goods to all parts of the world.

Like major cities in other parts of the country, Jersey City is having its face changed. Thousands of low- and middle-income housing units are already going up. Others are planned. The city boasts one of the country's outstanding maternity hospitals and the state's only college of medicine and dentistry.

Paterson (population 143,663). The face of Paterson has changed considerably since Alexander Hamilton's day. But it is still primarily a manufacturing center. During its history Paterson's economic life has centered largely upon a single industrial activity: either cotton textiles, locomotives, silk, or airplanes. As a silk center, for example, Paterson won world-wide renown.

Today, Paterson's industries are highly diversified. The city is the home of many electronic, pharmaceutical, chemical,metal-fabricating, furniture, and footwear plants. Like Newark and Jersey City, Paterson, too, has an impressive urban renewal program.

Camden (population 117,159). Camden is South Jersey's leading manufacturing city. The Delaware River and proximity to Philadelphia have been largely responsible for Camden's growth. The

* Population figures are according to the 1960 Census.

Campbell Soup Company located in the city in 1869 to tap the nearby agricultural acres. The first phonograph was made in Camden by RCA. Leather goods, TV sets, and ships are also made in Camden. The United States' first atomic-powered commercial ship was made in Camden's shipyards.

Trenton (population 114,167). Trenton is the capital of the state. But the city also takes much pride in its transportation and industrial functions. The sign over the Delaware River Bridge reads, "Trenton Makes, the World Takes." Iron and steel, wire rope, and pottery were largely responsible for Trenton's growth. Walter Scott Lenox produced his famous china in Trenton. Peter Cooper and Abram S. Hewitt formed the Trenton Iron Works in the city and John A. Roebling introduced there the manufacture of wire rope for suspension bridges. Roebling cable was used in the construction of the Brooklyn, George Washington, and Golden Gate bridges.

Trenton's face is also changing. New state government buildings are rising on what will become a glittering new cultural center. There is also much building activity along the waterfront. Trenton's new port facilities are rising along the Delaware.

Elizabeth (population 107,698). Elizabeth is an old city. Its beginnings go back to 1664. It is one of New Jersey's leading manufacturing centers. The products of the Singer Sewing Machine Company are known the world over. Standard Oil of New Jersey and at least 300 other manufacturers are located in Elizabeth.

Port Elizabeth, part of the Port of New York Authority, began operations in 1962. It will soon be able to berth twenty-four vessels. Elizabeth will soon have a new view of the world. So will New Jersey.

DO/DISCUSS

1. Much can be determined about the origins, geography, and development of New Jersey by examining a road map of the state. Chart a toponomy (place names) study using the following general headings. Note the example provided for each topic.
    a. Occupance or settlement (Swedesboro)
    b. Original vegetation or flora (Oakland)
    c. Surface or topographic features (Summit)

    d. Commemoration of individuals (Edison)
    e. Commemoration of other places (New Egypt)
    f. Economic activities of the past (Glassboro)
    g. Military or historical sites (Washington Crossing)
    h. Unusual or interesting names (Jenny Jump Mountain)

    Select enough representative samples to draw some broad generalizations.

2. New Jersey is essentially a peninsula. Explain this and indicate how it has served as both an asset and a hindrance.

3. The regional setting of New Jersey tends to follow a southwest-northeast diagonal between the nation's first and fourth largest cities. How has this situation affected the transportation, commercial, and population orientation of the inhabitants of New Jersey?

4. Some feel that the reference to New Jersey as a "Garden State" is today a misnomer. Does our current land use dictate a more applicable name? Can you suggest a name for the New Jersey of the future?

5. New Jersey receives an ample rainfall; yet we are perplexed by an increasing water problem. Can you identify some of the reasons for this paradox? What steps are being taken to overcome it? Have you any recommendations?

6. The location of a commercial jetport has been a crucial concern for New Jersey leaders for quite some time. Select a site that you might recommend and be able to support your choice with well-thought-out reasons.

7. Why is the transportation problem especially significant to our state? What are the specific difficulties? What can you predict for the future?

8. Present a convincing argument the governor might use to persuade national officials to locate an aerospace center in New Jersey.

9. Refer to the most recent edition of the *Statistical Abstract of the United States* or an appropriate almanac, and bar-graph New Jersey's national rank in manufacturing for (a) establishments, (b) payroll, (c) value added, (d) number of employees, and (e) new capital expenditures.

10. An imaginary triangle drawn from Fort Lee to Princeton to Long Branch and return would house about 10 per cent of the country's research presently being conducted. How might one explain the phenomenon of the concentration of so many laboratories in this small area?

11. Endeavor to give reasons why each of the following trends are taking place on the New Jersey agricultural scene. (a) Less of the state's labor force is involved in farming (now only 3 per cent). (b) Each year more farmland is sold for housing developments. (c) Highly specialized crop growing is becoming a necessity. (d) New Jersey's agricultural industry has become increasingly dependent on migrant workers. (e) There are now fewer but larger farms—the most intensive farming in in the United States. (f) Poultry production, New Jersey's leading source of farm income 1946-1962, has been declining and is now second to vegetable growing. (g) Nursery products sales are ever increasing.

21 counties + 21 seats.

SECTION II
History

The first practical submarine, designed by John Holland, built at the Paterson Iron Works.

CHAPTER 2

The Colonial Period

The Indians of New Jersey

Any proper history of colonial New Jersey must begin with a study of its aboriginal inhabitants, the Indians, who both by their presence and stage of culture affected the lives of the Europeans who settled there.

The colonists erroneously named them Delaware, but the Indians called themselves Lenni-Lenape, or "original people." They belonged to the general family of Algonkian Indians who inhabited northeastern United States. The Lenape nation was divided into three groups, which were geographically distributed: the Minsi (or *wolf.* Munsee), or "people of the stony country," in the north; the Unami, *turtle* or "people down the river," in the central portion; and the Unalach- *turkey* tigo, or "people who lived near the ocean," in the south.

The Lenape were a peaceful and hospitable people, strong and healthy, above average in height, and considered by many to be very handsome. But it was not long after the coming of the white man to New Jersey that their numbers were depleted by disease, liquor, and migrations resulting from colonial encroachment.

The Indians had developed a Neolithic (New Stone Age) cultural level, using implements of stone, wood, and bone, making clay pottery by the coil method, and obtaining their food by the four basic methods of hunting, fishing, gathering, and agriculture. Hunting and fishing were the chief occupation of the men, and the forests and streams

27

were usually rich sources of game and fish. But there were times of famine when even the village dogs had to be eaten. A hunt was a group endeavor, usually undertaken in the fall, and lasting from several weeks to a few months. Fish were caught by hand, net, hook and line, bow and arrow, spear, harpoon, club, and weir. The last was a V-shaped dam of stones placed across a river with the point downstream.

Food gathering was engaged in mainly by the women and children, with nuts, herbs, roots, and wild fruits, such as grapes, crabapples, berries, and persimmons, important supplements to the diet. During the summer an entire tribe would travel to the coast for shellfish. These either were eaten or, before being carried home, were dried and smoked so the meat could be used for seasoning and the shells for ornaments, wampum, or binding pottery.

Agriculture, attesting to the Indians' settled life, was extensively practiced. The men cleared the land by burning the trees and brush and turning under the ashes, which helped fertilize the soil. Planting, cultivating, and harvesting were carried on by the women with digging sticks and crude hoes. Corn, squash, and beans were the principal food crops, although pumpkins, melons, sweet potatoes, sunflowers, and tobacco were also grown. Corn was usually roasted or ground into meal. The latter was used for making bread or a kind of porridge called "samp," which became the early settlers' mush. Meat and fish were boiled or broiled. Broiling was done over an open hearth fire; boiling was accomplished by dropping heated stones into clay pots holding the food to be cooked and water. Most foods were stored for winter use. Corn meal was charred and placed in storage pots sunk in the ground. Two meals a day were customary, but the food pot was always kept boiling for a traveller or returning hunter. Skins of the deer, elk, wolf, bear, beaver, and raccoon were used in making the Indians' scanty clothing. In the summer the men wore only a small loin cloth; in colder weather a robe was thrown over one shoulder, with hip-length leggings and moccasins of skin completing the costume. Their sparse beards were plucked out with mussel shells, and their hair was cut off with flint knives, leaving a scalp lock down the center of the head to which painted feathers were frequently fastened. Women wore short skirts, with a loose tunic fastened over one shoulder. Their hair, worn either loose or in two braids, was held in place by painted bands of deerskin. Both sexes decorated themselves with paint on body and face and wore jewelry of stone, wood, shell, and animal teeth and claws.

The Lenape lived in semi-permanent villages of from ten to twenty

semi- nomadic

families, each family generally occupying a separate house, or wigwam. The wigwam was formed by driving saplings into the ground at regular intervals and then binding their slender tops and lashing them together. This framework was covered with strips of bark or overlapping bundles of grass. A hole was left in the roof for smoke from an inside fire. The furnishings were simple. Pine boughs were used for beds, rush or corn-husk mats for bedding, and occasionally wooden benches served as seats. The wigwams were generally grouped around a Big House used for ceremonial functions.

Trade was generally conducted by barter, although the Lenape had a medium of exchange in the form of small tubular shells or painted wooden beads called "wampum." It was used either by the piece or by foot-long strings. The white settlers took advantage of this cheap currency and began manufacturing it in factories, one of which was set up at Pascack, near Hackensack. Wampum was legal tender among the colonists until it was outlawed. In addition to its use as money, wampum was woven into belts for ornamentation, for commemoration of events, and for messages.

The government of the Lenape was most democratic. Each division had its own king or chief called "sakima" or "sachem," whose powers were limited. All matters of importance were decided by a council of elders and braves, and during wartime the king was superseded by a war chief whom he appointed. Justice was based upon retaliation and restitution. Property was owned by the tribe as a whole or the family, not individually. Parents arranged marriage, but with the tentative consent of the principals involved. Men were at least 18 and women 14 at the time of marriage. The "bride price" was met by presents given to the girl or her family. Polygyny (marriage to more than one wife) was permitted, but generally only chiefs or the very rich could take advantage of this privilege. Divorce could be effected by either party, the younger children going with the wife.

The Indian religion was totemism, or belief in an all-pervading force or spirit called "Manito," which was everywhere, inhabiting both animate and inanimate objects. Each tribe believed that this force was most highly concentrated in a particular object or totem, which was thus to be venerated. Among the Lenape, the Minsi totem was the wolf; the Unami, the turtle; and the Unalachtigo, the turkey. In addition, each Indian had his personal spirit, which acted as his guide and guard throughout his life. The tribal ceremonies, dances, and feasts were forms of religious observance and usually took place at the Big House. The priest of the tribe, or "shaman," received his calling through a vision, and he based his predictions upon dreams. He was

entertainer

also responsible for curing the sick by driving away evil spirits, since illness was attributed to supernatural causes.

When Europeans first came to their area, the Lenape were friendly, hospitable, and co-operative. But as farms of the Dutch and then the English colonists were established on Indian hunting lands, as their free-roaming cattle destroyed Indian crops, and as increasing pressure of settlement mounted, relations grew less friendly. Raiding and retaliation were followed by sporadic massacring along the frontier. Treaty agreements were violated by the whites, and acts of duplicity — the "Walking Purchase" of 1718 in eastern Pennsylvania is a notorious example—cheated the Indians of much of their lands. The peaceable Lenape never offered any systematic resistance, so that by the end of the seventeenth century all but a few had migrated into Pennsylvania, the Midwest, and Canada. In 1759 most of those remaining in New Jersey were placed on a reservation in Burlington County called Brotherton, the nation's first. When this establishment was dissolved in 1801, the last full-blooded Indians left the state.

The Lenape had a number of able and colorful chiefs during colonial times. One was Oratam, who represented his people at numerous peace treaties and land transfers in northern New Jersey during the mid-seventeenth century. Tammany, whose name was adopted by the New York County Democratic Society because of his sagacity, was the chief who negotiated the famous treaty of 1683 with William Penn that ceded the lands for the establishment of the colony of Pennsylvania. Perhaps the most notable chief was Teedyuscung who, as described in the chapter on "The People of New Jersey," represented his people at the councils of Easton, where the Lenape finally gave up all their claims to lands in the East.

As for the permanent influence of these original inhabitants and their contributions to contemporary New Jersey, they are many and varied. They include such obvious things as place names: Hackensack, Ho-Ho-Kus, Passaic, Pompton, Absecon, Whippany, Parsippany, Metuchen, Wanaque, and Rockaway, as well as Musconetcong, Metedeconk, Raritan, Assunpink, Hopatcong, Ramapo, and Watchung. Terms of Indian origin, not all Lenape, that are part of our vocabulary include *tobacco, canoe, wigwam, moccasin, papoose, tomahawk, wampum, persimmon, hickory, chipmunk, sassafras, succotash,* and *hominy.* Some of the Indian trails, such as the Minisink and Assunpink, became the basis of colonial roads. Some of the earliest towns were placed in Indian clearings, and the method of clearing farm land by burning the forest cover, although wasteful, was extremely helpful to the colonists, short of manpower and equipment. Also adopted were such Indian products as corn, beans, squash, and tobacco, and their methods of cultivation. Corn in hills, with beans to climb the ripened stalks, and vines such as squash and pumpkins to hide in their shade, are commonly grown together today as then. Medicines derived from roots, herbs, and trees, such as the sassafras, are still in use.

Some early settlements would have died out if the Indians had not supplied the colonists with food or guided them to good hunting grounds. Training in woodlore and methods of warfare, along with the supplying of fur pelts for trade with Europe as a source of ready income, were also important contributions. Perhaps most fundamental, however, was the opportunity that the Indian provided the white man to live up to the basic principles of brotherhood and morality. That a few, like William Penn, treated the Indians honestly, fairly, and as fellow human beings, speaks well for them. Unfortunately, many did not.

Early Settlements

The early history of New Jersey was closely tied to the rivalry for overseas possessions that developed between European nations during the Age of Exploration. In the seventeenth century, three powers, England, Sweden, and Holland, established settlements in the Middle Atlantic area of what is now the United States. One result of the inevitable conflicts between them was the founding of the English colony of New Jersey.

The first European to see, and possibly to land on, the New Jersey shore is believed to have been the Florentine navigator Giovanni da Verrazano, exploring for France. In 1524 he is said to have anchored his vessel off Sandy Hook and with a small boat explored upper New York Bay as far as the Jersey shore. Almost a century later, in 1609, Henry Hudson, an English navigator in the employ of the Dutch East-India Company, sailed the *Half Moon* into Delaware Bay and New York Bay, dispatched as far as Newark Bay a sounding party that discovered the Passaic and Hackensack rivers, and then sailed up the river that now bears his name. The following year Captain Samuel Argall explored the Delaware Bay region and named it after his benefactor and the governor of Virginia, Lord Thomas de la Warr, a name subsequently transferred to the bay and the river. In 1614 a Dutch captain, Cornelius Jacobsen May, explored the lower Delaware River and gave his name to Cape May.

The Dutch Lead the Way. The Dutch were the first to take advantage of these explorations, sending out trading expeditions and establishing settlements throughout the area. Holland had developed the largest and most efficient merchant fleet in the world and had become the leading commercial power of Europe. Joint-stock trading companies were organized by its wealthy merchants to found colonies and promote trade. One, the Dutch West India Company, interested in the North American fur trade, sent an expedition to Manhattan Island in 1624, and from this there developed New Netherland. Small bands were sent out into the interior to locate trading posts; one such group founded Fort Nassau on the Delaware River in what is now Gloucester County.

On the whole, because it was the neglected child of a trading company whose main interests were elsewhere, New Netherland hardly prospered and grew. A halfhearted attempt was made to encourage agricultural settlements under feudal landlords called patroons, resulting in the establishment of manorial estates as far north as the upper Hudson Valley and as far south as what is now Delaware. One of these communities was founded on a tract on the Hudson shore opposite Manhattan, granted in 1629 to Michael Pauw, the Burgomeister of Amsterdam. His agent, Cornelius Van Vorst, began to develop an estate called Pavonia at what is now Jersey City. In addition, some scattered homesteads, or "bouweries," were established by independent farmers in the Hackensack, Passaic and Raritan valleys.

Sweden, under the leadership of its brilliant king, Gustavus Adolphus, was also contending for world trade and empire. In 1638 an expedition was sent to Delaware Bay, a region that the Dutch had not yet fully occupied, and founded Fort Christina at the present site of Wilmington, Delaware. A vast track of land between Cape May and Raccoon Creek was purchased from the Indians in 1640, and the earliest Swedish settlement in New Jersey was built at Fort New Elfsborg (near Salem) in 1643. Sweden's interest was tied mainly to the fur trade, and although some farmers took up land, New Sweden, as it was called, never included more than 400 souls or extended more than thirty-five miles along the Delaware.

The Dutch protested against the Swedish occupation, but did not seriously interfere, primarily because the two countries were fighting on the same side in the Thirty Years' War. Once that conflict was concluded, the Dutch attitude changed, and in 1655 Governor Peter Stuyvesant sent an expedition that easily forced the surrender of the Swedes. New Sweden now became a part of New Netherland, and the inhabitants were permitted to retain their lands or return to Sweden.

The Dutch possessed New Netherland for forty years, during which time its progress was relatively slight. Not only was it neglected by the homeland but its inhabitants were scattered and large numbers were not Dutch. It was most hampered by the autocratic and corrupt nature of the colonial administration, compounded by the mismanagement of Indian relations. As a result of a treacherous massacre of an Indian village perpetrated by one of the governors, William Kieft, there was a period of slaughtering on both sides during the early 1640's that caused the temporary closing of the Pavonia settlement and struck the colony a blow from which it never fully recovered. All efforts by the people to gain political and social rights met with failure, and this particularly caused discontent among the non-Dutch. Thus when a small English fleet appeared off New Amsterdam on a summer's day in 1664 with orders for the colony to surrender, nobody would fight, and New Netherland became New York without a blow or a tear. But the Dutch stamp, and to a more limited extent the Swedish along Delaware Bay, was already placed indelibly on the area. More significant than the perpetuation of place and family names was the introduction of varied ethnic and religious elements into the population.

Prior to this conquest, there had been an interest shown by some Englishmen in the area. Several attempts were made to establish settlements along the Delaware. One succeeded when the Puritan colony of New Haven (Connecticut) in 1641 planted an offshoot of itself at Varkenskill, or Salem Creek. Further migrations of settlers from New England were imminent and probably would have occurred even if the area had remained under Dutch control.

Proprietary New Jersey

The takeover of New Netherland by the English came about after Charles II in 1660 returned to the throne, following the Puritan Revolution and the Commonwealth. With the restoration of the monarchy in 1660, the English Government began to take a more active interest in American colonization and in outstripping its commercial rival, Holland. Charles appointed his brother the Duke of York (later to become James II) Lord High Admiral of the Navy and authorized him to conquer New Netherland. England had consistently protested against the Dutch possession of the section of the

Atlantic coast discovered by John Cabot and was now in a position to make the protest good. James was not without personal motivation in his conquest. The King conferred upon him in 1664 the most extensive English territorial grant of the century, including all the continent between the Delaware and Connecticut rivers, Long Island together with Martha's Vineyard and Nantucket, and Maine east of the Kennebec. As Lord Proprietor, he was master of this domain under the King.

James appointed Richard Nicolls as his deputy governor and commander of the expedition. As has been mentioned, the Dutch surrendered without a fight, and on September 8, 1664 New Amsterdam's name was changed to New York. Within a month the English had taken possession of the Dutch forts up the Hudson and on the Delaware. Before the conquest, while Nicolls was still at sea, the Duke of York, with a stroke of his quill, had granted to two of his favorites, John, Lord Berkeley and Sir George Carteret, the land between the Hudson and Delaware rivers as the Province of Nova Caesaria, or New Jersey. It was named in honor of the island where in 1650 Carteret as governor had sheltered the Duke during the Puritan Revolution.

The change in ownership was far more significant than the inhabitants of the area could have sensed. From their experiences with Virginia and Massachusetts Bay, the English were learning that permanent settlements were sounder commercially and politically than the trading posts established by Holland and Sweden as a short cut to riches. The territory became an important connecting link between New England and the Southern colonies, immigrants came in large numbers, and towns sprang up along all the rivers.

Although the Duke of York's powers were absolute, in actual practice the government was liberal and somewhat benevolent. The Dutch and Swedes were allowed to retain their citizenship, although provision was made for naturalization as Englishmen for those who wished it. Religious freedom was guaranteed. A liberal policy was followed in government and the distribution of land in order to attract new colonists. Such a policy was good business, and the proprietors' interest in the colony was first and always financial. This does not mean that New Jersey was free from difficulties. Right from the start it was to be plagued with problems and perplexities growing out of proprietary rule.

As an indication that colonization was to be the English policy, Nicolls, having established his authority, and unaware of the Duke's grant, issued the so-called Elizabethtown and Monmouth patents, providing for the founding of Jersey towns on the New England model. From this action there developed the settlements of Elizabethtown, Woodbridge, Piscataway, Shrewsbury, and Middletown, established by Puritans from New England and by adventurous Long Islanders. Meanwhile, another group of Puritans from Connecticut, at the invitation of the proprietary government itself, settled north of Elizabethtown and founded Newark in 1666. Berkeley and Carteret had commissioned Philip Carteret, the young cousin of Sir George, as New Jersey's first English governor. Confusion began when Philip arrived at Elizabethtown in 1665 and was surprised to find a settlement under the Nicolls grant. He came with a document that may be viewed as Jersey's first constitution, "The Concessions and Agreements of the Lords Proprietors." It provided for a governor's council, a general assembly chosen by the freeholders, trial by jury, and religious freedom. In return for these generous concessions, the colonists had to take an oath of allegiance to the proprietors and to pay a quitrent (a fixed rent on land payable in lieu of certain feudal services).

The smoldering controversy over the dual land grants broke out when the first assembly met at Elizabethtown in 1668. Many settlers, resenting the feudal demands of the proprietors, held that their grants from Nicolls and deeds of purchase from the Indians gave valid titles to their land, and that the proprietors did not have the right of government. Barred from the assembly for this stand, a number of delegates formed the basis of an antiproprietary party, which refused to pay their quitrents. The revolt spread, and in 1672 five of the settlements — Newark, Elizabethtown, Woodbridge, Piscataway, and Bergen — held a revolutionary assembly at Elizabethtown. They deposed Philip Carteret as governor and elected as "president" James Carteret, dissolute son of Sir George. Philip hastened back to England to explain to his employers that the settlers were insisting that the Duke's grant did not convey governing power and to aid them in presenting their case to the Crown. The latter upheld the rights of Berkeley and Carteret and disallowed the grants of Nicolls.

East Jersey and West Jersey. A sudden attack by Holland swept aside these technical wrangles for the moment. A renewed war between the Dutch and English in 1672 brought a fleet the following year to New York, and once again the territory, including New Jersey, was in Dutch hands. But this was short-lived. Following the cessation of hostilities, it was restored to England by treaty in 1674. Legally the colony had thus reverted to the Crown, so Charles II regranted it to the Duke of York, who reconveyed the eastern part to Sir George Carteret. Philip returned as governor.

Although these measures resolved for the moment the conflicting claims as far as eastern New Jersey was concerned, the situation in the western portion of the colony was completely confused. Before the King reissued the charter to the Duke, Berkeley sold his share for £1,000 to John Fenwick, acting as agent for a fellow Quaker, Edward Byllinge. Immediately these two quarreled over their shares, and William Penn in 1676 arbitrated the dispute, awarding nine-tenths to Byllinge and one-tenth to Fenwick. The former had financial trouble, so Penn and two other Quakers were appointed as trustees. Fenwick and some followers founded Salem, but he, too, subsequently got into difficulties, and most of his lands came under Penn's control. To officially clarify the division of the province, The Quintipartite Deed was signed on July 1, 1676 by Carteret, Byllinge, and the three trustees. A line on the diagonal was drawn northwest from Little Egg Harbor to just north of Delaware Water Gap, Carteret retaining East (northeast) Jersey and the Quakers obtaining West (southwest) Jersey. Thus West Jersey, and not Pennsylvania, was the first Quaker colony.

For the government of this new colony, Penn drew up the "Laws, Concessions, and Agreements," a remarkable document and the most liberal constitution of its time. It provided a representative government having complete control of taxation, with the inhabitants electing the assembly and the judges. The assembly was paid, guaranteed free speech, and selected ten "Commissioners of State" for the executive administration of the colony. The people were provided with complete religious freedom, secret ballot, right of fair trial including trial by jury, no capital punishment, and security of property.

The transference of West Jersey to the Quakers did not mark the end of proprietary difficulties. Upon the death of George Carteret, his wife sold East Jersey at public auction in 1680 to a group of Quakers that included the proprietors of West Jersey. At the same time, the governor of New York, Edmund Andros, claimed the right to rule the eastern province, jailed Philip Carteret when he refused to relinquish the governorship, and insisted that all trade should clear through New York. So much popular disapproval of his actions was aroused that Andros was recalled to England, and the Duke of York officially recognized the independence of the Jerseys from New York.

During the next twenty years the proprietors continued to encounter innumerable difficulties. The colonists, especially those who had migrated from New England and were accustomed to a clear title to their land, challenged through the assembly their authority to rule and exact feudal privileges, and on occasion resorted to rioting. The sale and resale of proprietary rights, accompanied by factional antagonisms, further undermined the proprietors' authority. In addition, the governments were suspended temporarily when New Jersey was annexed to the Dominion of New England from 1688 to 1689. Nevertheless, the population prospered and grew to an estimated 15,000 by the century's end, and nine counties were created — Bergen, Essex, Middlesex, Monmouth, Somerset, Cape May, Burlington, Gloucester, and Salem, in that order. The Quaker settlement of Burlington became the capital of West Jersey in 1680, and the capital of East Jersey was transferred in 1686 to Perth Amboy, which had developed into its principal port.

The Jerseys United. Finally, in 1702, the proprietors of both East Jersey and West Jersey, realizing that further assertion of their dubious claim to political authority was not worth the cost, voluntarily surrendered their governing power to the Crown, and New Jersey became a united royal colony. However, they retained their rights to the land, and this would prove to be a continued source of trouble for the colony. To this very day their successors maintain small offices in Perth Amboy and Burlington, where they meet annually.

The four decades of proprietary rule was an important formative period for New Jersey. The struggle between the colonists and the proprietors intensified in the former a desire for political and economic rights free from feudal restriction and made them recognize that their hopes lay in the assembly. All efforts at permanent political and commercial union with New York were ended. The variety of peoples in terms of religion, ethnic origin, and social background that came in increasing numbers to the colony gave it an energetic society with diversified institutions. Although subsistence farming was the economic base, there were the beginnings of such enterprises as fishing and whaling, pottery making, production of naval stores, and fruit raising, as well as the establishment of highway and ferry transportation. Lastly, it might be noted that although New Jersey was now united, the period of political division left its mark. Because it coincided with geographic and economic factors, the boundary line separating East and West Jersey cut through what is still the least developed part of the state, and down to the present the northeast sector looks to New York while the southwest looks to Philadelphia.

Expanding New Jersey

As a royal province New Jersey made notable progress. The eighteenth century was marked by a rapid growth of population and the development of a more settled existence, a flourishing agricultural economy making Jersey one of the "bread colonies," improvements in transportation, expanding commerce, and the beginnings of a significant iron industry. But it was also a period of unrest and conflict. Administration of the colony from New York was a source of difficulty for a time, proprietary land claims continued to plague the inhabitants, and friction developed between the colonists and the mother country over the issue of self-government.

The settlement of 1702 allowed the proprietors to retain their rights as landlords and guaranteed to the colony the privilege of free trade through Perth Amboy. Despite the merger of the two provinces, separate capitals were maintained, and the assembly met alternately at Perth Amboy and Burlington down to the Revolution. Until 1738, the successive governors of New York were also the governors of New Jersey, but they headed a separate Jersey council and held a special commission that recognized the political independence of the colony.

The governor's council, appointed with his recommendation, acted as an advisory body concerning the administration of government, establishment of courts, and spending of money. It also sat as a court of appeals. In general, the membership was able and included many of the most influential men of the colony.

The General Assembly was the branch of government representing the people, deputies being chosen by the freeholders from each county and the two capitals. But there were property qualifications for voting, and those for holding office were quite high. The assembly's ability to pass laws was limited by the veto power of both the governor and the English Government. But the lower house (so labeled because it represented the people) had the exclusive right to initiate legislation involving money, and this prerogative, as it did in other colonies, proved to be a potent weapon.

Political Friction. From the start of the new government, there were continual complaints by Jerseyans about not having their own governor. Agitation reached its height during the 1730's, and, finally, in 1738 Lewis Morris of Monmouth County was commissioned the first royal governor of New Jersey.

Another source of political unrest was the continued effort of the now-numerous proprietors, who were no more than land speculators, to establish their ascendancy over public affairs. They organized into a number of councils that contested with each other and an anti-proprietary party for control of the government. On occasion, these factions did not find it beneath themselves to resort to bribery and corruption to influence elections, the courts, and the governor's council.

The controversy over land grants that had started during the previous century flared up again. The settlers holding land under the Elizabethtown and Monmouth patents, involving a huge area, would not recognize the jurisdiction of the new proprietors and refused to pay their quitrents. What touched off the dispute was the action of a group of frontiersmen. A number of settlers had taken up unsurveyed land in the hills west of Newark, justifying themselves with the squatter philosophy that the land belonged to the one who used it. They ignored the proprietors and refused to pay quitrents. In 1745 a certain Samuel Baldwin was arrested for cutting trees on a proprietary tract. His neighbors rallied to his defense and set him free, whereupon they were arrested. They in turn were removed from jail by mob action perpetrated by a well-organized band of frontiersmen.

With violence of this proportion, it was time for action by the governor. Jonathan Belcher, previously a conservative governor of Massachusetts, was a New Englander who had little sympathy for quitrents and consequently did nothing to punish the rioters or suppress the unrest. The farmer-dominated assembly did nothing except offer pardons for those already jailed. When the proprietors attempted to dispossess settlers in other areas by court action, further riots broke out, and nothing was done to suppress them. The proprietors appealed to England for support, but before the Crown could take action, the French and Indian War began. The proprietors were now compelled to placate the settlers to enlist their support for the war, while the latter found a new outlet for their fighting energies. Nevertheless, Jerseyans had successfully sustained one of the most important colonial rebellions against feudal privilege.

None of these conflicts did anything to impair the loyalty of the colonists toward the mother country. But, nevertheless, the seeds of revolution were being sown. Each time the prerogative of a distant Crown conflicted with the needs and experiences of the people, each time the General Assembly had one of its laws vetoed by the royal governor or by the English Government itself, each time the colonists felt that they were being neglected rather than interfered with, the gulf between colony and homeland widened.

The only effective device at the disposal of the colonists in trying to overcome this opposition was the power of the purse. As has been mentioned, the assembly had the sole power of initiating financial legislation, which meant that money could not be appropriated without its consent. Several assemblies—New Jersey's was among the leaders in this—developed the practice of appropriating the governor's salary for only one year at a time, and at the end of the term rather than at the beginning. Thus, if the governor did not continuously thwart the colonial will, he was promptly paid; if he vetoed too many measures, he might find his salary unexpectedly delayed or reduced, or, on occasion, he might have trouble collecting it at all. This would not work against a strong, effective executive, but it could be a most potent weapon with a lesser man in office. For example, at the time of Lewis Morris' death, the Jersey assembly had not paid his salary for two years.

Economic and Social Progress. Although torn by political disputes, New Jersey advanced economically and socially during this period. Since the state was blessed with an abundance of land, some of the most fertile soil, and one of the most equable climates in the entire coastal region, a premium was placed upon the industry of the individual farmer. Small farms usually varying in size from ten to 200 acres dotted the landscape. Especially in western Jersey, people lived not in villages but on isolated holdings. Economic pursuits were highly diversified, most of the labor being performed by the farm family. The worker on the farm had to be a Jack-of-all-trades—a farmer, woodsman, and artisan. Thus an economic basis for social equality was present in the colony, and this attracted an extraordinary mixture of peoples—the descendants of the original Dutch and Swedes, English Quakers and Puritans, Finns, French Huguenots, and those who settled the frontier lands: German Pietists and Scotch-Irish. Population leapt forward; there were an estimated 135,000 inhabitants on the eve of the Revolution, with the western section all but doubling the eastern.

The major agricultural products were grains, such as wheat, corn, rye, barley, and oats; livestock, including cows, hogs, sheep, cattle, oxen, and horses; fibers, such as flax, hemp, and silk; fish, such as shellfish, shad, and sturgeon; and such fruits as apples, pears, plums, peaches, and cherries. Related enterprises were dairying, lumbering, shipbuilding, production of naval stores and charcoal, leather tanning, and cider making.

In addition, there developed several manufacturing industries, the principal one being in iron. Mines in what is now Passaic, Sussex, and Morris counties, plus the bog ore found in the southern Pine Barrens supplied the raw material for a number of flourishing iron works. The principal ones were the Mount Holly Iron Works and Batsto in Burlington County, the Ringwood Furnace near the New

York border, the Aetna Forge on Rockaway River, and Hibernia in Morris County. All would supply munitions for the Continental Army during the Revolution. Several of them were set up as manors, with the ironmaster ruling with near-feudal sway over the settlement that developed around the enterprise. The growth of the industry was checked by the restrictions legislated by the British Parliament on exports and the manufacture of certain finished products. Other industries were glass, brick, and pottery making; the famous Stiegel glass works operated during this time.

To facilitate the movement of these goods and improve travel, a number of advances were made in transportation. The principal waterways were the Delaware and its numerous tributaries, and the Raritan, which developed into the prime commercial river of eastern Jersey, with New Brunswick at tidewater and Perth Amboy as the chief port of entry. The Delaware's ports of Burlington, Salem, and Trenton were soon supplanted by Philadelphia, and western Jersey became commercially dependent upon it, just as the eastern section became dependent upon New York City. The principal ferries crossed the Hudson, Passaic, Hackensack, and Delaware.

New Jersey was the leading colony in the development of land transportation. A number of roads were built between the principal towns, and several served as intercolonial connections when linked to water transport. Several stage lines were set up, but the roads, built on early trails, were narrow, winding, stump-infested, and ungraded. Travel was so slow and uncomfortable that the friendly taverns along the way were welcome stopovers.

New Jersey made several important cultural contributions as well. It was the only colony to have more than one college. The College of New Jersey, later Princeton University, was chartered in 1746; Queens College, now Rutgers, the State University, was founded at New Brunswick in 1766. Both were designed to prepare young men for the ministry.

Because of the large numbers of Quakers in western Jersey, that region regarded Philadelphia as its social and cultural metropolis. The Quakers affected the social life of the colony by their strong regard for humanitarian reform. John Woolman, Quaker preacher of Mount Holly, helped to generate strong sentiments against the institution of slavery, and some restriction was placed upon the importation of slaves.

Of a more material nature, some of the finest examples of Dutch colonial architecture were built in the colony—comfortable, modest stone houses in harmony with their surroundings. In addition, the

Finnish settlers in Jersey are credited with the introduction of the log cabin into American frontier life.

Thus, as New Jersey was approaching the last third of the eighteenth century, it had developed into a flourishing colony. It had a diversified economy, expanding towns, and a varied and growing population. Although it was small in size and pulled in two directions, its location was strategic from every point of view. Its people had the benefit of more than a century of experience in dealing with those who would deprive them of what they felt were their rights. From the struggle they developed ideals and practices that helped to promote a sense of self-reliance, a desire for self-government, and a love of liberty. They continued to view themselves as Englishmen, and thoughts of independence from Britain were far from their minds. But a swift sequence of events would bring about an even swifter change of mind and heart.

DO/DISCUSS

1. The encroachment of the white man upon the Indian of New Jersey and his acquisition of some of the Indian's practices illustrate that advanced people can learn from others at a much lower cultural level. Cite some examples in our country and in the world today of where more privileged people can profit in their ways of living from culturally and economically deprived groups.
2. Simulate a meeting between an early New Jersey colonist and a Lenni-Lenape. What wares might each bring in order to interest the other in a trade?
3. What basic daily and institutional needs that confronted the Lenape seem to persist and face the New Jersey resident today?
4. New Jersey has a long history of being populated by various ethnic and religious groups. (a) How might you account for this? (b) In what ways does this serve to the state's advantage?
5. Why do members of the same national, racial, or religious group often tend to settle in the same section of a city or part of a state? Does this general rule apply to

New Jersey? Be prepared to support your position.

6. Between 1660 and 1702 New Jersey was the scene of a spirited economic struggle between colonist and proprietor. In many ways it was not unlike financial negotiations reported in today's newspapers. Each of the following terms is mentioned in this section. Use each word to write a summary sentence reviewing what happened then, and use the same word in a sentence dealing with some current business transaction. Try to find excerpts in your newspaper on: (a) proprietor, (b) ownerships, (c) patents, (d) grant, (e) rent, (f) purchase of titles, (g) charter, (h) issue, (i) shares, (j) transfer, (k) sale, and (l) trustees.

7. Explain the eighteenth-century factors and circumstances that would make the following statement valid: As New Jersey expanded, the time for revolt narrowed.

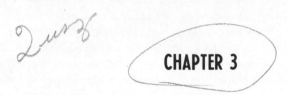

CHAPTER 3

The Revolutionary Era

The history of New Jersey during this period is closely tied to that of the other American colonies in their joint struggle for independence and their subsequent efforts at unification. Grievances against England were not as sharp in New Jersey as they were in other provinces, but an underlying desire and need for freedom caused its citizens to rise up when the moment came to break with the mother country. Few Jerseyans were aware of the central role that their state would play in the Revolutionary War, nor of the social, economic, and political consequences war and achievement of independence would bring. Certainly they could not anticipate the important part that the state would have in the formulation of the Constitution of the United States.

Road to Revolution

The year 1763 marked a turning point in the imperial relationship between England and her thirteen American colonies. Prior to this date, England had failed to control the economic and political life of the colonists in any systematic, thorough, and sustained fashion. As a result of distance, neglect, and accommodation, the colonists had learned to take care of their internal affairs and to ignore the restrictions placed upon their trade by the Navigation Acts. With the signing of the Treaty of Paris in 1763, concluding the Seven Years

44

War (French and Indian War) and marking the triumph of the British Empire, the differences in attitudes and objectives between mother country and colony became acute. With the French out of Canada and the Ohio Valley and their Indian allies neutralized, the colonists were less dependent upon England's protection. Furthermore, as a result of their participation in the fighting, they had developed confidence in their own military ability and a sense of self-respect. One can readily understand their resentment when it was decided that they be taxed to help pay for the huge cost of the war.

British Laws Provoke the Colonies. To enjoy the fruits of victory and establish a more efficient administration of its empire, Britain adopted a series of measures that increasingly provoked colonial opposition and detestation. The Proclamation of 1763 closed the trans-Appalachian West to settlement. The Grenville program enforced the various navigation laws cutting off the profitable trade with the West Indies and included the hated Quartering Act and Stamp Act. The Townshend Acts put more teeth in the regulation of colonial trade, and deprived colonial assemblies of the right to pay the salaries of British officials. These measures all served to incense the colonists, who felt that the freedoms they had previously enjoyed by neglect could never be taken from them. In addition to misjudging the strength of the Americans' desire to manage their own affairs, both King and Parliament fumbled badly in passing, then repealing, then repassing restrictive measures; in failing to immediately repress opposition to their program; and then, when it was too late, in punishing some as examples to the rest. It was these actions that forged a sense of unity among the colonies and made possible their revolt.

The year 1763 was important, as well, for New Jersey itself. It was the year in which the last royal governor of New Jersey came into office. He was William Franklin, the son of Benjamin Franklin, and a man of great ability and dedication to his office. Throughout his term he remained loyal to the Crown that had appointed him; meanwhile, he tried to prevent the alienation of the people from the mother country. In other times he would have succeeded and had a most fruitful administration, but, because of rising tensions and conflict, his initial popularity waned, his power diminished, and eventually he was arrested and banished from New Jersey.

Like the other colonies, Jersey had prospered during the French and Indian War, but, once it was over, began to feel the pinch of a post-war depression. Prices for agricultural commodities declined, and a large number of farm foreclosures occurred. In addition, the province had the largest war debt of any American colony and thus had to maintain a high level of taxation to pay it off. To make matters worse, the Currency Act of 1764 obliged the colonists to redeem all paper money issued during the war and forbade any further printing of such currency. This served to reduce the amount of money in circulation, aggravate the deflation, and make debts, which had been incurred when money was cheap and plentiful, more difficult to pay off. The end result for many was bankruptcy and financial ruin.

Besides economic distress, the situation brought social unrest to the colony. A debtor class of farmers and poor merchants became more evident during this time. As it suffered financially, it came into increasing conflict with the wealthier, more propertied, creditor class. One desired inflationary relief through cheap money, while the other supported the British policy of a sound and stable currency. With conditions worsening, the former grew hostile to the creditors and their supporters in the legal profession. Public demonstrations were held, and sporadic acts of mob violence occurred. On the whole, the public sympathized with the debtors, feeling that they were the victims of injustice and the callousness of those elements in the colony who were economically and politically dominant. The General Assembly responded to their plight by passing a bill in 1770 providing for the issuance of paper money, but it was promptly vetoed as a violation of the Currency Act. This increased the hostility of the lower classes toward the Crown.

Prior to this date, Jerseyans of all classes found themselves swept up in a controversy that affected all the colonies — the stamp tax. The passage of this revenue-raising measure requiring the use of stamps on all legal and commercial documents, newspapers, pamphlets, and playing cards outraged the Americans because it was an internal tax levied without their consent. They asserted that as English subjects they could only be taxed by their elected representatives, and, since they were not represented in Parliament, the Stamp Act was a violation of their basic rights.

Reaction to the measure took different forms. Conservative elements favored dignified petitions and remonstrances. Other groups refused to use the stamps, among them New Jersey lawyers who expressed willingness to sacrifice their income from legal business rather than obey the law. The more radical merchants, farmers, and workers formed loose patriotic societies called Sons of Liberty, which resorted to public demonstrations and acts of violence. When Governor Franklin tried to implement the act, public hostility was so strong that the stamp officer resigned and a replacement of appropriate prominence and influence could not be found.

The Colonies Act in Concert. Most important of all, opposition to the tax brought about the first concerted action of the colonies, the Stamp Act Congress of October, 1765. Initiative for the meeting came from the Massachusetts assembly. Nine colonies sent delegates; New Jersey's representatives were Robert Ogden, Speaker of the Assembly, Hendrick Fisher, and Joseph Borden. The Congress adopted a declaration of rights and grievances, petitioned the King and Parliament for a repeal of the act, and asserted that the colonists could be taxed only by their representatives in their own assemblies. When the Jersey assembly met for its fall session, it unanimously endorsed the action taken.

An important outcome of the Congress was the formation in the various colonies of committees of correspondence, which were instrumental in sustaining nonimportation agreements. So effective was the boycott of British goods that it was the British merchants who pressured Parliament into repealing the Stamp Act in March of 1766. But Parliament, wishing to assert Britain's supremacy, immediately passed the Declaratory Act, which reaffirmed the principle of parliamentary power to tax the colonies. Throughout the colonies the news of the Stamp Act's repeal brought about great rejoicing and a sense of accomplishment in having forced England to back down. For the moment, the Declaratory Act was ignored. The nonimportation agreements were dissolved, trade was resumed, the Sons of Liberty subsided, and peace was restored.

The calm was short-lived, however, for in 1767 the Townshend Acts were adopted. Once again the colonists resorted to a variety of acts of opposition. Constitutional arguments against the new tariff duties were formulated, the radicals retaliated against the customs regulations with acts of violence, and the merchants again turned to nonimportation agreements. In May of 1768, the New Jersey assembly petitioned the Crown reiterating the protest against taxation without representation. Tension and hostility mounted for the next few years, culminating in the so-called Boston Massacre early in 1770. Things did not come to a head, however, for at this very time the Townshend duties were repealed—all except the tax on tea, which was retained to assert Britain's right of taxation.

Most Americans considered the repeal to be a conciliatory action that justified a resumption of normal relations. In New Jersey, Governor Franklin handled things so well that the overwhelming majority of the people were not influenced by the handful who continued agitating, and the colony enjoyed several years of peace and calm.

This tranquillity was suddenly shattered by the famous Boston Tea Party, which occurred in December, 1773. This action touched off a renewed wave of patriotic fervor. A new committee of correspondence was promptly appointed by the Jersey assembly. Matters came to a head when England retaliated against the tea dumping with the passage of the Intolerable Acts, designed to punish the Bostonians and all citizens of Massachusetts and serve as a warning to the other colonists that defiance of the mother country would not be tolerated.

Rather than accomplishing their intended purposes, these acts created a wave of sympathy for the economic plight of the people of Boston, whose port was closed. Supplies were sent from sister colonies to aid in their relief. Beyond the commercial restriction was the more serious display of arbitrary and naked power shown by Parliament in depriving Massachusetts of much of its self-government. For American colonists this meant either abject surrender and the admission that they had no inherent rights or the taking of a clear-cut stand in self-defense, since every other colony could be treated in a similar fashion. Everywhere assemblies, town meetings, and committees of correspondence denounced the Intolerable Acts in speeches, resolutions, and pamphlets, while townspeople again staged demonstrations and dealt violently with British agents and their colonial supporters.

Governor Franklin did everything in his power to restrain the patriot leaders in his colony and to disunite the people. But his efforts failed, and once again New Jersey entered directly into actions of colonial unity. When the Virginia assembly sent out a call for a congress of all the American colonies, New Jersey was quick to respond. Initiative was assumed by the radical leaders of Essex County in arranging a meeting of elected delegates from all the counties for the purpose of selecting the colony's representatives.

The meeting opened on July 21, 1774 at New Brunswick and became Jersey's first Provincial Congress. A number of the delegates present were members of the General Assembly. Stephen Crane of Newark was chosen as chairman, and, after affirming their loyalty to the Crown, the delegates got down to business. They declared their support for Massachusetts, protested against parliamentary taxation, and pledged support of the actions of the forthcoming congress in obtaining relief from oppression, urging it to pass a new boycott of British goods. Five delegates were chosen to represent the colony at the First Continental Congress: Stephen Crane, William Livingston (later to be the state's first governor), John DeHart, James Kinsey, and Richard Smith.

Delegates from all the colonies but Georgia met in Philadelphia on September 5. Although united in opposition to the Intolerable Acts, the representatives were divided between the radicals, who wished to sever all but the lightest ties with Britain, and the moderates, who insisted upon colonial autonomy, or control of internal affairs, but accepted imperial regulation of external trade. The moderates prevailed, and there were adopted a Declaration of Rights and Grievances and a petition to the King. To put teeth into their demands, a Continental Association was established to supervise and enforce a stringent boycott of English goods. Local committees in each colony were formed and used every means from persuasion to force to assure that the nonimportation, nonexportation, and nonconsumption agreements were obeyed. The association worked in favor of the radicals by fanning the fires of rebellion and lawlessness abroad in the colonies. Refusal to participate in the campaign became synonomous with toryism. This compelled many moderates to go along with the rising tide and hopelessly widened the gulf between patriots and loyalists.

Jersey Catches the Rebel Spirit. The spirit of rebellion and lawlessness caught on dramatically in New Jersey and can best be exemplified by a "tea party" of its own that the colony experienced in December of 1774. It was brought about when the captain of a ship bound for Philadelphia with a load of tea decided that there might be some difficulties if he attempted to land his cargo there. Instead, he stopped at Greenwich in Burlington County and unloaded and stored the tea in the cellar of a local tory. When word of this spread, patriots from the area decided to take action and followed the example set for them in Boston just one year earlier. Disguised as Indians, the band broke into the storage cellar, seized the tea, and burnt it publicly in the Greenwich market square. One of the leaders of the tea party was Richard Howell, who later became governor of the state. The owners of the tea brought a damage suit against those of the band who could be identified, which caused the public to spring to their support. A subscription to raise money for their defense was instituted, and three prominent lawyers were engaged. One of them was Joseph Bloomfield, who also was later elected governor of the state. The defendants were found innocent in the civil action, and all charges were dropped because no jury could be found to convict them in a criminal case.

Governor Franklin's position now grew increasingly untenable. The situation in the colony was becoming more tense, and, although he still retained much of his personal popularity, Franklin's belief

in England's absolute authority clashed with the assembly's support
of colonial liberty. Early in 1775 the assembly unanimously approved
the actions of the Continental Congress, sent a separate petition to
the Crown for redress of grievances, and proceeded to choose a new
slate of delegates to the forthcoming Second Continental Congress.
With the outbreak of fighting at Lexington and Concord, the populace were aroused to the point where they were no longer satisfied
with a royal legislature under the control of the governor. A call was
sent out by the committee of correspondence for another Provincial
Congress to be held in Trenton on May 23.

Before they could meet, Franklin recalled the General Assembly
into session to consider certain supposedly conciliatory proposals
from England. After rejecting them, the assembly accused the governor of trying to split the colonists into factions, and promptly
adjourned. When the second Provincial Congress met, it declared its
allegiance to the King and then proceeded to set up a revolutionary
government. It declared that future delegates to any colonial congress would be selected by it and not by the assembly, it set up a Committee of Safety to act when it was not in session, and it took steps
to organize a militia and raise money for defense. Thereupon, a
succession of Provincial Congresses met, each one organizing the
revolutionary government of the colony on a firmer footing than before and making further preparations for war.

Meanwhile, the Second Continental Congress met in Philadelphia
on May 10, 1775 and proceeded to act. The Continental Army was
established with George Washington as commander in chief, a "Declaration of Causes of Taking Up Arms" was issued to explain why
the colonists were resisting the British military forces, and an "olive
branch" petition was dispatched to George III in a last effort to win
concessions. At the same time, military campaigns were initiated
by both sides, bloodshed increased, and a full-scale war was under
way. Yet more than a year would elapse before final independence
was declared, primarily because the vast majority of Americans, although they wanted liberty and self-government, were not willing to
break all ties with the mother country.

All the steps taken by the Continental Congress were supported
by New Jersey's Provincial Congresses, but the General Assembly
seemed to fall back under the influence of the governor. When the
assembly met late in 1775, Franklin was able to win over a number of
representatives to the loyalist side, and there was some fear that they
might come to terms with the Crown. This caused the Continental
Congress to dispatch a committee to Burlington to prevent such an

occurrence. The assembly finally adjourned on December 6 without taking any significant action either way, and this marked the last meeting of a royal legislature in New Jersey.

For all intents and purposes, the Provincial Congress was now the actual government of the colony. It organized three battalions of soldiers for the army, issued paper money for military supplies, and set up a new system of voting open only to those who pledged support of the American cause. At one point, in open defiance, Governor Franklin attempted to reconvene the legislature. For this he was declared an enemy and ordered arrested. When he refused to obey or appear before the Provincial Congress, the matter was turned over to the Continental Congress, which had him banished to Connecticut and placed under custody of the authorities there. This occurred in late June of 1776, making William Franklin one of the last royal governors to be removed from office, a tribute to his skill and initial popularity.

Independence Is Declared. As these events transpired in New Jersey, Americans in all the colonies were gradually accepting the necessity of independence. Military combat and mob violence became widespread. Thomas Paine's pamphlet *Common Sense* had a profound effect in arousing the patriotic zeal of the colonists and convincing them of the logic of open rebellion. In colony after colony, independent governments were set up. Finally, on June 7, Richard Henry Lee of Virginia proposed in the Continental Congress that it adopt a resolution of independence. A committee was appointed to draft a formal declaration, and an intense debate ensued on Lee's resolution. It was ultimately carried on July 2, and the Declaration of Independence, written by Thomas Jefferson, was adopted on July 4.

In preparation for this momentous step, New Jersey's Provincial Congress on June 22 selected five new delegates to the Continental Congress with authorization to vote for independence and organize a union of the thirteen colonies. They were Richard Stockton, John Witherspoon, Francis Hopkinson, John Hart, and Abraham Clark, all of whom signed the Declaration of Independence. At the same time the Jersey congress appointed a committee of ten headed by Reverend Jacob Green of Morris County to draft a new constitution in preparation for statehood. The document was drawn up by the committee and then debated with amazing speed. It was adopted by the Provincial Congress on July 2, two days before the Declaration. The congress continued to function through the summer, until elections under the new constitution were held and the state government established.

Cockpit of the Revolution

For more than a year, since Lexington and Concord, fighting between American and British forces had occurred on a number of divergent fronts, all distant from New Jersey. However, following the Declaration of Independence, the tide of war shifted to New York and Philadelphia, and from then on the strategic location of New Jersey made it a focal point of the conflict. On a line between these two principal cities, one the American capital, the state was a major target for British conquest. Furthermore, New Jersey was a principal link between New England and the South, and its continued occupation could have broken the back of revolutionary resistance. From the end of 1776 on, New Jersey was the scene of four major battles and close to 100 minor engagements, and was the site of three winter encampments of Washington's army.

Warfare in the state, as elsewhere, was not limited to engagements between the two military forces. New Jersey was plagued with a loyalist problem, for about half the population was sympathetic to England, if not outright hostile to the revolution. Although it is wrong to assume that division was solely on class lines, with all those of the upper classes in the tory ranks and all of the lower classes as patriots, the greatest strength of the former was found amongst the wealthier and more influential elements. These included some of the leading government officials, the proprietors and greatest landowners, Quakers and Anglicans, the conservative lawyers, and the wealthier merchants of Perth Amboy and elsewhere.

Many of these loyalists were a constant thorn in the side of the patriot cause. That they did not cause more serious harm can only be attributed to the fact that England did not organize them into military units until late in the war. When they did actively support British forces occupying a particular area, they quickly found themselves subject to swift reprisal by patriot committees as soon as the troops marched away. Nevertheless, throughout the war, the state experienced frequent raids by tory and patriot bands. Added to this was the loss and misery brought to citizens on both sides by the forays of the Hessians and the "pine robbers" of the shore region.

Washington's Victories at Trenton and Princeton. It was in the critical winter of 1776 that New Jersey first felt the full impact of the Revolution. Following the capture of New York City by the British, their victories in surrounding areas, and the seizure of Fort Washington and Fort Lee, George Washington withdrew the remnant of his forces across New Jersey in a series of moves that constituted a retreat in everything but name. Had General Howe pursued and engaged them, he might have crushed all American resistance. But once Washington had his army safely entrenched on the west side of the Delaware River, and with winter setting in, the exhausted troops were safe. Nonetheless, this was a low point in the patriot cause; public confidence had all but vanished, and the Continental Army was reduced to 3,000 men.

Once again Tom Paine rose to the occasion and with his pen supplied the needed boost to morale. The first of a series of essays entitled *The Crisis* appeared, with its ringing declaration, "These are the times that try men's souls." It was accompanied by a stroke of brilliance on Washington's part: the surprise attack upon the British garrison at Trenton. There were 1,400 troops stationed there, mostly Hessian mercenaries. They were unprepared for battle and held the American soldier in contempt; in addition, they were detested by the local inhabitants because of their plundering, which caused a number of lukewarm tories to join the patriot side. Washington chose Christmas night for the assault, certain that the garrison had spent the day in celebrating and carousing. His troops crossed the Delaware amidst sleet and snow at McKonkey's Ferry, eight miles north of Trenton, and swept down upon the town early in the morning. They surprised and defeated the enemy, killing their commander and capturing 1,000 men, and immediately recrossed the river, taking their prisoners with them. The quick victory was a stunning blow to the British and did a great deal to buoy up American hopes.

However, Washington's army was not out of danger. Lord Cornwallis brought up reinforcements and by January 2 had concentrated 8,000 troops around Trenton. Washington drew together every solder that could be found to defend his position. Fortunately for the Americans, when the attack came it was halfhearted and ended with nightfall. Although a minor action, this second battle of Trenton was of great importance. Once again, the British missed an opportunity to destroy the American army and perhaps end the Revolution. Instead, they gave Washington an opportunity to carry out another brilliant maneuver. Leaving their campfires burning, the rebels slipped away and marched on Princeton to the north. There they engaged three British regiments in pitched battle and finally defeated and routed them. The victorious Americans then rapidly withdrew from the region and took up winter quarters to the north at Morristown. Thus they eluded Cornwallis' effort to crush them and at the same time handed a segment of his forces a smart defeat.

The victories at Trenton and Princeton had very important results and are considered among the turning points of the war. They showed that British troops could be defeated in direct combat by American soldiers. The superior and hitherto-victorious invaders were reduced to acting on the defensive. Philadelphia was saved and Pennsylvania freed from danger. Most of New Jersey was spared enemy occupation, for Cornwallis was compelled to withdraw his forces from exposed positions and return to the environs of New York, keeping his advance units in the New Brunswick-Perth Amboy area. Washington proved himself to be an outstanding military strategist, causing the Continental Congress to give him full control of the army. Above all, new confidence was given to Americans that their cause could succeed.

Washington selected the rugged hill country around Morristown as the site for his army's encampment because of its geographic location. Only thirty miles from the main English forces in New York, the Americans could keep track of their movements and guard the main lines of communication connecting Philadelphia and New England. At the same time they were protected from attack by the ridges of the Watchung Mountains to the east.

During the months of 1777 that followed, Washington rested and reorganized his weary army and gathered supplies for the coming campaigns. A good part of the munitions used by the American forces came from nearby iron forges. Washington and his men remained at Morristown through the spring waiting to determine what action the enemy would take. The British abandoned their plan to conquer the capital at Philadelphia by means of an overland expedition through New Jersey. Instead, General Howe embarked the bulk of his army on transports, in order to attack the city from the sea.

Philadelphia Falls to the British. The British expedition chose the longest route, via Chesapeake Bay instead of the Delaware, because the latter was so well fortified. This gave Washington plenty of time to move his army from Morristown to a position south of Philadelphia. He met the enemy at Brandywine Creek, but could do no more than retard the advance of the vastly superior force. The British occupied the capital on September 27, 1777, and the gallant American attack at Germantown to dislodge them was a complete failure. The capture of Philadelphia was a hard blow to American prestige. Congress was forced to flee and spent the next years in one location after another. The British settled down to a comfortable winter in the city, while the Continental Army experienced hunger and cold some twenty miles away at Valley Forge.

The occupation of Philadelphia, however, did not have the military effects intended. As long as the Americans were able to retain control of the lower Delaware and bay regions, the British could not bring in supplies and reinforcements via the Atlantic Ocean. In addition to the natural obstacles to British navigation of shoals and mud banks patriot forces planted ingenious traps in the river channel designed to foul unsuspecting vessels. One type of obstacle erected was the *Chevaux-de-frise,* or barriers of sharp sticks, which anticipated modern tank traps. During the months of October and November several critical battles were fought. British and Hessian forces under Count von Donop on October 22 attacked the village of Red Bank (Gloucester County), seven miles south of Philadelphia. They were badly beaten in a bloody engagement, the Count was killed, and British and Hessian losses were close to 500 men. Fort Mifflin on Mud Island was surrounded and besieged from September to November 16. A gallant band of Americans defended the post until they finally were forced to evacuate after the walls were literally leveled by gunfire. Four days later Fort Mercer at Red Bank was abandoned and destroyed to keep it out of enemy hands.

It was another rough winter for the American troops, but the defense of the Delaware did prevent any further significant enemy action. The coming of spring brought renewed hope for the revolutionary cause. The great victory at Saratoga in the autumn of 1777 and the clever negotiations of Benjamin Franklin finally bore fruit: on February 6, 1778 a treaty of alliance was signed with France. The British became convinced that their position at Philadelphia had become precarious, for they would be unable to defend themselves if a French fleet came up the Delaware. General Howe was replaced by Sir Henry Clinton, who was authorized to evacuate the city. The British strategy was to concentrate forces in New York, and this was to be accomplished by an overland march through New Jersey.

Evacuation took place on June 18, and the British proceeded via Mount Holly, Crosswicks, and Allentown, to Freehold. Washington, alert to every enemy move, left Valley Forge and crossed into New Jersey three days later. He followed a course to the north of Clinton's and decided to attack at Freehold. What followed was the battle of Monmouth Court House.

The Battle of Monmouth. It was General Washington's intention at first not to have a pitched battle with the British Army, but the turn of events forced his hand. On June 28 an advance force under General Charles Lee attacked the enemy. Just when the Americans seemed to be winning, Lee ordered a withdrawal, which turned into a disorderly retreat. Washington arrived on the scene as the British were preparing a counterattack. He relieved Lee of his command

and dismissed him from the field, rallied the American troops, and checked the enemy. Following the day-long engagement fought in intense heat, Clinton withdrew his forces under the cover of night, leaving the Continental Army in possession of the field.

The battle was a victory for the Americans, who had stood up to the best that the British could throw into the field. Only the indecision or treachery of General Lee prevented a more decisive result, one that might have shortened the war. The enemy troops were forced-marched to Sandy Hook, where they were taken to the safety of New York City. All that Washington could do was move his forces northward through New Jersey, going via Paramus to Haverstraw, where he crossed the Hudson into Westchester County. He encamped at White Plains, fortified West Point, and waited for an opening to attack.

The battle of Monmouth was successful in producing the Revolutionary War's outstanding heroine. Mary Hays, the wife of an artilleryman, had been aiding the troops by providing them with spring water to slake their thirst caused by the heat of the day and of battle. When she saw her husband cut down by enemy fire, she quickly replaced him at his cannon. Mary helped fire the weapon throughout the battle, displaying great courage and skill. The next day she was presented to Washington and, it is reported, was rewarded for her valor with a sergeant's commission. This is how "Molly Pitcher" came into being.

Monmouth was the last general engagement of the war fought in the northern part of the country. For the next two years there was little significant military action. As far as New Jersey was concerned, sporadic guerrilla fighting continued, and a number of enterprising citizens turned to privateering. This combined the patriotic activity of destroying enemy shipping with the profitable venture of selling the goods seized in the process. Toms River and Little Egg Harbor were the centers for privateering, and the British had to divert much military effort to limit these harassments.

Final Phases of the War in Jersey. New Jersey was the site of another winter encampment of the Continental Army, in 1779-1780. Once again, Washington chose Morristown, establishing his headquarters at the mansion built by the ironmaster Colonel Jacob Ford and stationing the main body of nearly 10,000 troops in nearby Jockey Hollow. These were dark days for the revolutionary cause. The war had dragged on for a number of years, finances were in a state of collapse with Continental currency almost worthless and the states refusing to meet requisitions, and the troops were without proper food, clothing, or pay. To worsen matters, the country was in the grip of one of the severest winters of the century. The hardships, bitter cold, hunger, and disease — some would contend worse than at Valley Forge — reduced morale to the breaking point, and incidents of mutiny occurred.

When in the spring of 1780 the British heard of the unrest among the American troops, they sent a major force from Staten Island in the direction of Morristown. They were met first at Connecticut Farms, in what is now Union, on June 7 and then at Springfield on June 23. The stout defense of these points by the Americans discouraged any further enemy advance, and, after burning the towns, the British withdrew from New Jersey. These were the state's last military engagements of the war. However, once again, late in the summer of 1781, it was traversed by military forces. This time it was two well-equipped armies, the American under Washington and the French under Count de Rochambeau, on their way to Chesapeake Bay and the siege of the British at Yorktown.

Although General Cornwallis surrendered his entire force on October 17, 1781, two years elapsed before the final peace treaty between Great Britain and the United States was signed. During the interval, Jerseyans were constantly reminded that hostilities were not over. Privateering activities, British reprisals, "refugee raids," and general civil unrest continued to plague the state and make life miserable for its inhabitants. Monmouth County bore the brunt of internal discord, for here patriots and tories plundered one another without a halt. In addition, illegal trading with the British became widespread, and no effective means were found to suppress it. It can well be imagined with what joy and relief the official proclamation of the war's end was greeted.

The Internal Revolution

Second in significance only to the winning of independence from England were the domestic upheavals and changes wrought by the bitter struggle. The War of Independence can be looked upon as a two-fold revolution: the external one, which involved the successful breaking away of thirteen colonies from their mother country, and the internal one, which gave Americans the opportunity to express in concrete form their ideals as enunciated in the Declaration of Independence. The latter included the transformation of the colonies into states, the adoption of new political institutions, the readjustment of society to new conditions, and the formation of a durable union. Although there are some who contend that this second revolution has continued down to the present, all would agree that it completed an important stage of its development when the Federal republic was launched in 1789.

As might be expected, the changes that took place in New Jersey roughly paralleled those that occurred in her sister states. The parallel was less than exact because of differences in people, political traditions, and structure of society; because of the prolonged, bitter fighting that took place on New Jersey soil; and because of the state's unique geographic and economic status. Small in area, split into two sections with distinct historic, economic, and cultural attitudes, lacking in large cities or a frontier, and situated between the commercial centers of Philadelphia and New York, New Jersey was caught up in the sweep of events.

The New State and Its Constitution. New Jersey's transformation from a colony to a state in the summer of 1776 was accomplished speedily and without a hitch, although the process did not adhere too closely to the principles of popular sovereignty set down in the Declaration. As described earlier, the new constitution was drawn up, debated, and adopted as ordinary law by the Provincial Congress in a matter of days, even though that body had not been elected to act as a constitutional convention. Nor was the constitution submitted to the people for a popular referendum. There was no opposition to this method of constitution making; it was tacitly agreed that with the British fleet anchored off Sandy Hook, immediate action was necessary and the congress had the right to act in the name of the people.

The state constitution of 1776 was a simple, brief document, based mainly upon colonial models and experience. This was done on purpose, to make the form of government as similar to its predecessor as possible, so that adjustment to the new state government would be efficient and readily accepted. Political authority was vested in a governor and a legislature composed of two houses, the Legislative Council and the General Assembly.

Because of the bitter experiences American colonists had had with tyrannical executives (both kings and royal governors), New Jersey's governor, like those of other states, was given limited powers and bound by severe restrictions. He was completely dependent upon the legislature and subject to annual election by joint meeting of both houses. Although supposedly granted "supreme executive power," he had no control over appointments and lacked the veto power. In total, his duties were more judicial than executive. He was designated as chancellor and surrogate general and was presiding officer of the council, which acted as a court of appeals, the state's highest court.

The legislative branch enjoyed complete supremacy. It had the power to elect, in addition to the governor, the entire judiciary and the principal administrative officials on the state and county levels. Its actions were not subject to judicial review (the authority of the courts to determine the unconstitutionality of a law). The only restrictions upon its power were that it could not abolish annual elections, trial by jury, or freedom of religion.

The right of suffrage was extended to all inhabitants who were worth £50, eliminating the requirement of colonial times that one had to be a freeholder or landowner to have political rights. This greatly increased the number of eligible voters. However, the property qualifications for holding state office were kept quite high.

There were several other undemocratic features present in the constitution. No provision was made for amendments, nor was there a separate bill of rights. Some recognition was given in the body of the constitution to the people's rights. As mentioned previously, trial by jury could not be revoked and religious liberty was recognized. The latter, nevertheless, although an improvement over colonial times, was not complete. The right to hold office was guaranteed only to Protestants, and, while there could be no established church for the entire state, individual communities were not prevented from supporting with public funds the activities of a chosen sect.

Following the first elections under the new constitution, the state legislature convened in Princeton on August 27, 1776. At a joint session of the two houses William Livingston was elected governor, a position he was to hold for fourteen successive terms until his death in 1790. During the early stages of the Revolutionary War when the British were overrunning the state, Livingston and the legislature were forced to move from place to place to avoid capture. As the state was gradually reconquered by Washington's forces, it became possible for the elected officials to carry on the functions of government in as normal a fashion as could be expected during a life-or-death struggle for independence. Livingston was able to overcome the handicap of limited administrative power. His keen mind, intense drive, practical abilities, and great popularity enabled him to succeed to a marked degree in advancing the interests of New Jersey and in maintaining close co-operation with the central government.

Economic Problems. The problems faced by the state were legion. The physical consequences of prolonged warfare were widespread and serious. Added to the obvious loss of life, crippling of bodies, and destruction of buildings, crops, and livestock were a dislocation of business, paralysis of trade, and fluctuation in the value of currency throughout the war years. However, it would be wrong to assume that all sections and classes in the state were affected equally. West Jersey suffered less than the eastern part of the state, because it was removed from the major scenes of conflict, was primarily rural, and was more influenced by Quaker pacifism. At least 500 tory estates were confiscated and broken up or sold intact to those who had fought in or supported the Revolution. Proprietary claims were markedly reduced, especially those of the East Jersey group, whose leadership had been predominantly loyalist. Although all classes felt the effects of heavier taxes and inflation, the first was a heavy blow to the small farmers, and the second most directly injured the creditor group.

With the war's end, economic conditions grew worse rather than better. Industries, like that of iron extraction and manufacture, which had boomed during the war, experienced a sharp contraction. Agriculture also suffered from a loss of demand brought on by disbanding of the army. Efforts made to stimulate the state's foreign commerce failed; the merchants of Philadelphia and New York resumed their role as middlemen for Jersey's trade. Recovery was further impeded by the rush to purchase British goods being dumped at low prices in American ports. This checked the development of domestic enterprise and caused a further drain of hard money from the country.

Social and Cultural Changes. Less obvious, but of marked significance, were the changes that took place in New Jersey society. Orderly existence was disrupted, traditional patterns of social and political control were destroyed, economic shifts created new business opportunities, and a desire for a greater voice gripped the lower classes. The aristocratic elements were discredited because of active support for or passive identification with English colonial rule. Semifeudal privileges and restrictions were removed. Society became more dynamic, and a new leadership came to the fore. This leadership was not egalitarian or radical, nor did it come from the lower classes.

It was the rising middle class that took advantage of the opportunities presented by republican ideals and the practices of broadened suffrage, frequent elections, and increased numbers of elective offices. Where formerly many officials were appointed by the royal governor and the governor's council, now the popularly elected legislature in turn elected dozens of officials from the governor down to aldermen. Thus political authority was no longer monopolized by a group of aristocrats who could curry favor from king or governor, but was thrown open to those willing and able to gain public support.

Although social and cultural institutions were not subject to total upheaval, their post-war reconstruction brought about some important accomplishments. The various religious denominations had the task of rebuilding their churches and congregations. This was especially true of the Presbyterians, who had been the most ardent supporters of the Revolution and consequently suffered the strongest retaliation from the British. Some organizational changes were also made; most significant was the severing of the Anglican Church's ties with England and its establishment as the Episcopal Church. But The firm belief of the Quakers in pacifism and their general conservatism caused them to take no part in the conflict. Their property was seized and some were attacked, but that they did not suffer more serious consequences can be attributed to their strong position in West Jersey.

During these trying years, the Friends experienced a spiritual revival and increased their efforts in support of humanitarian reform. They were partially successful in a campaign for the abolition of slavery. Their efforts were reinforced by the social ferment brought on by the Revolution and the recognition of the incompatibility between slavery and the principles of the Declaration of Independence. In 1786 and 1788, legislation was passed prohibiting the importation of slaves and authorizing voluntary manumission, or freeing of slaves. In addition, certain abuses were outlawed, and a master was made responsible for teaching his slaves to read. Unfortunately, the tide of reform did not completely sweep away the evil of human bondage from New Jersey.

Another area of interest shown by the Quakers and others was the advancement of education. Restoration and expansion of schools were so rapid that they quickly outstripped their pre-war level. Most of them were private, supported by tuition and donations, but some of the towns had public schools. The number of grammar schools and academies also increased rapidly. The state's two institutions of higher education, however, were more drastically affected by the war. The College of New Jersey was able to make a strong comeback by 1790, but Queens College was plagued with a series of misfortunes and was forced to shut down in 1795 for a twelve-year period.

Although most historians do not accept the notion that conditions in the United States were so desperate as to warrant calling the 1780's "the critical period," it is recognized that the post-war years were trying times. New Jersey had its full share of difficulties. The derangement of the state's finances by the Revolution posed a most serious problem. Although Jersey had issued far less paper money than most other states, its citizens were stuck with large amounts of Continental currency and promissory certificates, which they had accepted in payment for the supplies and services given to the troops during the war. The significance of this will be recognized when one recalls the expression "not worth a Continental." To deal with the resulting inflation, the legislature sharply deflated the value of money and increased taxation to pay off the public debt.

These measures caused severe economic distress for many, especially those in the lower classes. Added to the decline in demand for farm produce was the drop in prices, resulting in an agricultural depression. Many farmers were unable to make payments on their mortgages and found their farms foreclosed by creditors. Jails were soon filled with debtors unable to meet their obligations. As conditions worsened, sporadic acts of mob violence broke out. Efforts were made to interfere with courts sentencing debtors to jail, and in some instances there was resistance to tax collections. Although the action taken was mild compared with Shays' Rebellion in Massachusetts, it did demonstrate that relief was needed. The legislature responded by passing laws to ease the plight of debtors and by issuing a moderate amount of paper money to lessen the impact of the deflation.

Conflicts with Neighbors.   New Jersey's internal problems were worsened by the difficulties it had with its neighbors. The printing of paper money caused the merchants of New York and Philadelphia to question the value of Jersey currency and refuse to accept it in payment for goods. The states of New York and Pennsylvania imposed a protective tariff on foreign commodities brought into their ports for the purpose of halting the flood of English goods pouring into America. This hurt Jerseyans, for they now had to pay higher prices for their purchases. As a further strain upon interstate relations, New York imposed entrance and clearance fees upon boats of all sizes bound to and from Connecticut and New Jersey, treating them like ships of a foreign nation. This incensed New Jersey to the extent that the legislature placed a tax on the lighthouse that New York had erected on Sandy Hook. Except for retaliation of this sort, Jerseyans were powerless to do anything about the harmful and discriminatory acts of their neighbors. They realized from the very beginning that their only hope lay in transferring the control of commerce to a central government.

When in June of 1776 the Second Continental Congress was weighing the momentous question of a declaration of independence, it recognized that some form of union of the thirteen states was necessary to carry on the revolution. A committee was formed to draw up a constitution, and its efforts resulted in the Articles of Confederation. Consideration of this document was delayed for over a year, and finally, on November 15, 1777, the Congress adopted it and urgently requested that the states ratify it as quickly as possible. The states, however, were not to be hurried in taking such an important step. New Jersey strongly urged a major amendment that would have given the central Government exclusive power to regulate foreign trade and levy a tariff. The state was persuaded to give up this change, and, for the good of the Union, it ratified the document on November 26, 1778. It was the eleventh to do so. The Articles of Confederation, requiring approval by all thirteen states, did not go into effect until 1781, when Maryland finally ratified them.

Jersey and the Articles of Confederation. Although, in the main, New Jersey co-operated with the Confederacy, it continued to press for a strengthening of the Confederacy's powers. In addition to the right to regulate trade, it wanted to see control over Western lands vested in Congress. These changes would remove the commercial restrictions of New Jersey's neighbors and provide enough revenue through land sales and a tariff on imports for the functioning of the central Government. Congress would not have to request money from the states, which New Jersey, lacking Western lands and foreign commerce, could meet only through increased taxation of its citizens. Every effort made to extend to Congress the power to levy a tariff was doomed to failure. Consent of all thirteen states was required, and unanimous support could not be obtained.

When in 1785 Congress requested money from the states, New Jersey refused to meet her share of the requisition until the other states accepted the tariff plan. This action struck a severe blow to the Confederacy and increased pessimism over the future of the Union. A special committee of Congress was sent to the Jersey legislature to plead with it to rescind its stand. Once again, an appeal to preserve the Union had its effect. The resolution of refusal to support the requisition was removed. However, the state never did make any payments, maintaining that it could not as long as its neighbors continued their trade restrictions.

Because it found itself at the mercy of larger and more powerful states unwilling to turn over any real authority to the Confederacy, it is not surprising that New Jersey was in the forefront of the movement to revise the Articles of Confederation. When invitations were extended to all states to attend a conference at Annapolis, Maryland, in September of 1786 to discuss the problem of interstate commerce, Jersey was one of the five to respond. The legislature instructed its commissioners to take up as well any "other important matters" necessary to the interest of the Union. These instructions became the keynote of the Annapolis Convention, but because so few states were represented, no action could be taken. It was recommended that all the states to be invited once more to another convention to be held at Philadelphia the following May to consider strengthening the Union. Congress supported this move, calling for a revision of the Articles of Confederation. Thus the spark ignited by New Jersey caught fire.

Jersey's Role in Drawing Up the Constitution. So anxious was the state to see a change of government, it was the first to appoint delegates. The four Jerseyans who actually participated in the convention were David Brearley, Jonathan Dayton. Governor William Livingston, and William Paterson, all excellent men. When the Constitutional Convention got under way on May 25, 1787, two things were immediately apparent. One was that rather than amending the Articles, a new constitution would be written. The other was that in control of the convention were those who wished a national government rather than a slightly stronger confederacy. Their proposals were contained in what became known as the Virginia or large-state plan.

The delegates from some of the smaller states were alarmed at the amount of power to be concentrated in the central Government and fearful that the larger, more populous states would dominate the new Union. They came up with a counterproposal. On June 15 William Paterson introduced the New Jersey or small-state plan, which opposed the basic elements of the other plan. Although the large states, outnumbering the small, were able to shelve the Jersey plan, they were forced to make a significant concession to the smaller states. Under the terms of the Great Compromise, it was agreed that the national legislature would consist of two houses: a Senate providing equal representation for the states and a House of Representatives based upon population. Another provision of Paterson's proposal that, with slightly different wording, became a key clause in the Constitution was the recognition of the supremacy of Federal law.

When the Federal Constitution was submitted to the states for their approval, New Jersey was the third to ratify. The legislature called for a special election so that the voters in each county could elect three delegates to meet as a ratifying convention. The convention so chosen assembled in Trenton, debated the Constitution section by section, and finally ratified it unanimously on December 18, 1787.

Before adjourning, the convention went on record in favor of offering a district ten miles square as the site for a permanent Federal capital. This was not a sudden inspiration. The Continental Congress had twice held sessions in New Jersey, at Princeton in 1783 and at Trenton in 1784. On two occasions it had voted to accept an offer from New Jersey to place the future capital near Trenton. But these efforts were blocked by rival states. The offer of 1787, followed by another the next year, came to naught. The Congress was unprepared to establish a permanent location and decided that New York would be the temporary capital when the new Government was launched in 1789.

In a number of states efforts to bring about acceptance of the Federal Constitution resulted in prolonged and bitter contests. In several cases ratification could only be achieved by the promise that a bill of rights would be added that would specifically guarantee the civil liberties of the people. When the first Federal Congress met, it quickly fulfilled the pledge by adopting on September 25, 1789 the appropriate constitutional amendments. On November 20 New Jersey became the first state to ratify the Bill of Rights.

Jersey in a Crucial Period. Thus the period between 1763 and 1789 was clearly a crucial one for New Jersey. It was converted in a few short years from a loyal colony desiring a measure of self-rule to an independent state with a new constitution. It experienced within its borders more than its share of the violence and destruction of a long and bitter struggle. Once the war was over, although faced with numerous problems, it underwent a successful reconstruction and established representative government on a firm footing. Its role in the transformation of the country from a weak, declining league to a strong, enduring union was decisive and noteworthy. Consequently, the contribution made by New Jersey to the nation's development during the revolutionary era cannot be overemphasized.

DO/DISCUSS

1. Select and perform one of the following activities relating to this era in New Jersey's history.
   a. Make a replica newspaper highlighting the news events of the revolutionary period in New Jersey.

Include editorials, feature stories, and advertisements. Select an appropriate name and masthead for a New Jersey gazette.

b. Construct a New Jersey event time chart or time line for the years 1763-1776.

c. Draw an appropriate cartoon depicting any episode, either from a loyalist's or a patriot's point of view, as it might have appeared in a New Jersey chronicle at that time.

d. Conduct a town meeting, "You Are There" program, or role-playing dramatization around some New Jersey problem of this period.

2. On a reproduced 8½" x 11" desk outline map plot the significant military sites and routes mentioned in this section. Use a color key and legend to highlight each place. What interpretations or conclusions can be derived? Was the strategy of the opposing general sound in view of New Jersey's terrain, and the geographic site and situation? Why? You may wish to use an opaque projector to enlarge your map when reporting.

3. List the five most pressing problems between the crucial years 1776 and 1789 in rank order of importance. Show how any two were interrelated. Were any unique to New Jersey?

4. What was the best single course of action taken by New Jersey during these troublesome years? Explain the reasons for your selection and picture some results for the state and nation had not the course been pursued.

CHAPTER 4

The Development
of Modern New Jersey

In 1789 New Jersey was a state with fewer than 185,000 inhabitants overwhelmingly rural in nature, divided into thirteen counties composed of small towns and scattered villages. Today it has well over six million in population, is highly industrialized, and is the most urbanized state in the nation. How it changed and grew economically and socially are dealt with in other parts of this book. The political developments that accompanied these changes will be described in this chapter.

The political history of New Jersey during this period reveals an interesting, if somewhat complex, interweaving of national and state issues. In the tug-of-war that is partisan politics, the state sometimes went along with national trends, while at other times it took an opposite course. In the main, the caliber of its government and public officials at any one time directly reflected that of the rest of the nation. There were periods of political reform and honest, efficient government, and times of corruption and machine politics. However, if developments of the past century and three-quarters are looked at as a whole—the establishment and refinement of democratic institutions, the constitutional changes, and the improvements in legislation, administration, and justice, despite the increased complexities of modern government—all must be credited to the desire of the citizens of New Jersey to enhance their political life.

The Early Period: 1789—1844

Federalists v. Anti-Federalists

Between 1789 and the outbreak of the Civil War, New Jersey experienced a number of significant advances in democracy. Political parties, for which the Founding Fathers made no provision, came into being early in this period. Actually, the nuclei of the parties had been formed prior to the launching of the national Government. The division of the country over ratification of the Federal Constitution caused the formation of two factions — the Federalists, who desired a strong central government and favored acceptance of the document, and the Anti-Federalists, who opposed adoption on the ground that the central government was made too strong. In New Jersey, where the people were so eager for a stronger government, the Anti-Federalists were unorganized and weak. They were unable to gain representation at the state's ratifying convention, and, as noted in the previous chapter, the Constitution was carried unanimously.

Federalists Predominate. Thus the Federalists were in power right from the beginning. They had the advantage of a head start, and most of those with wealth, education, and influence joined their ranks. The state's four delegates to the constitutional convention subsequently became Federalists, as did most of the political leaders of the period. New Jersey Federalists made a clean sweep of the first Congressional election in 1789 and succeeded in controlling the governor's office down to 1801. William Paterson was elected for three annual terms, and, when he resigned in 1793 to become an associate justice of the United States Supreme Court, he was succeeded by Richard Howell, who served eight terms.

Despite overwhelming Federalist dominance and near-absence of Anti-Federalist opposition, the state was sharply split. The old division between East Jersey and West Jersey still persisted. During most of the 1780's the former had controlled state affairs and fostered reform and popular measures. The adoption of the Federal Constitution marked a resurgence of conservatism and concern for property rights, and at the same time political authority shifted to West Jersey. The election of 1789 witnessed a bitter sectional clash over the new Congressional seats; the result was a victory for the entire "West Jersey ticket."

In one important respect the cleavage between the two parts of the state was overcome. This was on the selection of a permanent state capital. It will be recalled that prior to the Revolution, the seat of government was alternately at Perth Amboy and Burlington. This practice was interrupted by the war, when the legislature met where-ever it found a safe and suitable location. With the return to peace, there was rivalry among several cities for the privilege of becoming the capital. Trenton was finally chosen in 1790 as the location of a single capital for the whole state. Its selection probably was due to the fact that it had almost become the nation's capital and was readily accessible from all parts of the state. Three and three-quarter acres of land was purchased at the site of the present capitol, and by 1794 the legislature was able to hold its sessions in the new State House.

During the 1790's the Federalist and Anti-Federalist forces were each more firmly united and organized into political parties. The Federalists came under the national direction of Alexander Hamilton, Washington's brilliant Secretary of the Treasury. The Anti-Federal-ists, under the leadership of Secretary of State Thomas Jefferson, changed their name to Republicans to express their opposition to the aristocratic attitudes and policies of their opponents.

Republicans Rise to Power. In New Jersey, although the Federalists monopolized political office during most of the decade, the Republicans increased their support and cohesion. Republican societies sprang up in towns throughout the state, and a working relationship was developed with the newly created Society of St. Tammany (Tammany Hall) of New York City.

Hamilton's program, which favored the business elements, antago-nized the other classes of society and caused them to increasingly support the Jeffersonians. In New Jersey the Republicans began to win some political offices. The passage of the Alien and Sedition Acts of 1798 particularly hurt the Federalists. In Jersey, as elsewhere, there was a popular outcry against these repressive measures. In the elections of 1800, although the Federalists managed to retain control of state offices, the Republicans made a clean sweep of the Congres-sional seats. The following year the Republican Party was victorious, capturing control of the Assembly and electing its first governor, Joseph Bloomfield. Bloomfield was re-elected down to 1812.

Political control of the state for the first three decades of the nineteenth century was divided between the two parties. With the exception of Aaron Ogden, who was governor from 1812 to 1813, all those who occupied the office until 1817 were Republicans. Isaac H. Williamson served from that year until 1829 and was originally a Federalist. However, he was chosen by a Republican-controlled legislature and supported many of that party's policies. As for the state's representation in Congress, it was frequently split between the two parties. The state did lean to Republican candidates for the Presidency, but it twice went against the national trend. It supported John Adams against Jefferson in 1800 and De Witt Clinton against James Madison in 1812.

State Constitution Becomes an Issue. One of the political issues that came to a head in New Jersey before the end of the eighteenth century dealt with the Constitution of 1776. During the early years of operation under it, weaknesses had become evident. Lack of separation of powers between the executive, legislative, and judicial branches of the government, failure to grant the governor enough authority, and restrictions upon full popular participation in government were the aspects that came under sharp criticism. Demands for revision grew. Finally, in 1797, the Assembly called for establishment of a constitutional convention, provided that a majority of the votors in the election of 1800 desired it. The move for revision failed, primarily because of inertia and the unwillingness of the people to have changed what was familiar to them. With this defeat, the issues of constitutional reform remained quiet for another generation.

A matter that grew out of the constitution and was resolved, for a period of time at least, was the question of who had the right of suffrage. The Constitution of 1776 provided that all inhabitants having an estate of £50 could vote. No mention was made of sex, color, or citizenship. In 1790 an act was passed relating to suffrage that used the phrase "he or she." Very clearly, then, women had the right to vote, and there is evidence to show that many did. This made New Jersey the first state to have female suffrage. In addition, some Negroes were allowed to vote, as were large numbers of aliens. Unfortunately, these instances of liberality were short-lived. In 1807, because of certain election frauds, the legislature passed a law restricting the suffrage to "free, white, male citizens of the age of twenty-one years, worth fifty pounds."

The Slavery Issue. Another issue that stemmed from the revolutionary period was the continual problem of slavery. As described in the previous chapter, the importation of slaves had been banned, and voluntary manumission was permitted, beginning in the 1780's. Agitation was continued, however, by the Quakers and others. Governor Joseph Bloomfield was one of the advocates of compulsory emancipation, and he had the pleasure in 1804 of signing into law the Gradual Emancipation Act. It provided that every child born of a slave after July 4 of that year was to be free, but would remain the servant of the master of his mother until the age of 21 if a female and

25 if a male. Thus, although not slaves, these Negroes did not achieve complete freedom until adulthood.

Slavery was not eliminated by this act, but by 1830 the number of slaves was greatly reduced. The last traces of this institution were to linger on in the state until after the Civil War. In the bill of rights of the Constitution of 1844 there was a statement that all men are by nature free, but a court decision of 1845 held that this did not abolish slavery. This led the legislature the very next year to pass a law making slavery in the state illegal. However, the act provided that the emancipated slaves would continue bound to their masters as apprentices. As late as 1860 the Federal Census listed eighteen slaves in the state. Thus, if any remained slaves during the war, they were not completely freed until the ratification of the Thirteenth Amendment in December of 1865.

Hamilton-Burr Duel. The early period was witness to a sensational event of national consequence that directly concerned New Jersey because its tragic conclusion took place on the state's soil. This was the famous Hamilton-Burr duel. The two men had been in political conflict on more than one occasion. Their enmity came to a head in 1804 when Hamilton helped to defeat Burr, who was finishing a term as Vice-President of the United States, in his bid for the governorship of New York. The unstable Burr, who had been born in Newark, challenged his enemy to a duel and chose as the site a secluded grove of trees under the Palisades at what is now Weehawken.

The duel took place early on the morning of July 11, 1804. Hamilton, who had already proven his courage during the Revolution as a leader of troops under heavy fire, believed that it was murder to kill in a duel. It was his intention to hold fire and then throw away his shot, in the hope that Burr would miss and honor be satisfied. This was not Burr's intention. When the signal was given, he took deliberate aim, fired, and mortally wounded his adversary. So perished one of the greatest men of his times.

Burr was indicted for murder by a New York grand jury, but this was held illegal since the duel occurred in New Jersey. He was then indicted by a Bergen County grand jury, but fled to the South traveling under an assumed name. Republican leaders attempted to persuade Governor Bloomfield to suppress the charges against him, but Bloomfield, even though he had been an old friend of Burr's, maintained that he could not interfere. Eventually, the indictments lapsed, and Burr was allowed to continue on his erratic course through life.

The War of 1812. As mentioned earlier, the outbreak of the War of 1812 saw a sudden shift in the political control of New Jersey. There was strong opposition in the state to the nation's involvement in the life-and-death struggle between England and France, especially if it meant warring against the former and indirectly siding with Napoleon. Those sections that depended upon trade with Britain for economic prosperity were quick to blame the Republican Party for an unnecessary war. Disgruntled Jeffersonians teamed with the Federalists and Quaker pacifists in 1812 to win control of the legislature and governorship. The war was declared hopeless, and the legislature demanded that the United States enter into peace negotiations as quickly as possible.

Nevertheless, the state prepared to defend itself against possible attack. The militia was mobilized, and efforts were made to fortify the approaches to New York harbor and the Delaware Bay area to protect New York and Philadelphia. There was no land fighting of any consequence in the state, but after the British established a blockade of American ports, the Jersey coast was the scene of much privateering and blockade running. All together, over 6,000 Jerseyans served in the war, some of them outside the state.* The most famous was Captain James Lawrence, who was born in Burlington in 1781 and died a great naval hero on June 1, 1813. He had earlier commanded the *Hornet* and had met and sank the British vessel *Peacock*. After transferring to the *Chesapeake* and the command of a green and mutinous crew, he accepted a challenge from the *Shannon,* and sailed from Boston harbor to defeat and a glorious death. As he lay mortally wounded, he uttered the words "Don't give up the ship!"

By 1813 the innate patriotism and nationalistic feeling of most Jerseyans were rekindled, and the Republicans were restored to power. The Federalist Party became completely discredited for its opposition to the war, which at times approached treason. From then on no aspirant for political office could publicly acknowledge that he was a Federalist. To do so was to commit political suicide. The conflict between the two parties seemed to be at an end, which explains why it was possible for a Republican legislature, as mentioned earlier, to repeatedly choose as governor a former Federalist, Isaac H. Williamson. Most of this was during the period known as the "Era of Good Feelings." It would be wrong, however, to assume that the good game of partisan politics had been abandoned. If anything, it was reinforced on the local level by an intense factionalism that gripped New Jersey along with the other states.

*During the War of 1812 most of the militia called up in the various states refused to fight beyond the borders of their own state.

The Jacksonian Era *age expansion*

The Era of Good Feelings came to an end with the presidential election of 1824. It was a four-way contest between Andrew Jackson, John Quincy Adams, Henry Clay, and William Crawford, all running under the Republican banner. New Jersey favored Jackson in the regular election. When no candidate received the required electoral majority and the election was thrown into the House of Representatives, the Jersey delegation maintained its support for Jackson. However, Adams finally triumphed in the contest, as a result of Clay's efforts in his behalf. When the new President named Clay as his Secretary of State, Jackson and his followers charged that an underhanded deal had been made by the two men. The cry of "corrupt bargain" over the next four years served to split the Republican Party asunder.

Within New Jersey itself, local election contests for minor office were decided by the candidates' support of Jackson or Adams. In the presidential election of 1828, the state, which had four years earlier supported Jackson in defeat, turned against him by a narrow margin at his time of victory. However, in the state elections held the following year the Jacksonian supporters triumphed. They dropped the name Republican and began to be called Democrats. An outstanding lawyer, Peter D. Vroom, was their choice for governor. He served from 1829 to 1836, with a one-year lapse.

The 'Broad Seal War.' During the Jacksonian era, party battles within the state were fought with all the vigor and bitterness that characterized national politics. As a result of the panic of 1837, the Whig Party (as the opponents of the Jacksonian Democrats were known) triumphed in the state. Their gubernatorial candidate was William Pennington, and he managed to retain the office for six years. It was during his administration that political rivalry was most intense and there occurred the "Broad Seal War."

The Congressional election of October, 1838 was so close that all but one of the six seats were contested. Charges of corruption at the polls and submission of false returns in key precincts were leveled against the Whigs. Governor Pennington refused to go behind the face of the local returns, which gave all five disputed seats to the Whigs. He certified the returns, placing on the official commissions the Great ("broad") Seal of the State of New Jersey. Hence, the Broad Seal War.

Unfortunately, the contested election occurred just when the House of Representatives was so evenly divided between Whigs and Democrats that the body could not organize until the rightful holders of the five seats could be determined. For a short while the dispute in the House took on the appearance of mob action. Even with the restoration of order, a decision was not forthcoming until the end of the following February, when all the disputed seats were awarded to the Democratic candidates. This ended the Broad Seal War, but New Jersey politics were already gaining a national reputation for bitter fighting and disputed results.

The Constitution of 1844. Another effect of the political ferment of the Jacksonian era was the renewed agitation for revision of the Constitution of 1776, an agitation which this time reached a successful climax. In 1827 a convention had met in Trenton and petitioned the legislature to call a constitutional convention. The request was ignored, but the reform influence and crusading spirit of the time kept the issue burning brightly; for other states were reconstructing their governments to adapt them to the broadening concept of political democracy.

Finally, in 1840, things began to move forward. Governor Pennington complained to the legislature that the business of the courts was occupying all his time as chancellor and that he had no time for his other duties. A legislative committee, headed by Daniel Haines, appointed to study the matter came up with a thorough report on the defects in the constitution. When the legislature failed to take any action, popular resentment was aroused, and constitutional reform became the major political issue. Haines was elected governor in 1843, and soon afterward machinery was established for the writing of a new constitution. On March 18, 1841 each county elected delegates to the constitutional convention, which convened in Trenton on May 14.

The sixty delegates who drafted the Constitution of 1844 were of the highest caliber. Among them were three ex-governors, three state Supreme Court justices, seven former congressmen, and two governors-to-be. By June 29 the new document was adopted, and, when it was submitted to the people on August 13, it was overwhelmingly ratified by a six-to-one margin. It went into effect on September 2 and remained the Constitution of New Jersey for slightly over a century.

The document was a reflection of the times, strengthening popular government and providing greater democratic control. Property qualifications for voting and holding office were eliminated. A detailed and lengthy bill of rights was added, expounding principles of natural rights and popular sovereignty and drawing largely on the Federal Bill of Rights.

The body of the constitution incorporated the concept of separation of powers with the establishment of three distinct departments: legislative, executive, and judicial. The upper house of the legislature was divested of its function as the highest court in the state and had its name changed to "Senate." Equality of county representation in the lower house was abandoned in favor of representation on the basis of population. The total number of assemblymen could not exceed sixty.

The election of the governor was removed from the legislature and given directly to the people. His term was increased to three years, but he could not succeed himself. The governor's administrative powers were kept limited, and his appointive powers were moderately increased. Although he was given the right to veto, he could be overridden by a mere majority of the legislature.

The judiciary was reorganized, but the new structure was as complex as the old. At the apex was a newly created Court of Errors and Appeals, the highest court in the state. Judges for all state courts were to be appointed.

Another feature of the constitution worthy of attention was the amending process. Proposed amendments had to pass both houses by a majority vote in two separate sessions, and then be submitted to the people at a special election. In addition, a defeated amendment could not be brought up again for five years.

In the main, the Constitution of 1844 was a marked improvement over its predecessor, but it did not go far enough. The governorship was enhanced and legislative authority somewhat curtailed, but the latter body continued to be the most powerful of the three branches of government.

The Joint Companies Controversy. The years following the adoption of the new constitution saw the political life of New Jersey primarily influenced by two factors. One was of national signficance, the Mexican War; the other concerned transportation and railroad monopoly, an internal matter that had its beginnings in the 1830's. In 1831 the Delaware and Raritan Canal merged with the Camden and Amboy Railroad to form the Joint Companies. The following year the legislature granted the combine sole control of transportation across the state between New York and Philadelphia. In return, 2,000 shares of stock were turned over to the state, and a transit tax on through passenger and freight traffic was to be paid into the state treasury. From the income gained through these arrangements, the state was able to meet a good part of its annual budget. Thus other taxes were kept low, and the monopoly was allowed to continue.

As might be expected, the Joint Companies before long had a widespread and powerful influence on politics in the state. The monopoly aligned itself with the Democratic Party, helping its candidates win office. This naturally turned the Whigs into bitter enemies, and they vehemently attacked the combine and tried, unsuccessfully, to destroy it. In turn, the Democrats, when in power, saw to it that only favorable legislation was passed. The Whigs accused the Camden and Amboy of charging exhorbitant fares, of concealing some of its profits, and of blocking the chartering of several other railroads in the state. Despite their attacks, the monopoly persisted and in 1847 succeeded once again in electing Daniel Haines as governor. The two succeeding governors were also Democrats.

The only Whig to be elected governor by the people under the new constitution was Charles C. Stratton, in 1844. In that year the state also supported the Whig Party on the national level. Doubtlessly, a determining factor was that Theodore Frelinghuysen of New Jersey was vice-presidential candidate.

The Mexican War. Governor Stratton served during the Mexican War. Following a request from the Federal Government, he issued a proclamation calling for volunteers. The war was very popular in the state and was well supported. Five companies of troops were sent to Vera Cruz, and most of the demands and requisitions of the Government were met. The state had its share of heroes. General Stephen Kearny and Commodore Robert Stockton took prominent part in the conquest of California. Philip Kearny, who later would be killed in the Civil War and have the town of Kearny named after him, lost his arm as a cavalry officer in the Mexican conflict.

DO/DISCUSS

1. Why did the Federalists gain strong initial support in New Jersey? How do you account for the ascendancy of the Republicans (Anti-Federalists) by 1800?
2. Why is it necessary to have political parties in a democracy?
3. Did the choice of Trenton as the state capital prove to be advantageous for New Jersey? Explain. Would you suggest another site?

4. Generally the New Jersey rural and suburban citizen has voted Republican, while the city resident has tended to cast his ballot for the Democratic Party. How might you account for this? Is it a favorable sign for a democracy?

The Civil War and After: 1844—1896

The Pre-War Period

Political developments in New Jersey during the second half of the nineteenth century displayed a high degree of confusion and inconsistency. More often than not, the state was out of tune with the rest of the nation. The explanation for this can be found in the issues and conflicts brought to a head by the Civil War and the recognition that New Jersey, in many respects, was a border state.

New Jersey and the Slavery Issue. As the problem of slavery pushed all other issues off the national political canvas, the question of what to do about it profoundly affected developments within the state. Although, in a technical sense, slavery still existed in the state, New Jerseyans as a whole opposed its extension into new territories and doubtlessly favored its gradual extinction throughout the nation. The Quakers in the southwestern part of the state were staunch abolitionists, and the entire state was an important link in the "underground railroad."

Nevertheless, it must be recognized that the state had important commercial ties with the South and was closely bound socially with border slave states like Delaware and Maryland. A look at a map would show that a portion of South Jersey is below the Mason and Dixon Line. Prosperous manufacturing industries, especially in the rising cities of Newark and Passaic, had their best outlets in Southern states. The large number of immigrants who helped to nearly double the population of the state between 1840 and 1860 had mixed views on the slavery problem. They believed in liberty and opposed slavery as an institution and recognized that free labor could not compete with it. But they were interested in the continued sale of the products they produced and were fearful that war would curtail their livelihood. Thus there were compelling reasons why the majority of Jerseyans considered slavery an internal question to be settled by each state for itself without compulsion.

The emergence of slavery as the principal issue of the 1850's brought about a political realignment in the country. The Whig Party broke apart following its defeat in the national election of 1852. The Southern proslavery and northern antislavery elements could not remain united much longer. The Democratic Party did manage to remain intact until 1860. However, some Northern Democrats who were strongly opposed to slavery left their party and joined forces with antislavery Whigs and "Free-Soilers" to form the new Republican Party.* At the same time, a short-lived third party, the American, or "Know Nothing," Party, came into being. Growing out of "The Order of the Star-Spangled Banner," it was a secret organization opposed to the influx of Irish and German immigrants and to the supposed influence of the Catholic Church in American politics. Its program of hatred, bigotry, and secrecy had an immediate appeal to certain groups of voters in different sections of the country, but it soon collapsed because of its negativism and un-Americanism.

The 'Opposition' Party Emerges. These shifts in national politics had their effects in New Jersey. The Democratic Party was successful in winning the state in the presidential elections of 1852 and 1856; in the latter, Jersey was one of the few Northern states that did not support the new Republican Party, even though a native son, William L. Dayton, was its vice-presidential candidate. However, the Democrats were not so successful on the state level in 1856. The American Party captured a significant number of seats in both houses of the legislature and in the gubernatorial contest combined with Republicans to elect William A. Newell under the banner of the "Opposition Party of New Jersey."

Although the American Party quickly disappeared as an independent force in the state's politics, the Opposition Party was solidified and built up by Governor Newell into a strong state organization closely allied with the national Republican Party. In 1859 the Opposition Party succeeded in electing a United States senator and another governor, Charles S. Olden. This party continued to exist and flourish in the state because the name "Republican" was unpopular and seemed too radically antislavery even for those who supported its policies.

The presidential election of 1860 was as confusing on the state level as it was on the national level. The Opposition Party supported

*The present-day Republican Party.

Abraham Lincoln once he was chosen as candidate of the Republicans. The Democrats were faced with a national party split in two, each with a separate candidate, and a third candidate nominated by the Constitutional Union Party. Attempts were made to organize a unified fusion ticket, but they failed. With four candidates in the field, a strong, effective campaign was impossible, and there was extreme doubt as to how New Jersey would go. The election was so close that the result could not be determined until the official count was made by the state canvassers three weeks later. The final tally gave four electoral votes to Lincoln and three to Stephen A. Douglas, who received a total of twelve in the nation at large. New Jersey was the only state in the North that did not give its entire electoral vote to Lincoln.

Following the election of 1860 the name "Opposition" began to disappear and was replaced by the "Union" or "Union-Republican" Party. It supported Lincoln during the war years. The name "Republican" continued to be unpopular in the state until after the Civil War, at which time the people were able to realign their allegiances under the two major parties as we know them today.

Jersey's Divided Feelings. New Jersey was sharply divided as secession of the Southern states became more and more a likelihood after the election of Lincoln. Although there were some people and a few newspapers in favor of secession by New Jersey itself, the overwhelming majority were opposed to such a step. However, many held the states' rights view that the Southern states had a constitutional right to secede if they wished to, and that the Federal Government could not force them to remain in the Union. They were no less loyal than citizens of other states, but merely were more vocal in expressing their misgivings about civil war. Most of the opposition to war came from the Democrats, who constituted the nucleus of the "Peace Party" that came into being after hostilities began. Later they would come into power, making Jersey the only state in the Union to be under the control of the opponents of the war during part of the actual conflict.

However, the state was under the Opposition, or Union-Republican, Party from 1860 to 1863 and support was given to the policies of Lincoln. The legislature resolved that it was the duty of all loyal citizens to back up the national Government, and it held that the Union was more than a mere compact of states. Governor Olden supported Jersey's participation in a peace conference that was held in Washington early in 1861, but unfortunately this attempt to save the Union failed. When Lincoln passed through the state on February 21 on way to his inauguration, he was warmly greeted by the populace and given a series of receptions.

War

Following the firing upon Fort Sumter, the state was quickly unified, and the true loyalty and patriotism of New Jerseyans were displayed. Support was shown by leaders of both parties, there was an immediate response to President Lincoln's call for volunteers, and a special session of the legislature authorized a loan of money to repel invasion and suppress insurrection. It was declared that the state was making war against the South to maintain the Union and that the best way to restore peace was to vigorously prosecute the war.

Unfortunately, the feeling of enthusiasm was short-lived. The defeat of the Union Army at Bull Run on July 21, 1861 was a clear indication that subduing the South would not be an easy task. Public support quickly diminished, and criticism soon followed. Suspension of the writ of habeas corpus and other Federal acts in violation of civil liberties aroused local opposition in the states. In September, Colonel James W. Wall of Burlington County was arrested without charge by the army and imprisoned for a short time. Wall was a prominent Democrat and leader of the "Peace Party," whose newspaper editorials had been critical of the Government's handling of the war. Upon release, he was treated like a martyr to the cause of freedom of the press. This incident helped to solidify opposition to the Civil War.

"Peace meetings" were held throughout the state, with feelings running most intense in Bergen County. When Lincoln in September, 1862 announced his intention of issuing the Emancipation Proclamation, opposition was intensified. The proclamation was denounced on the grounds that the war was being fought to preserve the Union and not to free the slaves. It was declared an unconstitutional violation of states' rights. Copperheads (those who opposed the war to the point of giving aid to the enemy) aroused the prejudice of the populace by warning that New Jersey would be flooded with an influx of freed Negroes from the South.

Democrats Win on Peace. That year (1862) the state election campaign centered around the issues growing out of the Civil War. So strong were feelings against the war that the Democratic Party, at the forefront of the "Peace Party," swept into office. It captured the governorship, both houses of the legislature, and all but one of the Jersey seats in the House of Representatives. Elected as governor was Joel Parker, who had been a brigadier general in the state militia at the beginning of the war. A wise, sensible, and popular man, he was able to restrain the hotheads in his party who wished to terminate the state's participation in the war and directly negotiate a peace with the South.

Parker showed further statesmanship and able leadership in his handling of the issue of conscription. The Federal Government passed its first draft act in March of 1863, taking the process of raising troops out of the hands of the states. Again this was viewed in New Jersey as a violation of states' rights, and antidraft demonstrations occurred in various northern counties. Especially detestable to the poorer people was the provision that a draftee could pay $300 to hire a substitute. Violence comparable to New York City's draft riots was prevented by the action of Governor Parker, who appealed to the War Department in Washington to allow him the opportunity to furnish the state's quota by means of volunteers. His request was granted, and 6,000 men were recruited by an intensive campaign and the granting of bounties.

Another source of conflict between New Jersey and the Federal Government developed when the latter attempted to interfere with railroad transportation in the state. The War Department for military reasons tried to declare the Raritan and Delaware Bay Railroad a post and military line authorized to carry troops and supplies. This would have increased Federal power in the state and broken the lucrative monopoly granted back in 1832 to the Camden and Amboy Railroad. When a bill for this purpose was introduced in Congress, Jerseyans of all political persuasions protested so vigorously that the whole matter was dropped. Here was a clear-cut example of the interests of a state triumphing over what was considered necessary to the war effort. However, after the war was over, Congress did pass a general law making all railroads common carriers authorized to transport goods and passengers in interstate commerce.

Jersey Opposes Lincoln's Re-election. As the nation approached the presidential election of 1864, Lincoln's re-election appeared doubtful. This was because of the human and material losses sustained in the prolonged war and the President's strong leadership and efforts to preserve the Union at all costs. Many people were war-weary and wanted the conflict ended at any price, while others objected to what they felt were violations of the Federal Constitution, growth of military power in government, and invasion of the rights of the states. Within Lincoln's party, there was temporary opposition to his renomination. When the Union-Republican Party of New Jersey held its convention, however, it loyally supported the President, as did the Republican national convention, held in June in Baltimore.

The Democratic Party in New Jersey pledged itself to the defeat of the Administration. The national convention, held in late August in Chicago, declared the war a failure and advocated immediate cessation of hostilities. It nominated General George B. McClellan for President. McClellan had become a resident of the Oranges after having been relieved of the command of the Union forces.

Pride in its distinguished citizen and support for his views made McClellan a popular candidate in New Jersey. It appeared at first that he might be able to defeat Lincoln in the national contest. At that time it seemed as if the Confederate forces under General Robert E. Lee could never be vanquished. But the military situation and, along with it, the political picture changed suddenly. Union victories pushed morale sky-high, and Lincoln for the first time became a popular President. He was re-elected in November by a clear-cut majority of the popular vote and a sweeping electoral vote. Only three states supported McClellan: two border states and New Jersey.

Despite the state's opposition to Lincoln's handling of the war, it would be wrong to underestimate the contribution made by Jerseyans to the war effort. All told, close to 90,000 men from the state served under the Union banner, well over the quota set for it. Jersey was the first state to send a fully organized brigade of soldiers to defend the nation's capital when it was threatened in 1861. Its most prominent officers were Major General Philip Kearny, killed in battle in Virginia in 1862, and Major General Judson Kilpatrick, who served with distinction as a cavalry leader under General Sherman.

The Post-War Years

With the end of the Civil War in 1865, the Republican Party was openly established in New Jersey. The victory of the North justified the party's support of the war and discredited the Democrats' opposition. Returning soldiers gave their votes to the former. In addition, businessmen and industrialists were gradually won over to the Republican Party. In the state election of 1865, it was able to gain control of the legislature and elect its candidate for governor, Marcus L. Ward of Newark. An additional issue in the contest was the refusal earlier in the year of the Democratic-controlled legislature to ratify the Thirteenth Amendment abolishing slavery, making Jersey the only free state so to act. When the Republicans took over, they promptly ratified the amendment even though it had already been declared adopted and made part of the Constitution of the United States.

The Republican victory in 1865, after a period of Democratic, antiwar control, was hailed by the New York *Tribune* as signifying the state's return to the Union. In an editorial titled "New Jersey Redeemed," it asserted: "She is admitted to the Union with all the honors—let men and angels rejoice—let the eagle scream." The triumph of the Republicans, however, did not mean smooth sailing for them. Indeed, the state continued to be embroiled in bitter partisan struggles, with the parties alternating in victory and defeat. In addition, politics during this period turned sordid and selfish and at times was tainted with graft and corruption. Although Jersey did not go through any self-reconstruction, it experienced along with the rest of the nation a post-war letdown and moral weakening.

A Disputed Seat.   One of the struggles had important national implications and had to be settled, like the Broad Seal War, in the Congress. The term of a Republican United States senator was about to expire, and it was up to the state legislature to elect a new one. Prior to the time when the newly elected members took their seats following the election of 1867, the old legislature was divided. The death of a Democratic assemblyman gave the Republicans a one-vote control of that house, while the Democrats had a majority of two in the Senate. This meant that the Democrats could elect a senator by a one-vote margin, since Federal senators were chosen by joint session of the Assembly and Senate. The Republicans used every delaying tactic they could, even refusing to go into joint session. Finally, the election was held, and John P. Stockton, a Democrat, was elected.

When Stockton took his seat in the United States Senate in December, 1865, at the start of its new session, the Republicans protested that he had not been properly chosen. After a prolonged struggle and investigation, he was unseated by a straight party vote of twenty-three to twenty-one. Behind this move was the desire of the Radical Republicans to consolidate their strength for the forthcoming showdown with Lincoln's successor, Andrew Johnson.

Jersey and the 'Civil War Amendments.'   Another one of the state's internal political battles reached the attention of Congress. This involved the ratification of the Fourteenth Amendment, which guaranteed the rights of citizenship to the newly freed Negroes. A special session of the Republican-controlled legislature called in September, 1866 ratified the amendment. The Democrats bitterly opposed this step and made it an issue in that year's legislative election. They lost again. The Republicans, remaining in power, continued to support the Reconstruction program and attempted to change New Jersey's constitution to extend the right to vote to Negroes. This move was overwhelmingly defeated, and the Democrats made it the leading issue in the campaign in the autumn of 1867. This time they were able to gain control of both houses of the legislature and the following January promptly revoked the state's ratification of the Fourteenth Amendment.

In carrying out this revocation, the Democrats cited the fact that the amendment was still before the states, since three-fourths of them had not as yet ratified it. Republican Governor Marcus Ward vetoed their action, holding that a state having once ratified an amendment could not reverse itself. The legislature responded by repassing its resolution over the veto by an overwhelming vote and forwarding it to Congress. Both the Senate and House of Representatives attacked this maneuver and ordered:

> That the resolution of the Legislature of New Jersey purporting to withdraw "the assent of the said State to the Constitutional Amendment known as the Fourteenth Article," be returned . . . for the reason that the same is disrespectful to the House, and scandalous in character.

The Jersey legislature refused to be cowed and passed another resolution by overwhelming vote condemning the Congress for its action. Nevertheless, when the adoption of the amendment was proclaimed in July, 1868, ratification by New Jersey was included. The controversy became another issue in the state and national campaign of 1868. The decision to count a state's ratification of an amendment, despite subsequent negative action, became a precedent, which means it has been followed ever since.

The bitter partisan struggle over the "Civil War amendments" was not yet ended. The Democratic Party in New Jersey made a clean sweep in the elections of 1868. They retained control of the legislature, elected Theodore F. Randolph of Hudson County as governor, and won a majority of Congressional seats. They also carried the state for their presidential candidate, Horatio Seymour, who was defeated nationally by General Grant. When the Fifteenth Amendment, providing Negroes with the right to vote, came before the states for ratification early in 1869, Governor Randolph recommended that consideration be postponed by the legislature until after the state elections in the autumn. This would give the people an opportunity to express their will on the subject.

The election campaign of that year was centered on the issue of ratification. When the Democrats retained control of the legislature, they voted against the amendment. However, when the Republicans captured the legislature in the fall of 1870, they reconsidered the amendment and ratified it, even though it had already been adopted in March of 1870. Thus, they repeated the same action of five years earlier, when the Thirteenth Amendment was the issue.

The seesaw battle between the two parties continued unchecked. In the state election of 1871 the Democrats rode to victory with their candidate for governor, ex-Governor Joel Parker. They continued to retain control of the State House down to 1896. However, during most of this period, the Republicans dominated the legislature. Thus, on the state level, politics in New Jersey remained divided and bitter.

Republicans Attain Dominance in New Jersey.   In the presidential election of 1872 the state for the first time in a long time went along with the national trend. Grant's re-election was supported in Jersey by a decided majority, and he was swept into office, losing only six Southern states. For the first time New Jersey gave all of its electoral votes to a Republican presidential candidate. It supported Grant not in approval of his policies and leadership but in detestation of his opponent, Horace Greeley. As editor of the New York *Tribune,* Greeley had mercilessly attacked many Jersey Democrats during and after the war as Copperheads and traitors. Very few could forgive and forget so soon.

Before the Reconstruction era came to a close, two important political developments took place in the state. As described earlier in this chapter, the Camden and Amboy Railroad monopoly for many years had consistently supported Democratic candidates for office. This monopoly expired in 1869 and along with it the company's influence in state politics. The line came under the control of the Pennsylvania Railroad, which now gave active support to the passage of a general railroad act in place of the special charters that its rivals continued to seek. Such an act became law in 1873. As the Pennsylvania Railroad grew in strength and influence under the guidance of its agent, General William J. Sewell of Camden County, it increasingly threw its support to the Republican Party. This was one of the main reasons why this party was predominant in one or both houses of the legislature for nearly the balance of the century.

The other important development grew out of the issue of the general railroad act. With its passage, wide public support grew for the amendment of the state constitution to require general legislation in all fields and to forbid the passage of any special or private laws. A special Constitutional Commission made up of outstanding citizens was appointed by Governor Parker. Its recommendations went beyond the original intent, but twenty-eight of them received bipartisan support. After passing two successive sessions of the legislature, all of the proposals were adopted by the voters at a special election on September 7, 1875.

The most important of the new amendments provided for:
1. restrictions upon the passage of private, local and spe- ial laws;
2. assessment of property for taxes under general laws and by uniform rules according to its true value;
3. absentee voting for persons in the armed forces;
4. authorization of free public schools.

The sum total of the changes represented a marked advance in sound and honest government.

Reconstruction came to an end with the disputed presidential election of 1876. Although the Democratic candidate, Samuel J. Tilden, received a clear-cut popular plurality over his Republican opponent, Rutherford B. Hayes, the electoral votes in several closely contested states were all given to the latter. A special Electoral Commission declared Hayes the victor by a majority of one electoral vote.

As might be expected, New Jersey was well represented in the crucial political battle. Cortlandt Parker, a Newark lawyer, was among the Republican "visiting statesmen" who investigated the vote in one of the disputed states and assisted in formulating the method of counting that was entirely in the interest of Hayes. Two Jerseyans were on the Electoral Commission of fifteen, United States Senator Frederick T. Frelinghuysen and Supreme Court Justice Joseph P. Bradley. The commission was composed of seven Democrats and seven Republicans, with the fifteenth member nonpartisan. Justice Bradley was selected as the impartial member. On all questions, the commission divided along strictly party lines, and Bradley voted invariably with the Republicans. Thus it was he who named the next President of the United States.

The end of Reconstruction brought the gradual subsiding of tensions and hostilities that had grown out of the Civil War and had so profoundly affected political life in New Jersey. However, politics in the state down to the end of the century showed no improvement. This period was marked by selfish personal politics, corruption in both parties, boss rule, and the domination of government by big business. During these years there was a hairline balance between the two major parties. On the state-wide level the Democrats were able to win every gubernatorial contest and capture the electoral vote in each presidential election down to 1896. At the same time most of the state's congressmen were Republicans, and although its margin of control was often slight, the Republican Party dominated most of the sessions of the legislature.

Boss Rule. Starting back in 1869, the Democratic Party had unbroken control of the governor's chair. A number of the occupants were able and dedicated men, among them General McClellan, but they were thwarted by hostile legislatures, Democratic as well as Republican. In addition, they were subject to a small clique of men who operated behind the scenes and manipulated elected officials, many of whom they had hand-picked. Down to 1883 the Democratic Party was dominated by the "State House Ring," headed by Henry Kelsey, Benjamin Lee, and Henry Little. These men were the bosses of the party and acted as the "powers behind the throne."

The State House Ring eventually lost power, only to be supplanted by a man able to boss the state party machine by himself. Leon Abbett of Hudson County was a brilliant politician, a whirlwind campaigner, and an able administrator who captured the support of the common people by his opposition to the railroads and other large corporations. His actions combined elements of reform and demagoguery (the stirring up of popular feeling to gain office or influence). After many years in the legislature, he was twice elected governor, in 1883 and again in 1889. The only goal he was unable to achieve was that of election to the United States Senate.

The Republicans in the state had their political bosses, too. Most prominent among them was William J. Sewell, mentioned earlier, who all but ran the party for two decades. No measures were passed by a Republican legislature without his consent. At first a state senator, he was elected to the United States Senate in 1881 and served for twenty years until his death. As agent for the Pennsylvania Railroad and spokesman for big business in general, General Sewell was a prominent member of the "millionaires' club" of the Senate.

Big Business Thrives. As for the influence of business on government within the state, New Jersey during this time became known as the "home of the trusts." It had a very liberal policy toward corporations. Few restrictions were placed upon them, and the corporate tax rate was very low, especially for the larger ones. This attracted a host of businesses, particularly holding companies and other corporate giants. Of the 300 largest corporations in the nation, half were chartered in Jersey. This was beneficial from an economic standpoint, but it also brought about a wedding of politics to the interests of business. The result was bribery and corruption and the catering to special interests by public officials. Corporations frequently thought it necessary to pay for benefits received, and officials, both elected and appointed, often felt it only proper that they be paid for favors conferred.

Perhaps the biggest boon that corporations enjoyed was the virtual exemption from local taxes on their large property holdings. Since they were chartered by the state, they were deemed beyond local control and taxation. This was especially beneficial to the railroads, which owned extensive amounts of property along their rights-of-way and at terminals, but it was an overbearing hardship on the localities involved. This was particularly true for the cities in Hudson County, where all the lines with connections to New York had huge holdings. Under the leadership of Leon Abbett, the enemy of the railroads, a campaign was carried out to change all this. The full fruits were not achieved until after the turn of the century, but Abbett's efforts did succeed in establishing the beginnings of corporate property taxation.

The Temperance Drive.   Two social issues were injected into the politics of this period: temperance and race-track gambling. The question of the control or total prohibition of the manufacture and sale of alcoholic beverages had been fought over in America for more than a century. It came to a head in New Jersey in the 1880's. At this time the Prohibition Party polled enough votes in the state to show that it held the balance of power between the two major parties. The Republicans, recognizing this and in control of the legislature, attempted to gain the support of the temperance forces. They passed an act in 1888 for "local option" by counties, which meant that any county on its own could prohibit the sale of liquor within its borders. The measure was vetoed by Robert S. Green, the Democratic governor, but he was promptly overridden.

The prohibition movement spread like wildfire. The liquor interests, taken by surprise, mobilized their efforts in a war of self-defense. Leon Abbett, as their chief adviser, pledged the Democratic Party to support repeal. The legislative election of 1888 centered around this issue. The Democrats won control of both houses by slight majorities and promptly pushed through a repealing act. Thereafter, liquor interests were not apt to forget such loyal service from the Democrats. However, prohibition was to remain a bitterly divisive issue for many years to come.

The Race-Track Gambling Issue.   The problem of horse racing in the state also came to the fore in the 1880's. The tracks at Long Branch, near Camden, and at Guttenberg in Hudson County were the scenes of gambling and other offensive practices. Moral disapproval by the public reached such a pitch that in 1890 legislation was passed placing restrictions upon the activities of the tracks. Efforts to repeal these restrictions failed until the legislature of 1893, overwhelmingly Democratic, reversed matters entirely and passed bills legalizing race-track betting. Governor George T. Werts refused to support his party's position and promptly vetoed the bills. His vetoes were just as quickly overridden. The public's reaction was one of indignation; at the next election, the Republicans were swept into office on a tidal wave of votes.

The Democrats, however, did not give up without a fight. They were in the majority among the holdover members of the Senate, and so proceeded to lock out the new members and organize a "rump" session. This action was defended on the ground that the Senate was a continuous body and could judge the qualifications of its new members. Thus the holdover Democrats decided that the newly elected Republicans were not entitled to their seats. A bitter, prolonged struggle ensued, which was finally settled when the chief justice of the state Supreme Court ruled against the Democrats and held that the new senators were to take their places.

Actually, the triumph of the Republican Party in the state was attributable to more than the Democratic position on liquor and gambling. For too long a time the Democrats had been associated with political scandals and corruption. Election irregularities such as stuffing the ballot boxes, destroying unfavorable ballots, buying or threatening voters, using repeaters, and "voting the cemeteries" had become quite common. Elected officials had been no more than front men for political machines or bosses, or had been in the hire of special interests. Sessions of the legislature had been marked by disorder, acts of violence, falsification of votes, and outright bribery. Members of both parties bore guilt for this situation, but the Democrats had outdone their opponents. Thus it was against them that the public reacted.

The Brighter Side. Some efforts at political reform were made. The safeguards of the "Australian ballot" were introduced in 1890, providing for secret voting and an official ballot, identical for all parties. The movement for this reform was led by, of all people, Governor Abbett, who himself had benefitted from election frauds. In addition, bribery in connection with elections was made a criminal offense, but the measure was inadequate. Following the struggle over race-track gambling, a Commission for Constitutional Amendments was created whose efforts resulted in the submission to the people of several amendments in 1897. One prohibiting gambling in any form was adopted by a slender popular vote. Another would have brought about a significant social, as well as political, advance, but it was rejected. It would have given the vote to women in school elections.

One of the brightest spots for New Jersey in this long period of political decay was the election of one of its native sons to the highest office in the land. Although Grover Cleveland's early political career is associated with New York State, he was born in Caldwell, Essex County, and after his presidential terms spent his last eleven years in effective service in his native state. He had the double distinction of being the only Democrat in the White House from James Buchanan to Woodrow Wilson and the only President to serve two nonsuccessive terms. As might be expected, New Jersey supported him in his successful campaigns for office in 1884 and 1892, as well as in 1888, when he was defeated.

DO/DISCUSS

1. This section includes many political terms that frequently are mentioned during election campaigns. Select those words which seem ambiguous and make a partial dictionary (glossary) explaining the meanings of the words. Include your interpretation and observations.
2. Social issues (such as temperance and race-track gambling) have always played a key role in New Jersey's politics. Can you identify some present-day social issues that are controversial?
3. Check New Jersey's voting record in national elections under "Electoral College" in any encyclopedia or other reference source. Do you feel that New Jersey can be labeled safe for either political party? Why?

The Turn of the Century: 1896—1920

Republicans in Control

When John W. Griggs of Passaic County took office in January of 1896, he was the first Republican governor of New Jersey in over a quarter of a century. For the next fifteen years the Republicans held continuous possession of the governorship, captured the state in every presidential contest, and, except for one year, had unbroken control of both houses of the legislature. This monopoly was abruptly terminated by Woodrow Wilson in 1911.

The five Republican governors were men of outstanding ability and character, most of them with long and dedicated careers in public service. For example, Griggs was appointed by President McKinley to be Attorney General of the United States, a post in which he served with distinction. Following this, he was made a member of the Permanent Court of Arbitration at The Hague, a position which he held with honor for over ten years.

It was also during this time that a native son of New Jersey occupied the second highest office in the land. Garret A. Hobart, born in Long Branch and very active in state politics for many years, was elected Vice-President under McKinley in 1896. He exerted much influence and authority while in office, and his untimely death in 1899 was probably the only thing that prevented him from becoming the first citizen of New Jersey to become President of the United States. Hobart doubtlessly would have been nominated for re-election in 1900, and the assassination of McKinley would have meant his, and not Theodore Roosevelt's, elevation to the Presidency.

Progress Is Stifled. Despite the ability of these outstanding Republican officials, little in the way of constructive change was accomplished in the state. The various governors found themselves thwarted in their efforts to provide good administrations by the selfish claims and partisan maneuvering of petty politicians and the activities of special-interest groups. Republican-controlled legislatures were no more responsive to the public than their Democratic predecessors. New Jersey Republicans had more and more identified themselves with the business and industrial interests in the state. The triumph of big business at the close of the nineteenth century was one of the major reasons for Republican ascendancy during this period. As a result of these ties, however, most reforms and improvements were blocked by public officials under the control of business interests who favored a policy of *laissez faire,* or hands off.

Another important reason for Republican dominance was the sharp division that existed in Democratic ranks. Beginning with the nomination for President of William Jennings Bryan in 1896, the national Democratic Party was committed to an inflationary, or cheap money, policy based upon the free coinage of silver. This position was extremely unpopular in New Jersey and served to weaken the party's support within the state. New Jersey Democrats, unwillingly saddled with Bryan and free silver, went down to sweeping defeats in election after election.

The Democrats were, at the same time, unsuccessful in their attempts to identify the Republicans in the public mind with the growing trusts and monopolies. However, within the ranks of the Republican Party itself, a division developed over the issue of corporate domination of the affairs of the state. This domination was made increasingly evident during the first years of the twentieth century by the election of big businessmen themselves to high offices in the state.

The 'New Idea' Champions Reform.   The Republican division was brought on by a faction led by Mayor Mark Fagan and George L. Record of Jersey City and Everett Colby, Essex County legislator from West Orange. The program they advocated, dubbed the "New Idea," was an expression of the progressive movement then sweeping the country. "Progressivism" was the belief that progress toward social justice could be accomplished by making political life more democratic, economic life fairer and more truly competitive, and social life more moral and just.

The "New Idea" concentrated its efforts on the glaring evils of big business. An effort was made to limit the franchises issued to trolley lines and public utilities and to tax railroad property at the same rate as other property. For several years a number of bitter struggles were waged in the legislature, not only between the two parties but between the "New Idea" and "Old Guard" wings of the Republican Party itself. The outcome of all this was a series of compromises that provided for some degree of corporate regulation and modest increases in railroad taxation. An important accomplishment was the provision that the revenue collected from certain state railroad taxes be used for public education.

Other reform legislation that was adopted included pure food and tenement housing laws, weak child labor regulations, the establishment of a State Board of Children's Guardians, and the introduction of the merit system for state civil service. In addition, steps were taken to preserve the state's supply of drinking water and prevent its diversion to outside uses.

The most exciting controversy of the period arose over a matter unrelated to business regulation. It stemmed from an issue that had divided the state since the 1880's — prohibition. A new local option bill was introduced into the legislature in 1906 and was promptly defeated. This resulted in a state-wide movement led by the churches and climaxed by a meeting in Trenton. Among the prominent figures in attendance were bishops from the Episcopal and Roman Catholic dioceses. The conference drew up a bill, henceforth known as the "Bishops' Bill," that provided for regulation of the sale of liquor and rigid enforcement of the law. Heavy penalties were imposed for the sale of liquor to minors. The bill was enacted into law only after a bitter fight. From then on, the struggle between those who supported strict enforcement and those who attempted to modify or repeal the Bishops' Bill affected every election and plagued aspiring politicians down to the adoption of the Eighteenth Amendment.

The "New Idea" men failed to capture control of the Republican Party in 1906 and 1907, causing their movement to go into a decline. The conservative element aligned with the business interests and dedicated to *laissez-faire* policies remained in power. Although the reform movement thus accomplished only a small part of its program, it did awaken the people of the state to an awareness of the need for change and improvement. The Republicans in New Jersey fumbled the ball of progressivism; it was recovered by the Democrats and carried for a touchdown by Woodrow Wilson.

The Wilson Period

By the end of the first decade of the twentieth century, the state exhibited the effects of the great changes it had been undergoing over a short period of time. Its population had increased by one-third in the ten years since 1900 to over two-and-one-half million, placing it in eleventh position in the nation. Large cities came into being; urban residents now constituted three-fourths of the state's people. These dramatic advances were caused by the tremendous influx of immigrants into the United States at this time, with a goodly proportion settling in New Jersey. These newcomers represented a huge reservoir of manpower, talent, and energy, as well as a challenge to the processes of assimilation and Americanization.

Thus it can be seen that the state was no longer a small, rural corridor dependent upon the metropolitan giants of New York and Philadelphia. New Jersey was now big in every respect but physical size.

With bigness came problems and issues that could not be dealt with in the haphazard manner of the past. Dedicated politics and efficient and positive government became the order of the day. They were provided by Wilson in the two short years that he was governor of the state.

Woodrow Wilson was born at Staunton, Virginia, on December 28, 1856, the son of a Scottish Presbyterian minister. He grew up in various states of the South, but came to New Jersey to attend Princeton University, from which he was graduated in 1879. After practicing law for a time, he studied for his doctorate in history and political science at Johns Hopkins University in Baltimore. He taught at several colleges and then came back to Princeton as a professor in 1890. By 1902 he had become president of the university.

In that position Wilson showed a Jeffersonian democratic idealism as well as a strong, unswerving, dominating character. He reorganized Princeton's curriculum and administration and attempted to democratize student activities. Although his theoretical knowledge of government and politics was brilliant, he showed no practical interest in local or state affairs. He tended to be conservative and traditionalist in his outlook and very critical of progressivism at first.

The man who recognized his great future and brought Wilson into practical politics was George Harvey. Harvey succeeded in convincing the bosses of the state's Democratic organization, headed by James Smith, Jr., that Wilson would make an excellent candidate for governor. The party convention of 1910 was "steamrollered" by the organization into nominating him, but Wilson soon made it clear to all that he would not be boss-dominated. He carried on a vigorous campaign, making it a crusade for morality and justice, and by his eloquent and persuasive speeches won the support of the independent voters. The Democratic ticket was swept into office on election day. Wilson was elected by a sizable majority and the Assembly went overwhelmingly Democratic; only the Senate remained slightly Republican because of holdover members.

Wilsonian Reforms. Wilson soon had opportunity to prove his independence of the Democratic machine. James Smith was anxious to be chosen to the United States Senate, but Wilson blocked his bid by supporting the progressive candidate. Smith and his followers denounced the governor for his ingratitude and became his enemies from then on. This sharp break with the political machine that had made his election possible gave Wilson national prominence as a reform leader and turned him further toward progessivism.

Although he was governor for little more than two years, Wilson successfully carried out most of what reformers had struggled in vain to accomplish over the previous twenty to thirty years. As soon as he came into office, he took over the progressive program; to him it clearly envisioned the moderate regulation of big business and monopoly as the only democratic means of restoring competition and freedom of enterprise. He looked upon his election as a positive charge to exert executive leadership, and as head of his party he appealed over the heads of balky legislators directly to the people.

One of the first areas to which Wilson turned his attention was the conduct of elections. Some attempts had been made in the previous decade to reform the election machinery, but they were mostly ineffective. Wilson pushed through the legislature the Geran Act of 1911, which established the direct primary election of all candidates for state office as well as of the delegates to presidential nominating conventions. In addition, official uniform voting ballots were introduced and sample ballots were required to be sent to all registered voters. A corrupt practices act was also passed in the same year to regulate the conduct of campaigns and elections. It placed limitations upon expenditures, required the reporting of all contributions, and forbade contributions from corporations.

Another important innovation in government was accomplished through the passage of the Walsh Act of 1911. It permitted municipalities to set up a commission form of government.* Municipal elections were to be nonpartisan and conducted at a different time from elections on other levels of government. Commission government was looked upon by reformers as one of the best means of breaking boss rule of the cities.

In the economic sphere a public utilities act and an employer's liability act were passed. The first, designed to regulate utility operations, created a Board of Public Utility Commissioners with power to determine rates. The employer's liability act established the principle that an employer was legally liable for injuries to his employees incurred while at work, and set up a workmen's compensation system. Besides these laws, additional action was taken to provide more rigid factory inspection and tighten restrictions upon work by women and children.

The severest regulation of big business came from a series of laws sponsored by Wilson that were not actually passed until 1913, after he had already been elected President of the United States. There were seven measures in all, and they became known as the "Seven

*For a description of the commission form, see Chapter 6.

Sisters." They were antitrust laws designed to curb the operations of the giant corporations. Such forms of monopoly as holding companies and interlocking directorates were outlawed. The power to revoke charters under certain conditions was provided, and responsibility for violations of these regulations could be placed on individuals. The "Seven Sisters" were never strictly enforced and were finally repealed in 1920. They did serve, however, to drive many corporations out of the state and to end Jersey's reputation as "home of the trusts."

As significant as all these laws were, the effect of Wilson's short stint in New Jersey government went far beyond reform legislation. It gave to the state a new lease on life, revitalizing the democratic process and freeing politics from bossism and control by special interests. From that time forward political officials could not ignore the popular will, as they had in the past.

Wilson Moves On to the White House. During the latter part of his term as governor, Wilson began to devote more and more of his efforts to campaigning for the Presidency. First he had to win the nomination of the Democratic Party. To gather support he spoke in various parts of the country and went out to meet the people. At the national convention that met in Baltimore in June, 1912, Wilson was supported by the liberal wing of his party, but his chances at first were not too bright. However, William Jennings Bryan threw his support to him, and finally, on the forty-sixth ballot, Wilson was nominated. He was assured of election because the Republican Party had split in two, the regulars nominating President William Howard Taft and the progressive wing Theodore Roosevelt.

Wilson carried forty states with a total of 435 electoral votes. However, the popular vote showed: Wilson, 6,293,000; Roosevelt, 4,119,000; Taft, 3,484,000. Thus, in popular votes Wilson was a minority president, as Lincoln had been a half-century earlier. Actually, the progressive principles that Wilson and Roosevelt stood for were supported by three-fourths of the people.

Along with Wilson's triumph, New Jersey Democrats captured all but one of the state's seats in the House of Representatives, sent William Hughes of Passaic County to the Senate, and won complete control of the legislature. The year 1913 marked the last time down to the present writing that the Democrats have controlled both houses of the legislature. Later that year they elected James F. Fielder of Hudson County as governor. However, by 1914 the Republicans in the state were able to reunite and regain control of political affairs.

Several amendments to the state constitution were submitted to the people at a special election held in 1915, but all were defeated. One of them would have given the right to vote to women. Another was designed to simplify the amendment process itself.

President Wilson's first administration was an extremely successful one; many of the measures of his New Freedom program were outgrowths of his term as governor. However, during these years he gradually lost control of the New Jersey Democratic organization. The men he supported as candidates for governor and senator in 1916 were rejected by his party. Those nominated were defeated on election day by their Republican opponents. Wilson was humiliated further that day. Though his bid for re-election was successful, he lost New Jersey by a margin of close to 60,000 votes.

The voting nation-wide was so close that Wilson's Republican opponent, Charles Evans Hughes, went to bed Election Night believing he was victorious. It was not until the results were tabulated in California, giving Wilson a plurality of 4,000 and the state's electoral votes, that he was established the winner. Although his electoral margin was extremely narrow, his popular plurality of 600,000 and an increase in his total votes of almost three million over 1912 were better measures of the extent to which Wilson had won the support of the American people.

The Republican elected governor of New Jersey in 1916 was the president of the state Senate, Walter E. Edge of Atlantic City. Many advances were made in state affairs during his term. He was an excellent administrator and was one of those most responsible for the construction of the Holland Tunnel and the Delaware River Memorial Bridge. The state was particularly fortunate in having Edge as its wartime governor. He co-operated with the Federal Government in home defense, raising of troops, maintenance of military camps, and passage of emergency war legislation. He resigned his post in 1919 to run successfully for the United States Senate.

It was at this time that the states ratified the Eighteenth Amendment to the Federal Constitution, which prohibited the manufacture and sale of intoxicating liquors. The amendment aroused bitter hostility in New Jersey, one of the three states that refused ratification. As might be expected, the problem of enforcement became an immediate issue in the state. The Republicans stood for enforcement; the Democrats ignored the law and came out in opposition. This was shrewd politics, because the large foreign-born population in the state was vehemently against prohibition. The result was that starting with 1919, the next three governors elected were Democrats.

The year 1920 marked the close of the Wilsonian era, first as governor and then as President for two terms. Although he finished

out his career broken in health and defeated in his efforts to obtain
his country's support for the Treaty of Versailles and the League of
Nations, Wilson had made an excellent record both in peace and war.
New Jerseyans can be proud in the knowledge that when historians
rank all the Presidents in the order of their success in office, Woodrow
Wilson, the only citizen of the state who ever achieved the nation's
highest office, is placed among the first five.

DO/DISCUSS

Many streets and buildings in New Jersey memorialize
the name of Woodrow Wilson as a great President of the
United States, but no municipality or place in the state
bears his name. Read about Wilson's life and make a statement for or against such an honorary recognition.

The Recent Era: 1920—1964

An examination of political life in New Jersey from 1920 to the
present shows a mosaic-like pattern. During this time there was,
first, a period when the state's politics were dominated by one of the
last great "bosses" in the country. This was followed by the successful
culmination of a prolonged effort to write a new constitution, one that
gave the state a model form of government. In a span of little more
than forty years the country went through prosperity, then depression, then war, and again prosperity, accompanied this time by "cold
war." In some years the direction of the state's political life and the
party allegiance of its citizens paralleled those of the nation as a whole.
At other times Jersey went merrily along its own unique way.

The Hague Years

During the 1920's the Republicans were overwhelmingly successful
in New Jersey in every presidential election, and in all but one Congressional race. They also completely dominated the state legislature.

However, from 1920 to 1929 three Democrats in a row occupied the governor's chair This resulted from a combination of men of outstanding qualifications and the aforementioned prohibition issue.

Edward I. Edwards of Hudson County was a man of honesty and ability, but also a wily politician. He had promised to make the state as "wet" as the Atlantic Ocean and did everything in his power to prevent the enforcement of prohibition. When the Republican legislature passed the stringent Van Ness Act, he promptly vetoed the measure. However, he was easily overridden. The positive accomplishments of Edwards' term included the formation of the State Police Department and the creation of the Port of New York Authority, a bi-state commission of New Jersey and New York. After finishing his term he was elected to the United States Senate by a large plurality, conducting his campaign on the wet-and-dry issue.

Edwards was succeeded by Judge George S. Silzer of Middlesex County, who displayed outstanding courage, integrity, and business efficiency, comparable to Republican Governor Edge. Silzer was a skillful politician who was able to accomplish many worthwhile changes although faced with a hostile legislature. He did so by appealing directly to the public. He strengthened the administration of state government, enhanced public education, and developed a program for good roads. During his three years in office he maintained a sturdy independence from the Hudson County Democratic machine directed by Mayor Frank Hague.

Few men in the history of the state have had as much influence over political affairs for as long a period of time, have wielded as much power, or have had as fascinating a career as had Frank Hague. Mayor of Jersey City from 1917 to 1947, Democratic boss of Hudson County from 1915 to 1949, and leader of his party in the state from 1919 to 1949, Hague was also vice-chairman of the Democratic National Committee and exerted a strong influence on national politics for a time.

During Hague's reign the Democrats were able to elect six governors while the state was normally Republican. It has been said that no judicial or administrative appointment was made without Hague's approval. Not only did he dominate his own party, but many Republican leaders worked in close harmony with his wishes, to the point where they were known as "Hague Republicans." As for his own Jersey City and Hudson County, he was their absolute and dictatorial ruler, having built up one of the most loyal and efficient political machines this nation has ever known.

'Hagueism.'   Hague was able to compile such a remarkable record through a combination of energy and drive, keenness of mind, political skill, demagoguery, and dedication to public service. He cleansed city and county of racketeering and vice, greatly improved welfare conditions, and provided superb public medical facilities. To this day people in the area revere his memory. What Hague's reign cost them in monetary terms probably will never be known, but its effects upon the democratic process have been evident. Not only was there the absence of a functioning opposition during his time, but the heritage of "Hagueism" still effects politics in the area. During the three decades that his machine provided such huge Democratic pluralities in Hudson County, the party's organizations in other parts of the state withered and declined. Furthermore, Republicans constantly used the issue of "Hagueism" to keep independent voters as well as their supporters in line, at the same time drawing attention away from any bosses in their own party.

Progress Under Moore.   A man whose name was often associated with Frank Hague's was A. Harry Moore of Jersey City. He was a close and loyal friend who consistently co-operated with Hague; yet he displayed personal honesty and integrity throughout his lengthy public career. Moore was the best vote-getter this state has had in modern times. Three times elected governor, in 1925, 1931, and 1937, he also was elected to the United States Senate in 1934. Moore's great personal popularity resulted from his outstanding abilities as a public speaker, his attractive personality, his sympathies for the plight of the laboring class and the needy, and his accessibility at all times to the people of the state.

During each of his three times as governor, Moore had to deal with Republican legislatures. Therefore, any positive measures had to be the result of compromise and concession. The following were the major accomplishments of his administration:

1. the prohibition of child labor and the elimination of sweatshops;
2. the creation of a State Planning Board and a State Housing Authority;
3. the establishment of a complete state highway system and a Department of Motor Vehicles;
4. the start or completion of the Holland Tunnel, the George Washington Bridge, the Camden-Philadelphia Bridge, the Staten Island bridges, and the Lincoln Tunnel;
5. the establishment of a county parks system;

6. the creation, after the repeal of prohibition, of the Alcoholic Beverage Control Commission to regulate the sale of liquor;
7. the launching of a program for the care and education of physically handicapped children;
8. the establishment of a tenure system for public school teachers and administrators.

Moore's second term was sandwiched between those of two Republicans, Morgan F. Larson of Perth Amboy and Harold G. Hoffman, also of Middlesex County. Although both had legislatures controlled by their own party, neither had administrations that were as successful as had been anticipated. Larson was handicapped by the passage of a number of "ripper" bills. This was a legislative tactic used to reduce the governor's power, either by eliminating existing bureaus and thus legislating out of jobs those appointed by the governor, or by creating new bureaus and providing that their officials be chosen by the legislature. "Ripper" legislation grew very serious during this period and caused a loss of unity and efficiency in state government, as well as a wasting of public funds.

Governor Hoffman served during the later years of the Great Depression of the 1930's. Like Moore, much of his attention was devoted to the problems of unemployment and public finance. Under the direction and support of the Federal Government, broad programs of social security, public health, and public works projects were inaugurated. Many municipalities had gone bankrupt because they could not collect taxes due them. In turn they were unable to pay their teachers and other workers. The state took the lead in helping them and the counties to reorganize their budgetary practices and to develop refinancing plans. This was done under the supervision of the State Department of Local Government.

The event during this period that gave New Jersey national — even international — notoriety had nothing directly to do with the depression or efforts to overcome it. It was the kidnapping and murder of the child of Colonel Charles A. "Lindy" Lindbergh, on the night of March 1, 1932 near Hopewell in Mercer County. Bruno Richard Hauptmann was charged and found guilty of the crime in a sensational trial. The affair was not climaxed until April 3, 1936, when Hauptmann was executed.

The depression years witnessed a resurgence of Democratic strength on the national level. Starting in 1932, Franklin Delano Roosevelt was elected to four successive terms, and, strangely enough, New Jersey supported him each time. Yet during this entire time the Democrats in the state could not once win control of the state's Con-

NEW JERSEY'S MAJOR ROADS AND HIGHWAYS

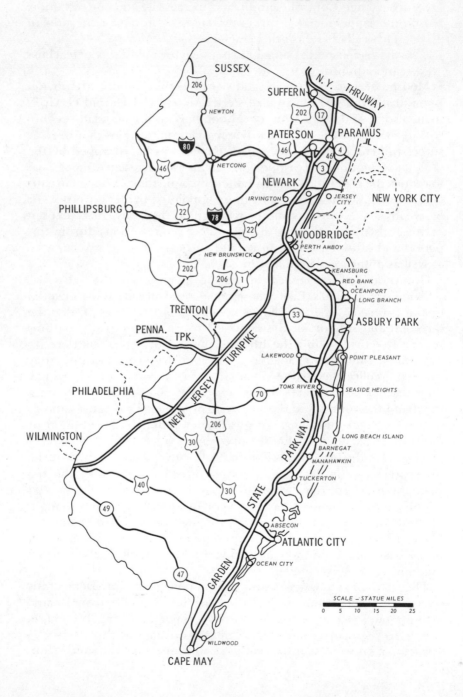

gressional delegation and were able to elect only two United States senators, Moore and William H. Smathers of Atlantic County. However, they did succeed on the state level in electing in 1940 another Democratic governor, Charles Edison of Essex County.

Governor Edison Fights in Vain. Edison had been Secretary of the Navy under President Roosevelt, and he rode to victory with his chief, who won a tradition-breaking third term. Edison had been the choice of the Hague machine, and it was thought by all that he would "play ball" with it. But Edison was a man of courage and independence and, like Woodrow Wilson a generation earlier, soon made it clear that he would be free from dictation. He refused to act on Hague's recommendations for judicial appointments and broke with him over the problem of railroad taxation so important to Hudson County. As the split widened, Edison tried to bring an end to "Hagueism" and rid the state of bossism. But his strong, honest leadership was not matched by sufficient political "know-how" to break such an entrenched machine. The voters failed to respond and give him their support, and the Republican-controlled legislature was more interested in benefitting from the division in the Democratic Party than it was in ending boss rule. Thus when Edison's term expired, Hague returned to power, but his rule was no longer as absolute as it had been formerly.

Edison's chief contribution to the development of the state was his efforts to bring about a complete revision of the constitution. A special commission was appointed made up of leading citizens and legal experts and headed by Robert C. Hendrickson of Gloucester County. The commission came up with a draft of a new constitution. Public hearings were held by the legislature, but no further action was taken until 1943, a year later. At that time a referendum was approved by the people directing the legislature to draft a new constitution for submission to the voters. The document developed was modeled after the one drafted by the Hendrickson commission, but it was rejected by the voters in the general election of 1944 after a bitter campaign. Opposition to the document was whipped up by Mayor Hague for personal reasons, but the chief cause of its defeat was the feeling that since it was drafted by the Republican-dominated legislature, it was not a well-balanced constitution.

Edge and Driscoll Make Gains. Although the movement to revise the constitution failed for the moment, efforts were continued by Edison's Republican successors, Walter E. Edge of Atlantic County, who had served his first term during World War I, and Alfred E. Driscoll of Camden County. In addition, rather than do nothing until a new constitution was adopted, both governors proceeded within the limits of their powers to overhaul and revitalize the state's administration. Their target was the tangle of bureaus and agencies with overlapping functions and indefinite lines of responsibility that had developed over many years as the need for state services increased. Major departments like education, economic development, law, and finance were reorganized.

Other significant action taken by Edge and Driscoll included the establishment of a Labor-Management Institute in 1947, the trebling of state aid to local school districts, and the creation of the Turnpike Authority in 1948. The last-named agency has been responsible for the construction and operation of the New Jersey Turnpike, which has proven to be the most successful limited-access toll highway in the nation. Another major development was the passage of the Fair Employment Practices Act of 1945, which created the Division Against Discrimination in the Department of Education. It was charged with preventing discrimination in employment because of race, creed, or nationality. In 1949 the jurisdiction of the division was increased to include discrimination in public places such as restaurants and amusement parks. In 1963 the division was transferred to the Department of Law and Public Safety.

The Constitution of 1947

Constitutional revision was once again brought to the forefront of public attention in January, 1947, when Governor Driscoll stressed its necessity in his inaugural address. Working closely with leaders of both parties, he helped set up the machinery for writing a new constitution. Delegates to a convention were nominated on a bipartisan basis and were people of very high caliber. They were elected by the voters of the state in June, at which time the vote to authorize the convention was better than five to one in favor. The convention met at Rutgers University, New Brunswick, to reduce as much as possible any political atmosphere. The only limitations placed upon the delegates were that they could not alter the territorial boundaries of the counties or change the undemocratic basis of representation in the Senate or the Assembly. These restrictions were designed to appease the rural counties, which feared urban domination.

Most of the work of the convention proceeded very smoothly during the summer months, primarily because the issues had been analyzed and refined over the years during which the struggle for revision had been carried on. However, two somewhat minor matters were so controversial that the outcome of the convention hinged upon their solution. One involved the question of gambling. There were groups that wanted to eliminate all forms of gambling in the state; there were others that wanted to legalize games like bingo, provided the profits were used for charitable purposes; there were still others that wanted to keep intact the constitutional provision that permitted only pari-mutuel betting at race tracks. Eventually, a compromise was worked out, leaving things as they were, but providing that the legislature in the future could take action on the subject following a referendum by the people. The issue was finally resolved in 1953 when the voters supported a constitutional amendment authorizing bingo games and raffles.

The other controversial matter was the persistent problem of railroad taxation. Led by Frank Hague, Hudson County, where most of the railroad property was located, fought for the elimination of preferential tax treatment for the railroads. A bitter behind-the-scenes struggle took place, with Hague threatening to block constitutional revision, as he had done three years earlier. An agreement was finally hammered out stating that all local and state real estate taxes "shall be assessed according to the same standard of value; and . . . at the general tax rate of the taxing district in which the property is situated."

The Constitution's Changes. The convention finished its work early in September, 1947, and the new constitution was submitted to the voters on November 3. It was overwhelmingly adopted by a vote of 653,000 to 185,000. The Constitution of 1947 was a vast improvement over its predecessor. The position of the governor was greatly enhanced; his term of office was increased to four years and he was permitted to succeed himself once. To strengthen his veto power a two-thirds vote of the legislature was made necessary to override, instead of a simple majority. The legislature was forbidden to elect or appoint on its own any administrative or judicial official except the state auditor, and the governor's power to remove appointees was broadened. His authority as chief executive was spelled out more fully, and provision was made for major reorganization of administrative departments.

The terms of assemblymen were increased from one to two years and those of senators from three to four years. Authorization was granted for increasing their salaries. The constitution provided for the complete reorganization of the judicial system in the state, making it one of the best in the nation. Another important change was a liberalization of the amending process. If three-fifths of each house of

the legislature approved, an amendment would be submitted directly
to the people. If only a majority of each house approved, then the
amendment had to be accepted by a majority again the next year be-
for it could be submitted to the voters. In addition, the state bill of
rights was expanded to include a provision for the prevention of discrimination because of religion, race, color, ancestry, or national
origin, and a provision to guarantee the right of collective bargaining
for persons in private employment.

Shifting Party Fortunes

The Constitution of 1947 went into effect on January 1, 1948.
Alfred Driscoll was the first governor eligible under it to succeed
himself. In the election held in November, 1949, he won by a plurality
of 75,000 over his Democratic opponent, Elmer Wene, state senator
from Cumberland County. The closeness of the vote, accompanied
by a sharp split among the Democrats of Hudson County that denied
to Wene the customary huge plurality, cast strong doubt on Driscoll's
popularity. Nevertheless, in his second term, a four-year one, he
served the state well.

During these years the people of New Jersey shifted their allegiance
on the national level in favor of Republican candidates. They had
supported Thomas E. Dewey in 1948 when he tried to defeat Harry
Truman's bid for re-election. They continued to vote Republican in
1952 and 1956, helping the ticket of Dwight D. Eisenhower and
Richard M. Nixon to victory. In fact, Jerseyans supported Eisenhower
for a second term by giving him a phenomenal vote nearly double that
of his opponent, Adlai Stevenson. In addition, the citizens of the state
consistently elected Republicans to the United States Senate and gave
that party control of the state's delegation to the House of Representatives.

However, the Democrats continued to show their ability to occupy
the governor's chair more often than not. At the end of Driscoll's
second term, his party chose Paul L. Troast of Clifton, prominent
businessman and first chairman of the New Jersey Turnpike Authority. His Democratic opponent was Robert B. Meyner of Phillipsburg, former state senator from Warren County. Meyner won the
election held in November, 1953 by the sizable margin of 150,000
votes. Four years later he was re-elected over Malcolm Forbes of
Bernardsville, state senator from Somerset County, and became the
first governor to serve two four-year terms.

Slim Margins. As noted earlier, the Republicans had had almost unbroken control of both houses of the legislature since Wilson's time. This near-monopoly of power was broken in 1958, when the Democrats captured the Assembly by a margin of two to one. Since then, they have maintained a substantial control of the lower house and have reduced the gap between themselves and the Republicans in the Senate. Beginning in 1960, the Senate margin has been narrowed to one seat. In November, 1962 a Senatorial contest took place in Union County to fill the vacancy created by the resignation and subsequent death of Robert C. Crane, Republican senator. The Democrats spared no effort in trying to win the seat, for victory would have meant their first control of both houses of the legislature in half a century. However, the Republican candidate, Nelson F. Stamler, Union assemblyman, won a clear-cut victory.

More recently, the pendulum of legislative control swung the other way. The election in November, 1963, which centered around a proposal for a $750 million bond referendum, brought a sharp reversal of Democratic fortunes and returned the Republicans to undisputed control of the legislature. At the time of this writing, the Senate is divided, fifteen Republicans and six Democrats, and the Assembly is divided, thirty-three Republicans and twenty-seven Democrats.

The gap also was narrowed in the state's Congressional delegation. The party division in the House of Representatives was reduced to eight Republicans and six Democrats in 1955 and again in 1961. With the addition of the fifteenth Congressional district in Middlesex County and its capture by the Democrats in the 1962 election, the division in the Eighty-eighth Congress, 1963-1965, became eight Republicans to seven Democrats. The state's two Senate seats were equally divided between the two parties since the election in 1958 of Harrison A. Williams, Jr., of Westfield, the first Democrat since 1944. Williams was formerly a congressman from the sixth district, comprising Union County. The Republican senator, Clifford P. Case of Rahway, was first elected to his position in 1954 and was subsequently re-elected in 1960. He had been congressman from the sixth district as well, serving from 1943 to 1952.

The development of New Jersey into a "swing state" with a fine balance between the major parties was further shown by three electoral contests in the early 1960's. In 1960 the Democrats were able to deliver the state's sixteen electoral votes to the national ticket headed by John F. Kennedy and Lyndon B. Johnson. The margin was extremely close, as it was nation-wide: only 22,000 votes separated Kennedy and Johnson from Richard Nixon and Henry Cabot Lodge.

In the same election, Senator Case was re-elected by a huge margin of more than 300,000 votes over his opponent, Democratic Party leader Thorn Lord of Princeton. The next year another closely contested election took place. It was the gubernatorial race between Republican James P. Mitchell, former Secretary of Labor under President Eisenhower, and Democrat Richard J. Hughes, former Superior Court judge. Although Mitchell was the favorite, Hughes showed himself to be a tireless and effective campaigner. He defeated his opponent by under 35,000 votes in November, 1961.

Referenda. Since the adoption of the present constitution, a number of important issues have been decided by the voters in referenda submitted to them at general elections. Reference was made earlier to the adoption in 1953 of the bingo and raffles amendment; further changes in gambling regulations were made in 1959 and 1961, affecting amusement games. In 1957 a significant constitutional amendment was adopted that decreased residence requirements for voters to six months in the state and sixty days in a county. This was further modified by an amendment in 1963 that reduced the county residence to forty days and eased requirements for absentee ballots in presidential elections.

A number of the referenda have dealt with bond issues designed to raise revenue for special state projects and services. The largest of these—a $750 million proposal for highway construction, institutions and agencies, and education, tied to surplus toll revenue from the New Jersey Turnpike—was defeated by the electorate in 1963.* The most significant of those adopted were:

1. Higher education—$15 million in 1951, $67 million in 1959;
2. Garden State Parkway—$285 million in 1952;
3. Institutions—$25 million in 1952, $40 million in 1961;
4. Water supply—$46 million in 1958;
5. Green Acres—$60 million in 1961.

Two other important political developments of this period were the reapportionment of seats in the state Assembly and the geographic shifts in strength of the two major parties. The first is described in detail near the beginning of Chapter 5. After years of delay and then only to avert action by the state Supreme Court, the legislature in 1961 readjusted the number of Assembly seats held by each county to more closely reflect recent shifts in population. Three seats each were taken from Essex and Hudson counties and distributed equally

*For a fuller description of this referendum, see the end of Chapter 8.

among six other counties that had shown the most growth. The shift in party strength was most dramatically illustrated by the lessening importance of the Democratic Party in Hudson County and its re-vitalization in Burlington, Camden, Essex, Mercer, Middlesex, and Passaic counties. At the same time, although Republican support con-tinued to come from the rural counties of the northwest and the south, the rapidly growing suburban counties of Bergen, Monmouth, and Morris have given that party much of its strength.

Thus, as New Jersey approaches the last third of the twentieth century, it can do so with a form of government that is, in the main, well suited to its needs and with a political system better balanced and more dynamic than ever before. It is well that these attributes exist, for the problems that must be dealt with have already made their chal-lenge and will demand the highest degree of interest, dedication and effort by all the people of the state. As Jersey's population leaps ahead, as her cities grow larger and her suburbs spread, as industry expands, the problems of human relations, education, urbanization, transpor-tation, water resources, and land use become greater and more com-plex. As the people demand more services from their municipalities, counties, and the state, the cost of government rises and the prob-lem of finding additional revenue becomes more acute.

DO/DISCUSS

Many students of political science today feel that the day of the powerful political boss is now past. If this be true, how do you account for the passing? What factors in American life could aid in the return of "bossism"?

SECTION III
Government

The State Capitol at Trenton, New Jersey's seat of government.

CHAPTER 5

The Structure
of State Government

The government of a state is based upon its constitution, which is a set of fundamental, organic laws or principles whence is derived the framework of government and the authority to pass and enforce ordinary laws. The Constitution of 1947 was the third one adopted in New Jersey's history and is presently in force. It overcomes many of the weaknesses of its predecessors and is reasonably short and flexible. It provides an effective separation of powers among the three branches of government — legislative, executive, and judicial. Reflecting the tendency of industrialized, urbanized America to strengthen the power of its chief executives, the authority and responsibility of the governor are markedly enhanced. In addition, administrative structure is streamlined and a judiciary system established that is serving as a model for other states to follow. Furthermore, additions to the bill of rights are designed to prevent discrimination against individuals because of race, color, religion, or national

111

origin and to guarantee the right of collective bargaining in private employment.

The Legislature

The legislature is the branch of government constitutionally authorized to determine state policy and enact it into law. It is bicameral (consisting of two houses), with an upper house, or Senate, and a lower house, or General Assembly. The former is composed of twenty-one senators, one from each county, and the latter of sixty assemblymen apportioned among the counties according to population, making the legislature one of the smallest in the nation. Assemblymen represent the entire county from which they are elected, and not the municipalities in which they live. A senator must be at least 30 years old, a citizen, and a resident of the state for four years and of the county he represents one year before election. An assemblyman must be at least 21, a citizen and a resident of the state for two years and his county for one year. Members of both houses receive annual compensation of $5,000. Because of their additional duties the President of the Senate and the Speaker of the Assembly are paid an additional one-third. Legislators may not hold any other state or Federal office, but they may hold county or municipal positions. All have legislative immunity, which means that they cannot be arrested while attending a session or going to or from one, nor can they be held accountable for what they say on the floor. These privileges are to insure that they will be free to speak and act in carrying out their legislative responsibilities and subject to no intimidation.

Apportionment Problems. As is true with many states, the issues of legislative representation and apportionment have been sources of continued difficulty in New Jersey's political life. The constitutional requirement of equal representation in the Senate has traditionally meant that the sparsely inhabited, agricultural counties have controlled that body, to the detriment of the more thickly populated industrial counties. So entrenched are rural interests that the possibility of amending this provision is almost nonexistent. However, as cities and suburbs continue to grow and spread, bringing industry and people to formerly rural areas, the disparity of representation will gradually diminish.

The problems of Assembly apportionment are different from what they are in most states, since members are elected on an at-large basis in each county rather than from individual districts. It is diffi-

cult for the voters in a populous county to choose wisely when they
are confronted with the task of electing a large number of assemblymen. Furthermore, since the minority voters often cannot elect a
single candidate, the assemblymen from each county are usually all
of the same party. This means that the majority party is generally
overrepresented in the Assembly as a whole. The constitution includes a limitation of sixty on the size of the house, a guarantee that
each county have at least one member, and a provision that there be a
reapportionment of seats after each Federal Census. This last requirement has been the source of delays and intense partisan struggle for a number of years. Counties with a large number of seats are
reluctant to lose any to counties experiencing population increases,
especially if the shift strengthens the opposing political party. Thus,
there was no reapportionment following the 1950 Census.

The issue came to a head again in 1960, after a decade of rapid
population growth in certain sections of the state, when efforts to
realign seats were blocked. This renewed failure to fulfill a constitutional requirement was brought before the state Supreme Court,
which held that if the Assembly did not agree to reapportionment by
a certain date, the court would enforce its own plan. Finally, on February 1, 1961, the day of the deadline, those who opposed the change
were overwhelmed, and the new apportionment was adopted. It
deprived Essex and Hudson counties of three seats each to provide
for one additional seat each for Bergen, Burlington, Camden, Middlesex, Monmouth, and Union counties. The new apportionment of
seats in the Assembly, effective in 1962, is as follows:

Atlantic 2	Gloucester ... 1	Ocean 1
Bergen 7	Hudson 6	Passaic 4
Burlington...... 2	Hunterdon ... 1	Salem 1
Camden 4	Mercer......... 3	Somerset ... 1
Cape May 1	Middlesex ... 4	Sussex 1
Cumberland ... 1	Monmouth ... 3	Union 5
Essex 9	Morris 2	Warren...... 1

Workings of the Legislature. The legislature meets each year at the
State House in Trenton, the opening session occurring on the second
Tuesday in January. Before hearing the governor's annual message
in joint session, each house meets separately to organize. By the custom of "moving through the chairs," the majority leaders of the previous year are invariably chosen as President of the Senate and Speaker of the Assembly. As presiding officers, they wield considerable

power in their respective houses. They recognize members who desire to speak, an effective device in silencing debate or cutting off the minority; they decide parliamentary questions, subject to appeal, and have general direction of matters; they appoint all committees, determine to which one a bill should be referred, and have a strong voice in establishing the order in which bills come to the floor.

In recent years regular sessions have lasted into late spring (an exceptionally long period for a state legislature meeting annually). This is because it is the custom to meet once a week, on Monday, and work into the evening, a practice made possible by the short traveling time from all corners of the state. This permits legislators to engage in other occupations at home when they are not in Trenton on committee business. When he deems it in the public interest, the governor may call a special session—either of both houses, to enact certain legislation, or of the Senate alone, to confirm appointments. Although the governor may request that particular action be taken, there is no limitation on what may be done, nor is there any assurance that the legislature will give serious attention to what is asked of it.

Each house has its own committees, which, like those of the Federal Congress, are designed to divide among small groups the work of preparing legislation and to give individual legislators the opportunity to develop special competence in a few fields. Unfortunately, the committee system in New Jersey, as in many states, has not been successful. Even though in 1954 major changes were made and the number of standing committees reduced to twelve in each house, only a few committees meet regularly, hold public hearings, or study bills thoroughly. The basic cause of failure is the dependence of the rank-and-file members upon party leadership. If the leaders of the party in power approve a measure, it generally passes; if they oppose, then it dies. The device used to maintain party regularity is the caucus. This is a secret meeting in each house of the legislators of the majority party to determine what action should be taken on bills that are coming up for consideration. The caucus is more effective in the Senate, where it is possible, if the majority holds eleven of the twenty-one seats, for six senators to block a measure from reaching the floor, despite the wishes of the other fifteen. Although there were some modifications made in the system during the 1950's, and it is claimed by legislators that the caucus no longer operates, there is much to support the belief that this undemocratic device still exists.

Lawmaking Powers.   The legislature of New Jersey has, essentially, the same broad scope of lawmaking powers as do other states.

Because of the growing complexity of economic and social life, these powers are on the increase. However, there are, besides those listed in the Federal Constitution, a number of limitations on the legislature's authority that are specified in the Constitution of New Jersey. The most important prohibitions are:

1. passing bills on more than one subject by putting "riders" or additions on them;
2. appointing any executive, administrative, or judicial officer, except the state auditor;
3. granting a divorce;
4. authorizing gambling of any kind without a referendum or vote of approval by the citizens of the state;
5. passing general laws applying only to particular persons, places, or corporations.

Although this last prohibition was put into effect in 1875, the state was plagued with private and local bills for many years. The legislature adopted the practice of classifying counties and cities in such a specific fashion that a carefully worded measure would only apply to a particular situation. In recent years, the governor has vetoed a number of these special bills, the courts have found some others unconstitutional, and the legislature itself has assumed a greater degree of restraint. Thus, special legislation has been significantly curtailed.

Legislative Procedure. The process by which a bill becomes a law in the New Jersey legislature is similar to that of other state legislatures and the Congress. Bills may be introduced in either house, except for revenue measures, which must originate in the Assembly. All bills go through what is called three "readings." "First reading" occurs when formal introduction of a bill takes place, and the clerk of the house records and reads its title and number. Following this, the bill is printed and referred by the presiding officer to an appropriate committee. If a majority of the committee supports the measure, it will be reported out, either in its original form or with changes, called amendments. If the majority opposes it, they will not refer it out to the whole house, but allow it to "die in committee."

When a bill is favorably reported, it is placed on the house calendar and waits its turn to advance to "second reading." At this stage, changes in the bill may be made from the floor by any of the members. If the measure surmounts this hurdle, it can be brought up for "third reading," or final passage, after the lapse of one day. This delay can be disregarded provided three-fourths of the membership agree to suspend the rules and declare the bill an emergency measure. Further debate may take place at third reading, but for most measures only the sponsor will speak, stating in a few words why the bill should be passed. Following this, the presiding officer authorizes a roll-call vote. In the upper house the roll is read by the clerk, and each senator casts his vote orally. In the Assembly the voting procedure is speeded by use of electrical roll-call machinery. Two large scoreboards behind the Speaker's rostrum record each member's vote as he presses a switch at his desk, and the final count is tabulated electronically. Final passage requires the approval of a simple majority of all members in each house, thirty-one votes in the Assembly and eleven in the Senate.

When a measure fails to pass, the sponsor, if he feels that he can subsequently persuade some of its opponents to change their minds, can obtain another vote at a later time simply by having the clerk record him as opposing the bill. This allows him to bring it up again for reconsideration at a future date, since he is officially an opponent. If a bill is amended and passed in one house in a form different from that in which it was passed in the other house, it must be sent back to the house of origin for reconsideration. Only when a bill is passed in identical form by both houses is it forwarded to the governor for his consideration.

As many as 1,000 bills and resolutions may be introduced in a single session of the legislature. To make sure that they are worded in appropriate legal language, conform to the constitution, and do not overlap or conflict with existing statutes, there exists the Law Revision and Legislative Services Commission. In addition to these functions, the commission and its staff carry on a continuing revision of the state's laws and recommend the repeal of obsolete laws.

Lobbying. All the measures that are introduced in the legislature are not necessarily drawn up by their sponsors. Many are written by the administrative departments of the executive branch, by various civic organizations, and by other special-interest groups. These organizations employ individuals to attend legislative sessions and protect their interests. Such individuals are known as "lobbyists," because they congregate in the halls or lobbies of the legislature and there attempt to win members over to the viewpoints they represent. Lobbyists seek support for measures their groups are sponsoring or opposition to those they consider harmful.

Much lobbying is neither sinister nor hurtful to the legislative process. Some lobbyists are highly qualified professional personnel who provide much-needed technical information; others represent groups that act to promote the public good, such as the League of Women Voters. Unfortunately, there are pressure groups concerned only with promoting their own selfish interests. These may employ lobbyists who supply distorted information. In recent years many state legislatures and Congress have taken steps to regulate the activities of lobbyists, but, in general, these controls have not proven very effective. Aside from prohibiting outright bribery, New Jersey has not taken any steps in this direction.

The Executive

The chief executive of New Jersey is the governor, whose main functions are to put into effect and enforce the laws passed by the legislature and, by appointing key officials and assuming responsibility for the thousands of workers in the executive branch, to supervise the administration of the state's government. In addition, he participates in the legislative process, has several judicial powers, and is commander in chief of the state militia. He is the leader of his political party and, as the only state officer elected by all the people, represents all Jerseyans. He is one of the most powerful state officials in the nation.

The constitutional qualifications for the governorship are quite simple. A candidate must be at least 30 years of age, a United States citizen for twenty years, and a resident of the state for seven years. The yearly salary is $35,000, plus an expense account of $20,000. Starting in 1956 the governor had been provided with an executive mansion, Morven in Princeton.

The governor is chosen at a general election held every four years in an odd-numbered year, so as not to conflict with national elections. He may succeed himself only once. If he wishes to run again, he must wait at least one full term. This is a vast improvement over what existed before the adoption of the present constitution. Prior to 1947, the governor had a three-year term and could not succeed himself, which prevented him from developing any long-term program. The present arrangement, nevertheless, still denies the voters the right to continue in office a two-term governor they feel is the individual best qualified for the job.

The governor is inaugurated on the third Tuesday in January following his election and is sworn in by the chief justice of the state's Supreme Court. His oath consists of a pledge to support the constitutions of the United States and of New Jersey and to faithfully perform all the duties of his office. The state is one of the few that does not have a lieutenant governor. In case the office is vacated for any reason, the first to succeed is the President of the Senate, followed by the Speaker of the Assembly. It has been the practice in recent years for these two officers to take turns as acting governor when the governor is out of the state on business or a vacation.

Executive Powers. As chief executive, the governor has the power to appoint the officials of the various executive departments, bureaus, and agencies, as well as the judges of the state courts. The only restriction upon his authority is that a majority of the Senate must approve his appointments. It is here that there occurs the custom of "Senatorial courtesy," according to which senators co-operate with one another by refusing to approve a nominee who is opposed by the senator from the nominee's home county. To get around this check, governors may make interim or recess appointments after the legislature has adjourned, such appointments expiring at the end of the next session. The only restriction is that the appointee cannot be a person already refused confirmation.

The governor also has the power of removal. He can dismiss all the executive officials he has the power to appoint, except the secretary of state and the attorney general, whose terms of office coincide with the governor's. All other individual heads of principal departments are removable at the governor's pleasure. Other officers are removable only "for cause," which means formal charges, a hearing, and a determination of guilt.

The Constitution of 1947 did much to overcome the confusion, overlapping, waste, and lack of centralized responsibility that existed in the executive branch of the government. At one time, there were ninety-six independent departments, bureaus, boards, and commissions, making it impossible for any governor to properly supervise the administration of government. Although the new constitutional restriction allowed as many as twenty principal departments, the commission established to reorganize the administrative structure was able to allocate all existing agencies into fourteen departments. They are shown on the chart on page 119. Nine of these departments are headed by an individual; the other five are under a board or commission. Although the governor's constitutional authority over all the departments is not complete, the reorganization and on-going revisions make the administration of New Jersey one of the best structured in the nation.

Legislative Powers and Influence. In addition to his executive functions the governor has very important legislative powers. His inaugural address upon taking office, his annual messages at the opening sessions of the legislature, and any additional special messages he

EXECUTIVE BRANCH OF THE NEW JERSEY STATE GOVERNMENT

ELECTORATE

GOVERNOR

DEPARTMENTS

OFFICE OF THE CHIEF EXECUTIVE
SECRETARY
COUNSEL
EXECUTIVE ASSISTANT
PRESS SECRETARY

AGRICULTURE
BOARD OF AGRICULTURE
SECRETARY
DIVISIONS:
Animal Industry
Markets
Plant Industry
Information
Administration
OFFICE:
Milk Industry

BANKING AND INSURANCE
COMMISSIONER
BANKING ADVISORY BOARD
BUREAUS:
Banking
Savings and Loan Associations
Insurance
Actuarial
REAL ESTATE COMMISSION

CIVIL SERVICE
COMMISSION
PRESIDENT
CHIEF EXAMINER
DIVISIONS:
Examinations
Administrative Services
Executive Services
Classification and Organization, State Services
Classification and Organization, Municipal Services
Research and Planning

CONSERVATION AND ECONOMIC DEVELOPMENT
COMMISSIONER
DIVISIONS:
State and Regional Planning
Veterans' Services
Water Policy and Supply
Shell Fisheries
Fish and Game
Administration
Resource Development

DEFENSE
CHIEF OF STAFF
DIVISIONS:
Adjutant-General
Personnel
Operations and Training
Logistics
Engineering
Fiscal and Finance
State Maintenance
War Records and History
U.S. Fiscal and Property
Civil Defense and Disaster Control
Army National Guard
Air National Guard
Naval Militia

EDUCATION
BOARD OF EDUCATION
COMMISSIONER
DIVISIONS:
Administration
Controversies and Disputes
Curriculum and Instruction
Higher Education
Vocational Education
Business and Finance
State Library, Archives, and History
State Museum
NEW JERSEY SCHOOL FOR THE DEAF
SURPLUS PROPERTY AGENCY

HEALTH
COMMISSIONER
PUBLIC HEALTH COUNCIL
DIVISIONS:
Constructive Health
Environmental Health
Laboratories
Local Health Services
Preventable Diseases
Vital Statistics and Administration
Chronic Illness Control
Special Consultation Services
COMMISSIONS:
Air Pollution Control
Radiation Protection

LABOR AND INDUSTRY
COMMISSIONER
DIVISIONS:
Labor
Workmen's Compensation
Employment Security
STATE BOARD OF MEDIATION
REHABILITATION COMMISSION

STATE
SECRETARY OF STATE
STATE BOARD OF CANVASSERS
OFFICE OF ATHLETIC COMMISSION
ELECTIONS UNIT
LEGALIZED GAMES OF CHANCE CONTROL COMMISSION
DIVISION OF THE AGING
DIVISION OF LAWS AND COMMISSIONS

THE TREASURY
TREASURER
DIVISIONS:
Budget and Accounting
Taxation
Tax Appeals
Local Government
Purchase and Property
Investment
Administration
Pensions
Racing Commission

INSTITUTIONS AND AGENCIES
BOARD OF CONTROL
COMMISSIONER
DIVISIONS:
Welfare
Mental Health and Hospitals
Correction and Parole
Mental Retardation
Administration
Business Management
STATE PAROLE BOARD
BUREAU OF LEGAL AFFAIRS

LAW AND PUBLIC SAFETY
ATTORNEY GENERAL
DIVISIONS:
Law
State Police
Motor Vehicles
Weights and Measures
Professional Boards
Alcoholic Beverage Control
Civil Rights
Administration

PUBLIC UTILITIES
BOARD OF COMMISSIONERS
PRESIDENT
EXECUTIVE OFFICER
DIVISIONS:
Rates and Research
Engineering
Accounts and Finance
Railroads
Street Transportation
Administration
Legal Affairs

STATE HIGHWAY
COMMISSIONER
HIGHWAY ENGINEER
DIVISIONS:
Planning, Research, Soils and Tests
Roads, Design and Construction
Bridges, Design and Construction
Maintenance and Operations
State Aid and Federal Aid Secondary Roads
Administrative Services
Right-of-Way Acquisition and Titles
Personnel
Railroad Transportation

wishes to send contain his views on the condition of the state, his ideas on the operation of government, or recommendations of specific measures to carry out his ideas. He is also required to deliver each year a budget message, which is a detailed statement of the state's finances, including the sources and amounts of revenue expected and the anticipated expenditures for the coming fiscal year. (The fiscal year runs from July 1 to the following June 30.) The budget recommendations are turned over to a joint appropriations committee of the legislature for thorough study and the drawing up of bills to authorize the expenditures. Additional taxes may have to be provided, because of the constitutional prohibition on expenditures exceeding revenue.

Over and above the issuance of messages and the authority to call special sessions (discussed earlier in this chapter), the governor plays a direct role in the legislative process. All bills passed by both houses of the legislature must be submitted for his consideration. If he approves a measure, it becomes law. If he disapproves, he may veto it and return it, with his objections, to the house of origin. If both houses can each muster a two-thirds vote, the bill automatically becomes law; if either fails, the bill is dead. The governor has the power to veto a bill conditionally, which means that he may return it with recommendations for specific changes. If his suggested amendments are agreed to and repassed by both houses, the bill is submitted to him again for his approval. In addition, he is authorized to veto individual portions of an appropriation bill while approving the rest of it. This is called an item veto. Although there are constitutional time limits set upon the governor for his action on bills, it has become the practice to have them presented to him at his convenience. This means that several months may go by before he acts on certain measures, saving him from making quick decisions when scores of them are passed at one time.

The governor's authority is not limited to those constitutional powers specifically granted to him; instead, there are a number of ways that an occupant of the office who has a definite program for the state, a positive conviction of the importance of the governorship, and a strong personality can exert his influence. As the only state official elected by all the voters, he is the spokesman for the whole people, which means that the legislature must adhere on most occasions to his requests. In any executive-legislative dispute, he can more effectively arouse public opinion through press releases and speeches and thus gain support than can individual legislators.

The governor can also exert a great amount of authority as the leader of his party, especially when the party has a majority of the seats in both houses. It is quite common for a strong executive to apply political pressure on those who oppose his policies. By means of patronage, the power to appoint hundreds of important and lesser officials in the executive and judicial branches, he can "reward his friends and punish his enemies." No legislator wishes to be deprived of his share of these positions for those who support him at election time and for prominent individuals in his country.

Limitations on Executive Power. This does not mean that the governor's power is absolute. Despite the application of all forms of pressure, the legislature may not pass the measures he wishes. His program cannot be put into operation without funds, and all appropriations must be granted by that body. Confirmation by the Senate is required for his appointments. In addition, the governor may be impeached and removed from office if found guilty of crime. Impeachment, or the formal accusal of wrongdoing, is accomplished by a majority of the Assembly. This is followed by a hearing of evidence in the Senate, which acts as a court. A two-thirds vote is required for conviction, which results in removal from office. Of course, this extreme action has hardly ever been used, but it is available as a constitutional safeguard against executive tyranny or criminal action.

The Governor's Aides. Because of his numerous responsibilities and the tremendous demands made upon his time and energy, the governor has several kinds of assistance. The administrative heads of the fourteen executive departments act as a cabinet that aids him in developing policy and carrying out his program. He has a personal staff, headed by an executive secretary, who is in charge of all the professional and clerical workers. One of the secretary's responsibilities is to act as a screening agent of all those who seek appointments with his chief or extend invitations for him to speak or attend ceremonial functions. The governor also has a personal counsel, who serves as legal advisor on legislation, veto messages, and such matters as pardons, clemency, and extradition (the surrender of an alleged criminal by one state to another). In addition, such matters as relations with the press, radio, and television, public relations in general, responding to a heavy load of mail, and conducting research are handled by members of the executive staff.

The Judiciary

The judiciary is comprised of a system of courts and is the branch of government responsible for the administration of justice. Any citizen who feels that his rights are in danger from any source can appeal for justice. The courts protect the individual from wrongdoers by sentencing those who have broken the laws; they protect him from unjust accusations of wrongdoing by providing a fair trial; they settle legal disputes between individuals.

Essentially there are four types of legal actions for which the courts are responsible. Criminal actions are those cases in which violations of law have been committed and the state is seeking to convict the alleged offender. Civil actions embrace disputes between private individuals or groups, generally involving damage suits or violations of contract. The party initiating the suit is called the plaintiff, and the one being sued is the defendant. A third type of action is called equity, which consists of cases in which an individual has been or may be wronged, even though no crime or breaking of contract is involved. An example is a matrimonial dispute. A fourth type of action is probate cases, which deal with wills and the administration of estates. In addition, there are two forms of jurisdiction, original and appellate. A court is said to have original jurisdiction when a case may start in it. Courts with appellate jurisdiction hear cases that are referred to them from lower courts.

Prior to the Constitution of 1947, New Jersey had probably the most complicated and cumbersome judicial system in the nation. There was such a patchwork of courts with overlapping jurisdictions that the average citizen was baffled, and even expert lawyers could not always untangle the legal maze. Worst of all, there were long delays in the handling of cases, and individuals found legal costs prohibitive. The changes wrought by the new constitution climaxed a century-long struggle for reform. Much of the credit for bringing this fight to a successful climax and for the changes that make the state's judicial system a guide for other states to follow is given to Arthur T. Vanderbilt, former dean of New York University's Law School, a lawyer of national repute, and New Jersey's first chief justice under the new system.

The structure of the court system is shown on the chart on page 123. The supreme, superior, and county courts are specifically provided for by the constitution, whereas the inferior courts are established and may be altered or abolished by the legislature. New Jersey, unlike New York State, but like our Federal Government, follows the practice of appointment of judges (except for surrogates). The hope behind this method is to keep the judiciary out of politics. It is true that the custom has developed of making bipartisan appointments to courts with more than one judge, but every effort is made to

NEW JERSEY'S COURT SYSTEM

SUPREME COURT

CHIEF JUSTICE AND 6 ASSOCIATES
Has final decision in all appeals from lower courts; broad powers
of administration over all state courts.
First Term – 7 years, Tenure on reappointment, retirement at 70;
salary – $26,000, additional $1,000 for C.J.

SUPERIOR COURT

44 JUDGES; Term, Tenure, and retirement same as
Supreme Court; salary – $22,000

Law Division	Appellate Division	Chancery Division
Civil and criminal cases	Decides appeals from other two divisions and lower courts	Equity cases

COUNTY COURT

69 JUDGES, at least one in each county;
Term – 5 years, tenure after 10 years;
salary – $20,000.

INFERIOR COURTS

May be established, altered, or abolished by law. All judges appointed
by governor, except municipal judges and surrogates, latter elected.

COUNTY DISTRICT COURTS	MUNICIPAL COURTS	JUVENILE AND DOMESTIC RELATIONS COURTS	SURROGATE COURTS

insure that justices of the three constitutional courts are free from political obligation or financial temptation. They must have had at least ten years of legal experience in the state to be eligible, their salaries cannot be diminished during their terms, they cannot practice law or hold another position of profit—state, Federal, or private—and they must resign if they run for elective office. In addition, they are subject to impeachment.

Higher Courts.   The Supreme Court, which meets in Trenton, is the highest court in the state. Cases that come before it are generally in the form of appeals from decisions in lower courts. Procedure here differs markedly from that in the trial courts. Briefs, which are written arguments drawn up by counselors to support their positions in a case, are submitted ten days in advance so that the justices can familiarize themselves with the issues. Public hearings are held on Mondays, and each counselor has forty-five minutes to present oral arguments, during which time he may be subjected to probing questions by any justice. Following this, the court will confer privately on the cases just heard, and the chief justice will appoint, for each case, a justice to write the majority opinion. As a case is completed, the court's decision in the form of a majority opinion is announced as the first order of business on a subsequent Monday. If there has been disagreement, a dissenting justice may submit a minority opinion.

The Supreme Court has broad administrative powers over the state's judicial system. It makes the rules of procedure that the other courts must follow, and it has jurisdiction over the admission of lawyers to the bar and supervises their professional conduct. The chief justice is the administrative head of the judiciary and has the authority to assign judges from one court to another as needed. He is assisted in this function by an administrative director and a staff whose duties are to keep him informed on the status of judicial business throughout the state and to handle operational details. They also compile and publish statistics which are valuable in the study of crime and delinquency. In addition, an annual judicial conference is held that makes proposals for enhancing the efficiency of the courts and improving law enforcement.

Below the Supreme Court is the Superior Court, as shown on the chart on page 123. It has both original and appellate jurisdiction. The divisions indicated are functional and not rigidly structured; judges are shifted from one to another and each division can exercise the authority of the whole court. The Chancery Division primarily handles controversies dealing with property and trusts, as well as matrimonial cases. Divorces in New Jersey are granted on three grounds: desertion for more than two years, adultery, and extreme cruelty. Judgments do not become final until three months after the decree.

County courts were retained under the new system to provide original jurisdiction on a level close to the people. For administrative purposes, the county courts are divided into a probate division, which handles wills and estates, and a law division, which handles the other civil actions and all criminal cases. The county surrogate serves as clerk of the first division, and the county clerk is the clerk of the latter one. A county judge may try any criminal case, except murder, without a jury, if the defendant wishes to waive his right to trial by jury.

Lower Courts.   One of the inferior or lower courts is the county district court, which handles civil actions involving not more than $1,000, except automobile liability, which can go up to $3,000, and criminal cases that are not of an indictable nature. Some of the district courts have a small-claims division, which handles contractual disputes not exceeding $50. District judges are appointed by the governor for terms of five years, with salaries, payable by the county, that vary according to the county's classification and number of judges. The district courts as a whole have a tremendous volume of business: about 50 per cent of all civil cases are decided here.

With the elimination of the office of justice of the peace by the new constitution, municipal courts headed by magistrates came into being. There are about 500 such courts in the state. If they are within the confines of one community, the magistrates are appointed by the local government. If two or more municipalities set up a single court, the magistrate is appointed by the governor. All magistrates serve three year terms, with salaries determined by the local government. Municipal courts have jurisdiction over minor civil actions, violations of municipal ordinances and motor vehicle laws, and certain criminal offenses not classified as misdemeanors. The costs and fees set by the magistrate go into the municipal treasury.

Two other types of inferior courts that are specialized in nature are the surrogate court and the juvenile and domestic relations court. The former is presided over by the surrogate, who is the only elected judicial officer in the state; he serves a five-year term, with a salary fixed by the county. He has jurisdiction over wills, trusts, guardianships, and the like. Juvenile and domestic relations courts have been set up in the counties to deal with a wide range of offenses committed by juveniles, those under 18 years of age. All cases are heard privately without a jury to protect the youth from harmful publicity.

The court also has jurisdiction over matters involving the neglect or abuse of children, their temporary custody, and the support of a wife and family.

DO/DISCUSS

The Constitution of New Jersey (1947), Article I, guarantees twenty-one separate rights and privileges. Review this document and compose an original short story including obvious or subtle violations of one or more of the mentioned rights. This is called a case study. Read your story in class and have others attempt to detect the specific infringement.

CHAPTER 6

Local Government

An analysis of the government of New Jersey must include a study of the nature and function of its counties and municipalities. Although there are only twenty-one of the former, a small number by comparison with most other states, there are 568 municipalities. The network of counties, cities, towns, townships, boroughs, villages, and special districts—some large in size and population and others extremely small, some urban and others rural, some partly both—grew out of geographic factors, conditions of transportation and communication, and issues of local pride that were appropriate to "horse-and-buggy" days but not to the modern scene. Such multiplicity is unnecessary and may be undesirable, for the piling up of jurisdictions results in duplication, waste, and confusion. Worse still, it may be an obstacle to effective self-government. True democracy is not achieved by increasing the number of governments or of elective officers, but rather by the adaptation of government to modern community needs and by the selection of a few officials responsible to an intelligent, informed, and alert electorate.

Local governments do not exist by any original or inherent right, nor do they have any reserved or residual powers. They are created by the authority of the state in which they are situated, and by it are endowed with whatever powers and functions they possess. They are instruments of the state, employed in the enforcement of its laws, the collection of its taxes, and the performance of many of its administrative functions. Individual states can handle their localities in any way they see fit, giving or denying them home rule (a broad control

127

over their own affairs), trying out new forms of government, or consolidating existing units. Thus, the picture of local government in New Jersey is bound to be different from what it is elsewhere, and an examination of it is essential to an understanding of the state.

The County

The county as a governmental unit may be traced back through the Colonial Period to England, where in Anglo-Saxon times there existed its predecessor, the "shire."* It is a territorial and administrative subdivision of a state, competent to acquire and dispose of property, make contracts, and sue or be sued in court. In New Jersey the county plays an important role in the governmental affairs of the state, having obtained a renewed lease on life in the last quarter of a century. Much of this has come from Federal assistance programs that started with the depression and are administered on the county level. It might be added that thirteen of the counties were in existence before the state was created, nine of them before the end of the seventeenth century; therefore, one must also take into account the significance of tradition and local pride.

In New Jersey the county is an arm of the state, lacking constitutional authority, having no charter, and possessed of only those powers granted to it by the legislature. Each one falls under one of six classes, depending on population and location. The classification as determined by the legislature, based upon the 1960 Census, is as follows:

> First class—more than 600,000 population (Bergen, Essex, and Hudson)
>
> Second class—200,000 to 600,000 (Burlington, Camden, Mercer, Middlesex, Morris, Passaic, and Union)
>
> Third class—50,000 to 200,000 (Cumberland, Gloucester, Hunterdon, Salem, Somerset, and Warren)
>
> Fourth class—less than 50,000 (Sussex)
>
> Fifth class—bordering the Atlantic Ocean and with more than 100,000 population (Atlantic, Monmouth, and Ocean)
>
> Sixth class—bordering the Atlantic and with less than 100,000 (Cape May)

Board of Chosen Freeholders. The governing body in each county is called the Board of Chosen Freeholders, a unique title in the United

---

*The term sheriff derives from the combination of shire and "reeve," which was the name given to the chief agent of the king in the shire.

VITAL STATISTICS CONCERNING ALL NEW JERSEY COUNTIES

COUNTY	POPULATION	NUMBER OF HOUSEHOLDS	EFFECTIVE INCOME PER HOUSEHOLD	RETAIL SALES PER HOUSEHOLD	EDUCATION PEOPLE OVER 25 HIGH SCHOOL	COLLEGE	SQUARE MILES FOREST & FARM	INDUSTRIAL	RESIDENTIAL	TOTAL	NUMBER OF MANUFACTURING ESTABLISHMENTS	COVERED JOBS IN MANUFACTURING	COUNTY
ATLANTIC	160,880	48,400	$6,380	$5,032	45.0%	9.8%	78.6%	3.5%	8.4%	565.55	204	7,911	ATLANTIC
BERGEN	780,255	244,800	8,898	4,365	41.3	16.4	32.5	9.6	48.3	235.08	1,588	85,416	BERGEN
BURLINGTON	224,499	60,400	8,189	3,177	39.0	11.1	82.2	1.1	4.6	819.30	202	17,281	BURLINGTON
CAMDEN	329,035	118,500	7,279	4,112	40.4	9.9	64.6	3.0	25.0	222.16	440	50,659	CAMDEN
CAPE MAY	48,555	16,200	5,385	5,646	37.0	8.7	53.0	3.8	34.9	265.34	52	1,525	CAPE MAY
CUMBERLAND	106,850	32,000	5,962	4,547	34.1	8.3	84.0	0.8	7.3	502.40	225	21,417	CUMBERLAND
ESSEX	923,545	277,200	8,285	4,846	38.2	14.3	27.2	11.9	51.7	127.44	2,419	133,919	ESSEX
GLOUCESTER	134,840	41,500	6,834	3,382	36.9	11.0	75.4	2.4	16.5	328.60	125	10,993	GLOUCESTER
HUDSON	610,734	176,000	7,324	3,679	42.5	8.9	3.6	58.1	20.0	44.10	2,254	118,702	HUDSON
HUNTERDON	54,107	16,800	5,891	3,189	34.7	12.8	77.1	0.5	18.9	437.00	66	4,301	HUNTERDON
MERCER	266,392	72,900	8,498	5,030	41.7	17.6	58.8	5.8	29.5	226.00	380	37,697	MERCER
MIDDLESEX	433,856	131,400	8,028	3,943	47.3	14.6	57.8	14.6	17.9	308.79	598	69,966	MIDDLESEX
MONMOUTH	334,401	103,800	7,501	4,292	42.3	13.3	69.8	0.8	18.5	477.01	400	15,947	MONMOUTH
MORRIS	261,620	76,000	8,373	4,470	38.8	17.7	69.3	3.7	20.6	477.70	341	22,696	MORRIS
OCEAN	108,241	37,700	5,313	5,487	40.7	11.3	81.3	0.5	3.5	641.00	90	2,544	OCEAN
PASSAIC	406,618	130,200	7,343	4,364	45.4	11.0	62.4	3.7	29.1	192.20	1,431	77,517	PASSAIC
SALEM	58,711	18,000	6,877	3,774	44.5	20.2	70.8	2.9	22.2	343.02	45	11,664	SALEM
SOMERSET	143,913	41,300	7,950	3,574	36.7	15.1	58.5	3.2	34.2	305.10	139	18,868	SOMERSET
SUSSEX	49,255	15,400	5,525	3,839	36.2	12.8	74.9	0.1	13.5	526.30	61	2,867	SUSSEX
UNION	504,255	150,000	8,884	5,194	42.0	16.2	18.4	15.7	55.9	103.39	1,091	84,028	UNION
WARREN	63,220	19,700	6,143	3,496	37.5	9.5	77.1	0.3	19.4	362.00	104	11,248	WARREN
THE STATE	6,066,782	1,828,200	7,837	4,347						7,509.48	12,282	807,785	THE STATE

States. The name comes from the fact that during earlier times only those who were freeholders, that is, owned property, could vote and hold office, and those from among them who were chosen to administer the government were called "chosen freeholders." Prior to 1912 a county board consisted of members elected on a representative basis from each municipality. In that year the legislature passed a law enabling counties to establish small boards of from three to nine members depending upon population, elected at large, that is, by all the voters of the county. Since that time, all but Atlantic, Cumberland, Gloucester, and Salem have adopted small boards; membership in these four ranges from fourteen to thirty-four. All freeholders serve for a three-year term.

A Board of Chosen Freeholders operates like the commission form of government in a city, with both legislative and executive powers. Thus, the same group that determines policy also carries it out. One freeholder is chosen by his fellow members to act as director or presiding officer; usually he is the most widely known and influential member and a leader in county affairs. The board carries on its business by means of committees, with each member a chairman of one committee and a member of several others. The director makes the appointments. The set-up in a first-class county, however, varies from this, for such a county also chooses a county supervisor to act as chief administrative officer under the board. He is also elected for three years, but generally is returned to office as long as his party retains its majority in election years.

To do its work, the county must have sources of revenue. The principal ones are property taxes, fees, and payments from the state, with the first representing about three-fourths of the total. New Jersey is one of the few states whose counties do not levy a tax directly on the inhabitants within the county. Instead, property owners pay one tax bill to the municipality, which turns over a certain amount to the county. This procedure is simple and efficient, but it means that the average citizen, unaware of his contribution to its support, knows little and cares less about his county's government. Public hearings, even the one in which the annual budget is discussed, are poorly attended, unless some controversial issue of the moment has aroused intense interest. The major areas of county expenditure are for welfare, penal and correctional institutions, and roads and bridges. When expenditures grow particularly heavy, a county may issue bonds to spread the burden over a number of years.

Functions of County Government. The citizen who drives his automobile over local roads is frequently made aware of one of the long-standing functions of the county, the construction and maintenance of the highways under its jurisdiction. To carry out its responsibilities, it has the power to acquire property for road building by condemnation and purchase. Some counties, but not all, carry on such other public works functions as establishment of park systems and recreational facilities, preservation of shade trees, and extermination of the infamous Jersey mosquito through a Mosquito Control Commission, as well as water supply and sewage disposal services.

Another important concern of the county is welfare, the administration of which is supervised by a welfare board comprised of two freeholders, the county adjuster, public welfare officer of the county, and five laymen. It is responsible for the required programs of aid to dependent children, aid to the totally disabled, and old-age assistance. It is further required to provide financial support for the state program for the blind and for the foster home care program. Some counties also maintain specialized institutions such as hospitals for the tubercular, the chronically ill, the mentally diseased, and maternity cases, as well as homes for the indigent aged.

As an arm of the state, the county has the age-old responsibilities of law enforcement and, as described in Chapter 5, maintenance of a system of courts. The chief law enforcement official of the county is the prosecutor. He is appointed by the governor for a five-year term and comes under the supervision of the attorney general. His salary, however, is paid by the county. He is aided by a legal staff and a force of detectives and investigators, the numbers of which are determined by the size of the county. It is up to the prosecutor's office to bring about the detection, arrest, indictment, and conviction of those who break the laws. When a suspect is arrested, the prosecutor or one of his assistants presents the charges to a grand jury so that it can determine whether or not there is a case against the individual. If the charges are groundless, the suspect is freed; but if the grand jury feels that there is enough evidence to warrant a trial, it returns an indictment. It is the prosecutor's office that represents the state at the trial and any subsequent appeal.

The grand jury differs markedly from the trial jury, with which most people are familiar. It consists of twenty-three citizens selected from a special panel of thirty-five and is the highest judicial body in the county. It may make investigations on its own initiative with or without the assistance of the prosecutor's office. It may call witnesses and place them under oath. It may disregard the evidence presented by the prosecutor and the instructions it receives from the judge when it is impaneled. It may do all of these, but rarely does. In fact, a major criticism of grand juries in New Jersey has been that they are usually too subservient to the prosecutor. The testimony taken by a grand jury is secret and in most instances may not be employed in a trial unless the defendent waives his right. In any event, there are two possible actions that a grand jury can take, besides dismissing the charges. It may return either an indictment or a presentment. With the first, the accused must stand trial. The latter is returned when it is felt that although there is insufficient evidence for a trial, a situation exists that needs correction; for example, when gambling is known to be going on but there is not enough evidence to place any individuals on trial.

Besides the prosecutor's office and the juries, there are other county law enforcement agents. The sheriff, who is elected for a three-year term, has some police powers, but is primarily an officer of the county court. With his deputies, he is responsible for maintaining order in court, taking custody of persons awaiting trial or detained in the county jail, serving warrants and summonses, transporting prisoners to state institutions, and conducting the sale of property seized under court order. The chief probation officer, appointed by the county judges, and his assistants investigate convicted criminals before they are sentenced, as well as supervising convicts released on parole. The county coroner, physician, or medical examiner is concerned with the investigation of violent or suspicious death, to determine the possibility of homicide or suicide.

The county assists the state in another important field, public education. The county superintendent is an agent of the state who handles certification of teachers, distributes state money, collects school records, and exercises general supervision of county schools. Attached to his office are child-study supervisors, attendance officers, and helping teachers who aid teachers in schools of more than one district. Some counties have vocational and technical schools, and several more are in the process of establishment. These are designed to provide occupational training for secondary students and may include more advanced post-graduate evening programs.

The county exercises a number of other functions. It serves as a center for the recording of documents such as deeds, mortgages, wills, and veterans' discharge papers. In most counties this is handled by the county clerk, but several have a register of deeds. The county also has important responsibilities in the election process, as described in Chapter 7. In addition, it supervises weights and measures, maintains health clinics and blood banks, and provides agricultural and home economics extension services.

NEW JERSEY COUNTIES AND MAJOR CITIES

The Municipality

Municipal government directly affects more people at more points and more frequently than any other type of government. Yet a municipality, as mentioned earlier, has no inherent powers of its own and owes its legal existence to the state. As a chartered corporation, it has power to sue and be sued, to acquire and dispose of propety, to make contracts, to tax, and to enact ordinances, all these corporate privileges coming from the state. A New Jersey municipality can choose its form of government, combine with neighboring municipalities, divide in two, or change its name, but only within the framework laid out by the legislature. There is no constitutional home rule in the state.

Since the passage of a constitutional amendment in 1875, there are five categories of municipalities recognized by law—cities, boroughs, towns, townships, and villages. Traditionally speaking, a city refers to a densely populated community, a borough and a town connote less congested urban areas, a township is pictured as a sprawling rural region, and a village is considered to be a small rural community. These images, however, have little relation to fact, at least in Jersey, for there is a city with only 271 inhabitants, a borough with twenty-two, a township with over 40,000, a village with over 16,000, and so on. In other words, the label attached to a municipality may have no relation to its physical appearance or population. Of the five categories, only cities have been classified by the legislature. The four classes are: first class, with a population exceeding 150,000; second class, from 12,000 to 150,000; third class, less than 12,000; fourth class, all those bordering on the Atlantic Ocean.

Mayor-Council Government.   No matter what category a municipality falls under, it has essentially one of three types of government— mayor-council, commission, or council-manager. The mayor-council form has always been the most widely used in the state. Based upon the principle of separation of powers followed on the state and Federal levels, it is characterized by a sharp division of authority between an elected mayor as chief executive and an elected council as legislature. The number of councilmen varies from three to nine. In the smaller communities they are elected at large; the more populous localities are divided into wards, and the voters of each elect their own councilman. The council adopts the yearly budget and enacts ordinances or laws for the municipality.

The mayor is the official head of government and has a term of from one to four years. He presides over council meetings, makes appointments, supervises the work of the various municipal departments, and represents the community at ceremonial functions. Whether or not he has any real authority or power depends upon which of the two variations of mayor-council government is followed — the "weak mayor" system or the "strong mayor" system. Under the first, he can make but few appointments and only with council approval, he has no veto power over council actions, and the management of municipal affairs is largely in the hands of departments and boards subject to little mayoral control. The "strong mayor" type is just the opposite.

Commission Government. The commission form of government was introduced in this country at the beginning of the century as a reform measure to overcome the political corruption that characterized many cities at that time. In 1911 the New Jersey legislature passed the Walsh Act authorizing the adoption of the commission form by popular referendum, and many of the larger communities acted accordingly.

The principle behind this form is the elimination of the divided authority and diffused responsibility of the mayor-council type. In place of mayor and council, one finds a small board of commissioners elected at large every four years, in what is supposed to be a nonpartisan election. In localities with less than 10,000 inhabitants, there are three commissioners; in those with more than 10,000, five.

The commissioners are the only elected officials and have all legislative and administrative authority. They choose one of their number to have the title of mayor, usually the one who received the highest vote in the general election, but his legal authority is the same as the others. If there are five commissioners, each one becomes the head of a municipal department. The departments are public affairs, revenue and finance, public safety, public works, and parks and public property. Each commissioner has complete authority in his own department. He appoints all subordinates, supervises their work, and prepares the annual budget. The combined departmental budgets, when approved by the board of commissioners, become the municipal budget. All actions are taken by majority vote.

The so-called township plan is in reality a variation of the commission form. The governing body is referred to as the township committee and has three or five members depending on population, but it functions like the board of commissioners. The only significant difference is that such officials as the township clerk, the tax collector, and the magistrates are elected by the voters rather than appointed by the commissioners.

Council-Manager Government. The council-manager form of government was first adopted at the time of World War I, also for the purpose of reform. Although it is viewed by experts in municipal management as the best of all forms of government, Jersey communities have been slow in turning to it. At present, there are only nine municipalities so governed.

Essentially, the council-manager form combines the better features of the commission and mayor-council forms. There is an elective council of from five to nine members that serves as the legislative and general supervisory authority, choosing one of its own members as mayor. Instead of handling all administrative detail, however, it selects a new type of official, called a "manager." He is a professional, nonpolitical administrator, usually with training and·experience in public affairs, who serves as the council's agent in directing the municipality's activities and services. He has the power to appoint and remove most departmental officials, he acts as chief executive to enforce local ordinances and supervise all administrative work, he prepares the annual budget for council approval, he attends all council meetings but has no vote, and he stands ready to carry out all functions assigned to him.

This arrangement provides for centralization of administrative authority in the hands of an expert. If municipal affairs are conducted properly, this means that the manager is doing well, and the members of the council are credited by the electorate with having made a good selection. If things go badly, the council, as ultimate authority, may fire the manager, for he has no fixed term of office. Under such a set-up, municipal government has the opportunity of becoming more efficient, scientific, and businesslike.

Optional Charter Law. Despite the fact that the governments of all municipalities in New Jersey follow one of the above patterns, there are enough variations and modifications of form to make the picture a confused one. For more than a century the legislature granted charters to individual communities without concern for uniformity. Then it began to pass general laws, only some of which superseded previous actions and were truly universal. By mid-twentieth century, the need for one, uniform, general municipal charter law was recognized. Therefore, in 1950 there was passed the so-called Faulkner Act, or Optional Municipal Charter Law. There is no compulsion in this law; a municipality may alter its form of government, but only if its citizens so wish. The change can be brought about by a petition and direct referendum of the electorate or by the establishment of a charter commission to make a thorough study of the existing government and the possible alternatives. The commission may recommend making no change, adopting one of the optional plans, or developing a special charter. In any event, the citizenry have the final word on election day.

The Optional Charter Law provides municipalities with the choice of essentially three forms—the strong mayor-council plan, the council-manager plan, and a small municipality plan, the last open to localities of under 12,000 population. There are a number of variations of each plan made available by the law, but they differ only in regard to whether councilmen are elected all at once or on an overlapping basis, whether at large or representing a ward, and whether on a partisan or nonpartisan basis. Not included as a possible plan is the commission form of government. This once highly regarded form has been discredited by experience with it. In too many communities the five-headed board of commissioners prevented the unity of public policy and focus of responsibility essential to good government. When things went wrong, the commissioners would squabble among themselves and try to shift blame. In addition, few of them had any special qualifications for administering the departments placed under their control. Consequently, in recent years a number of larger municipalities in the state have taken advantage of the Faulkner Act to drop the commission form. Following the lead taken by Newark in 1953 were such communities as Camden, Trenton, Jersey City, Bayonne, West Orange, and Irvington.

Municipal Services. Nevertheless, no matter what the form, category, area, or population of a municipality, its prime function is to provide its people with services. These undertakings might involve the exercise of powers neither necessary nor peculiar to government; rather, they might well be carried on by private individuals or businesses. Thus a municipality's main concern is for good management, just as if it were—as it indeed is—a corporate business enterprise. Furthermore, the kinds and quality of services provided by a particular locality depend upon the needs of its inhabitants and their willingness to pay.

One obligation that every municipality must meet is to provide for public safety, the protection of life and property. For this, it must have both police and fire fighting and prevention facilities. The size of these forces depends, naturally, on the size of the community. In recent years police departments have grown rapidly, not only because of increasing population but because of the impact of the automobile, making traffic regulation one of the major responsibilities of the police. Only the larger communities have full-time, paid fire departments. All the others depend upon volunteer manpower, although some of these have at least one salaried staff member. Money for the equipment of volunteer companies comes from taxes, but the firemen are expected to supply their own uniforms. A number of communities hold firemen's fairs and similar fund-raising activities.

Another area of service is public works, which, although there is an element of protection in it, is primarily designed for the convenience of the citizenry. The most common forms have to do with water supply, waste disposal, and streets. Of great importance is provision for an adequate water supply for domestic and industrial purposes. The storage and distribution of water is an engineering enterprise, but one which many municipalities have made a public rather than a private business. This is because a good water supply is closely related to community health and effective fire protection. Some localities have their own reservoir system, while others obtain their water on a contract basis from a neighboring community or from a private water company. In some communities, however, the individual consumer must buy directly from a private concern.

The collection and disposal of wastes is a vital service, and one that is developing into an acute problem in many areas, what with growth of population, diminution of unused lands, and pollution of waterways. Garbage and sewage disposal may be provided by the municipality itself, by joint action with others, or by contract with a private agency. For example, a number of communities in northern Jersey are handled by the Passaic Valley Sewerage Commission. A service provided solely by the municipality is the construction and maintenance of streets and sidewalks. Involved here are such operations as planning and surveying, curbing, paving, repairing, cleaning, and lighting the streets, and laying sidewalks.

Few municipal services contribute more to public well-being than the work of the agency charged with protecting the people's health. Since 1887, every municipality, large and small, has been required to have a board of health. Because of advances in medicine and sanitation, most attention today is given to preventative measures. Inspections of water and milk supply, and of every establishment and operation through which articles of food reach the consumer are carried on; vital statistics are gathered to afford a continuous picture of the community's health; communicable diseases are quarantined and emergency orders issued; and close co-operation is maintained with other municipal agencies in carrying out health measures (for example, arrangements by the board of education for medical and dental inspection of schoolchildren). However, local health efforts are far from uniform throughout the state. In the majority of communities, those with sparser populations, there is, as would be expected, no qualified, licensed health official.

Educational activities are among the oldest of municipal functions in the country, and for New Jersey communities represent their largest responsibility. A description of the role of the locality in public education may be found in Chapter 10. Another service is public welfare, but here Jersey municipalities are limited to providing general assistance to the needy. In addition, they may provide hospitals, airports, parks, playgrounds, libraries, and museums.

Sources of Revenue. To furnish this wide variety of compulsory and optional services and meet steadily increasing demands of all sorts upon them, municipalities must collect and spend huge sums of money. The principal source of revenue comes from real and personal property taxes, which is followed by state aid. Additional income is derived from licenses and permit fees, fines, parking meters, proceeds from municipal enterprises, and interest on delinquent taxes. A locality cannot itself spend all the revenue that it collects, for payments to the school district and the county are mandatory. It handles what is left for local purposes.

Municipalities are free to determine for themselves the kinds of taxes to be employed and the amounts to be levied, as well as how the money is to be spent, subject only to expressions of political opposition by their taxpayers. They must, of course, undergo a certain degree of budgetary supervision and control by the state. They must follow the procedural rules established by the Division of Local Government of the Department of the Treasury. In instances where a community gets itself into an unsound financial condition, the state may appoint an administrator of finance to straighten things out.

Special Districts. Because of the increasing demand for services, and their rising costs, a number of municipalities have been authorized by the legislature to join together into special districts to increase efficiency and reduce expenditures. The most common of these are school districts, a number of which maintain regional high schools. But special districts have also been created for fire protection, water supply, police radio service, sewage disposal, lighting, and health services. In addition, a municipality may establish special taxing districts within its own boundaries to provide certain services to particular sections of the community, or it may set up local authorities to operate specialized facilities such as housing or parking. Thus, as one can see, the multiplicity and variety of local governments are boundless.

DO/DISCUSS

Give close attention to the current events in your local or area newspaper illustrating major functions and powers of your municipal or county government. Make a scrapbook of news items that best represent (a) taxation, (b) elections, (c) governmental appointments, (d) budgets, (e) public works, (f) welfare, (g) law enforcement, (h) public education, (i) recording of documents, and (j) any other power or function. Attempt to write an appropriate caption under each clipping.

CHAPTER 7

Political Parties
and the Election Process

Essential to an understanding of the state and local government, as well as history, of New Jersey is an examination of its politics. It is through politics that the people in a democratic society rule, by expressing themselves on what they want done and selecting from their own ranks those to do it. A study restricted to the formal governmental institutions as described in constitution and statute would leave one poorly informed about the actual workings of government. These institutions do not operate as one would be led to suppose or as they may have originally been intended, the reason being the existence of partisan politics. It is politics that puts the flesh upon the skeleton of governmental structure and gives the organism its motive power. Rather than the corrupt and sordid conflict and manipulation for offices and other spoils that unfortunately too many think it, and that it sometimes can be, politics is the entire range of civic activities associated with determining public policy. It is the means by which constitutions are made and amended; by which governments are created, endowed with powers, and limited in authority; by which public officials are chosen; and by which broad objectives of public action are determined.

Without any agencies to give coherence and direction to the political wishes of the people, there would exist only the confusion and futility of separate, discordant individual wills. To determine the collective will and translate it into action, there have developed such institutions as public opinion, pressure groups, political parties, and nominations and elections. It is with parties and nominations and elections in New Jersey that this chapter will be concerned.

141

Political Parties

A political party in a democracy may be defined as a portion of the voters consciously bound together by at least a traditional belief in certain political principles and some common attitudes toward public issues, as well as by the desire, through peaceful, institutional methods, to gain control of political office and run the government in such a manner as to carry out the party's program. A party may be large or small, national or local, tightly knit or loosely organized. It is true that parties have been suspected and criticized in the country since the time of George Washington, but they are both inevitable and necessary.

Parties help keep the electorate informed on public affairs and, even though they may be biased, give the voters an opportunity to hear different sides and make up their own minds. By selecting candidates for office and developing platforms, parties enable voters holding the same general views to unite so as to enhance their chances for victory. Parties stimulate political action and provide the incentive for many to vote. They provide the little-known aspirant for office with the vehicle to achieve popular support. To some extent they must bear the consequences of the success or failure of those elected under their sponsorship. The party or parties out of power serve as watchdogs and critics of the party in power. In addition, parties help to bind together peoples of divergent occupation, race, religion, and ethnic background throughout the nation.

Despite their importance to the democratic process, political parties in this country have traditionally been nongovernmental, voluntary, self-sufficient, autonomous organizations. Since the start of this century, however, many Federal and state laws have been passed investing parties with a public status. Thus, there are lengthy and complex regulations that a party must obey, such as, when and how it must choose its candidates, how much it may spend in campaigning, and how it is to select officials for its local subdivisions as well as representatives to the national organization.

County and State Committees. The keystone of a party's structure is the county committee. It is comprised of one county committeeman and one county committeewoman from each district, elected annually at the primary election by members of the party. This is the "grass-roots" level. Following the primary, the county committee meets to elect a chairman and vice-chairlady, who are responsible for maintaining the party organization. The committee also selects two persons to serve, with the two selected by the opposition party, on each of the election district boards that supervise the voting on election days. The municipal committee consists of the members of the county committee resident in the municipality; they choose one of their number to be municipal chairman or leader.

The state committee is comprised of one man and one woman elected every four years from each of the twenty-one counties. Chosen at the gubernatorial primary, they meet the following week to choose the state chairman and vice-chairlady, who also serve for four years. An executive director hired by the chairman becomes the administrative officer of the state committee. The chairman also annually nominates for the governor's appointment one member of each county board of elections to serve a two-year term.

The principal functions of the state committee are to maintain the state party organization, to choose one committeeman and one committeewoman to serve on the national committee, and to call the state party convention. This convention is held annually following the primary, and its main purpose is to adopt the party platform on which its candidates will campaign. The platform is a declaration of political principles and a statement of position on current public issues.

The prime goal of these committees, of course, is to bring about first the nomination and then the election of their party's candidates. Their activities begin long before the primaries, but the greater part of their work comes just after nominations are made. New residents and first voters must be properly registered, aliens assisted in becoming naturalized, voters instructed in the mechanics of balloting, campaign funds raised, literature distributed, public meetings and rallies arranged, challengers appointed to enforce the election laws, and party supporters urged to vote and assisted in getting to the polls.

Two-Party System.   Although the bulk of New Jersey's voters are not declared members of any party and thus claim to be independents, over the course of time most of them support the same party election after election. Technical membership in a party is achieved when a citizen, wishing to vote in a primary election, declares before the election board that he is a member of a particular party. In addition, an individual may join a voluntary political club for the opportunity of participating in year-round partisan activities. Yet there are many people who do neither, but consider themselves to be Republicans or Democrats. This is because party membership in this country is, for most, a rather vague and elusive matter, and because the parties themselves require no payment of dues, attendance at meetings, or adherence to rules. Thus, aside from technical declaration, a person is considered a party member when he says he is one.

The two major parties, Republican and Democratic, are favored in New Jersey by the requirement that to be officially designated on the election ballot with a column of its own, a party must have polled at least 10 per cent of the vote cast in the preceding election for members of the General Assembly. This discourages the development of third or minor parties; their candidates are not given a column, but appear on the ballot in the section labeled "Nomination by Petition." In recent elections, candidates for such parties as the Socialist Labor Party, the Socialist Workers Party, and the Conservative Party have so appeared, but their support has been insignificant.

The most effective means by which the party in power can build up a nucleus of faithful supporters is through patronage. This is the practice of bestowing public office and favor upon party regulars or potential adherents. Officials appointed under the "spoils system" are expected to be the active party workers and to contribute liberally to the party's "war chest." The party out of power strives to counteract this potent device by holding out the promise that when it triumphs, it will reward its supporters in like fashion.

Ever since their formation, the modern Democratic and Republican parties have exclusively shared the support of the majority of the voters. If one examines the results of the elections for President and governor for the past 100 years, one can see that the Democrats were dominant prior to 1900, while the Republicans have been more successful since. Totals show a fairly equal number of victories for each.

In sharp contrast to state-wide elections have been those involving Congressional districts, counties, and municipalities. During the first half of the present century, Democratic control of the state Assembly was infrequent and of the Senate, rare. Most of the time Republican majorities were overwhelming. In addition, New Jersey sent far more Republicans than Democrats to Congress.

There were several reasons why the Republicans fared so much better than the Democrats in the latter group of elections. An important factor was that Democratic strength was concentrated in a few populous, industrialized counties, while Republican strength was more widely distributed, providing control of the larger number of rural counties. Since the counties, regardless of population, have equal representation in the Senate, that body was consistently rural-dominated and Republican. With assemblymen elected on a county-wide basis, urban pockets were frequently outweighed by suburban and farm population, denying city Democrats their representation. Explanation for the Congressional imbalance may be found in the unequal representation in Congressional districts throughout the state and in some use of the gerrymander. The latter is the practice whereby the party in control of the legislature sets up districts in such a manner as to concentrate the opponent's strength in as few as possible and spread its own majorities over as many as possible, thus assuring itself a maximum number of seats.

It is recognized by all but the most partisan that prolonged, one-sided control of the state by either party is not conducive to healthy politics and good government. In recent years, because of rapid population growth, decentralization of industry, and movement from city to suburb to once-rural areas, this one-sidedness has been diminishing. There is less concentration of Democratic strength in, and therefore dependence upon, such counties as Hudson and a greater diffusion elsewhere. This resulted in Democratic Party control of the Assembly from 1958 to 1963, while the Republicans have retained an edge in the Senate. The Democrats also have been successful of late in gubernatorial elections and have gained more seats in Congress, but New Jersey continues to be a "swing" state in presidential races. County and municipal elections as well are much closer now. Thus there seems to be a trend in the state toward a resurgence of the two-party system.

Nominations and Elections

Just as party activities are left essentially to be regulated by the states, so are the nomination and election processes almost entirely under state control. This is not only true of state and local elections but applies to Congressional and presidential ones as well. Thus, all states have collections of election laws so voluminous and complex that they are rarely studied by their citizens. New Jersey's Title 19 is a thick volume of about 300 pages. State control of elections, however, is subject to some Federal regulation. There are the familiar constitutional restrictions of the Fifteenth and Nineteenth amendments, which prevent the denial of a citizen's right to vote because of race, color, previous condition of servitude, or sex. In addition, there are several statutory regulations concerning election of Federal officers.

Voting Qualifications. The qualifications for voting in New Jersey are quite simple and liberal. The state constitution, as amended, requires that a person be registered, a citizen of the United States, 21 years old, a resident of the state for six months and of the county for forty days, and, in addition, not be an idiot, insane, or disqualified as a criminal. Attendance at a college or being stationed at a military post within the state does not in itself establish residence. For those who are to be absent from the state on election day because of military service or for other reasons and for those in the state who are unable to cast a ballot at the polling place, there are provisions for absentee ballots. Furthermore, there is no literacy test, which means that ability to read or write is not a qualification for voting.

The requirement of registration before voting is to insure that only qualified persons exercise the franchise. The state has a system of permanent registration, which means that once a citizen has registered as a resident of an election district, he does not have to register again unless he moves out of the county, changes his name, or fails to vote in four successive general elections. This system eliminates one factor that contributes to nonvoting: the requirement that a person must register each year in order to vote. Registration is held before the municipal clerk or at the office of the county board of elections and may take place up to the fortieth day before an election. In addition to supplying information about himself, the registrant must take an oath and sign his name. Each time he votes thereafter, he must sign his name so that it can be compared with the signature in the register. The original registers are held by the county at all times, but shortly before the election the duplicate or signature-copy registers are turned over to the municipal clerk for distribution to the election boards.

Nominating Primaries. The first stage in the electoral process is the selection of candidates. Although many people ignore this and feel that voting in the final election is enough, the choice of candidates is of prime importance. Whether or not we have honest and efficient public officials depends upon the character and qualifications of those who receive nominations. Thus, those who fail to participate in the nominating process are left with the limited choices of others, often those belonging to a political machine.

A candidate seeking nomination for office must file a petition signed only by qualified voters—1,000 if it is a state-wide election. At the time of the primary he will run against others who are seeking the nomination of their party for the same office. The direct primary was introduced into New Jersey in 1903 as a substitute for the nominating convention. It is a preliminary election or, actually, several elections at once. Each party has a separate ballot listing all of its candidates for public office.* Its supporters hold their own election to choose one nominee for each office to run in the general election against the choices of the other parties. In addition, party officials—the committeemen and committeewomen—are elected at the same time. Primaries, with all the parties participating simultaneously, are held annually on the third Tuesday in April and are conducted just like general elections. They are presided over by the regular election officials, are held at the accustomed polling places, are financed by public funds, and are subject to careful state regulation.

New Jersey has a "closed" primary, which means that participation is confined to those who declare their party affiliation, with voting limited to that party's candidates. By contrast, in an "open" primary the voter does not declare his party and can, therefore, vote for any party's candidates. The closed type is designed to develop party responsibility and prevent raiding. In New Jersey a person, having declared himself, cannot switch allegiance and vote for the opposing party's candidates until he has not participated in two successive primaries. One disadvantage of the closed type is that many people stay away because they do not wish to declare their party preference, whether through fear of possible loss of business or through a mistaken notion of independence. It goes without saying, of course, that how a person votes on primary day has no binding effect on how he may vote in the regular election.

As is true of other reforms in the machinery of political democracy, the direct primary has not improved the nominating process to the extent that its advocates had hoped. It does afford the rank and file of the party opportunity for more direct and decisive influence than under the old convention system, and it may weaken machine control. But, in most instances, the turnout at primaries is poor and most of the votes are cast by party "regulars." Often the candidates selected by the party leaders run unopposed, reducing the primary to a rubber-stamp approval of the professionals' choices. The primary is effective only in those instances when party adherents are aroused against conspicuously unfit candidates. Thus it serves as a potential check against flagrant irresponsibility and corruption.

Mechanics of Elections. General elections are held on the first Tuesday after the first Monday in November, with even-numbered years set aside for national offices and odd-numbered years for state offices.

*When voting machines are used, each party's slate appears on a separate section, and the machine is locked by an election official in such a fashion that the voter can manipulate only the levers for the candidates of his party.

This permits concentration on one level of government at a time and assures that state candidates do not ride into office on the coattails of the presidential candidate. Further separation occurs in those municipalities that have nonpartisan elections and therefore no primaries. Their elections are held on the second Tuesday in May, while the other municipalities hold theirs at the time of the general election. All elections, whether primary, general, municipal, or special, and whether they are for state or Federal office, are conducted at the expense of the state and its subdivisions.

Although the state and the municipalities have certain responsibilities, most of the detailed preparation for and the actual administration of elections are in the hands of the counties. In each there is a county election board consisting of four members, equally divided between the two major parties. They are selected by their respective parties and commissioned by the governor for two-year terms. This board has charge of all elections within its county and also serves as a board of canvassers. Among other duties, it must advertise an election and provide sample ballots for all registered voters to familiarize them with the names of candidates and the wording of any public question. It selects the polling places—usually, but not necessarily, located in school houses or other public buildings. It appoints for one year the district election boards, each composed of four members, two each from the Republican and Democratic parties.

The district boards are directly responsible for the management of the polls on election day. There are approximately 4,000 such boards throughout the state. Each board chooses one of its members as judge or chairman and another, of the opposite party, as inspector. The remaining two serve as clerks and handle the signature-register books. All members are granted the authority of constable to insure the maintenance of order at the polls, and at least three must be present at all times. They are paid $30 for their day's labors.

At the present time, all but eight counties use voting machines. Although their initial cost is great, machines have the advantages of absolute secrecy, greater protection against tampering with votes, and speed and accuracy of tabulation. Results in state-wide elections are delayed by the rural counties that must count their paper ballots by hand.

The polls throughout the state are open from 7 A.M. to 8 P.M. If a voter arrives near closing time, he is entitled to vote provided he was on line prior to the time of closing. Besides the four-member board, there also may be present at the polling place a policeman to aid in maintaining order and a number of challengers. Each party and each candidate on the ballot may appoint two challengers for each election district. These individuals have the power to challenge the right to vote of any person whom they feel is ineligible. If a person is so challenged, he may be permitted to vote after he takes an oath affirming that he is qualified. Any falsification, however, is a criminal offense.

The procedure that the registered citizen must follow in voting is quite simple. He is asked his name and address, and one of the clerks opens the register to his page. The voter signs his name, and this signature is compared with the one already there. If all is in order, he is permitted to enter the voting-machine booth, or, if paper ballots are being used, he is given a ballot to mark secretly in an enclosed booth. With a machine, he must turn down a lever for each candidate for whom he wishes to vote; with a ballot, he must make a mark opposite each candidate he favors. It is not possible to vote for a complete party slate by moving one lever or making a single mark. If a citizen wishes to vote for a person whose name does not appear on the ballot, he can do so by writing in his name in the appropriate place. When the voter finishes casting his ballot, he may leave the polling place.

As soon as the polls close, the board makes an open and public count of the votes and prepares the tally sheets showing the results. The machines or ballot boxes are locked and delivered to the municipal clerk, who must keep them sealed for ninety days in case a demand for a recount is made. On the Monday following the election, the official canvass takes place. Each county board of elections meets as a board of canvassers to certify the results submitted by the district boards. Certificates of election are issued to each victorious candidate. For elections involving a President, governor, or congressman, the board of state canvassers, consisting of the governor and two state senators from each major party, certifies the results.

As can be seen, the election process, although fairly simple for the voter, is an elaborate, expensive operation involving officials on many levels of government. Despite the costs in time, energy, and money, there is no questioning its value. Democratic self-government would be impossible without giving the people opportunity to express their political will.

Flaws in the Election Process.   There are, however, several weaknesses in the election process that need to be corrected. The practice in New Jersey of placing primary responsibility for elections on county agencies creates an unnecessary decentralization that results in inefficiency, undue expenditure, and a lack of proper enforcement of the election laws. Advocates of reform recommend the establishment of a state agency to superintend all elections, thereby providing centralized responsibility, uniformity of practice, and rigid enforcement.

Another weakness, not limited to Jersey elections, but true of those of most states, is the use of the long ballot. This device confronts the citizen with a lengthy list of candidates to be voted on, as a result of the mistaken notion of earlier times that the greater the number of elective officials, the more democratic the government. It is extremely difficult, if not impossible, for the average person to form an intelligent opinion as to the merits of all the candidates, and thus there is a great deal of blind voting and voting a straight ticket. The remedy is to shorten the ballot used in county and municipal elections in a fashion comparable with that of national elections, where the voter is asked only to choose a President and Vice-President and members of Congress. In other words, only policy-determining officials should be elected. Officials with narrow, administrative duties, like county clerk, register of deeds, sheriff, surrogate, tax collector, and magistrate, should be appointed.

The most serious shortcoming in the election process is the failure of American citizens to meet their responsibilities. In addition to being inactive in party politics and failing to participate in primaries, there are many who do not even vote or only go to the polls during presidential elections. There are a number of reasons for nonvoting, but the most common cause is simple indifference and laziness. There is no question that this situation ought to be remedied. One solution frequently proposed is compulsory voting, but its advocates are misdirected in their zeal. There is no particular virtue in numbers. In fact, a disinterested, uninformed voter is more harmful than a nonvoter. What needs to be done is to increase the number of those who vote intelligently, objectively, and purposively. This means a greater stress upon citizenship education, both within and without the schools, from kindergarten through adulthood.

DO/DISCUSS

Use a panel discussion to offer a critique or review of New Jersey's political parties and the election process. The moderator should focus the commentary on such topics as (a) voting qualifications, (b) the merits of political parties, (c) voting apathy, (d) the primary system, (e) the referendum trend, and (f) voting practices.

CHAPTER 8

Taxation and Finance

A study of the other chapters of this book should make it apparent that the activities and services of government—state, county, and local—cost money. In fact, raising and spending money is the most important functional aspect of government, for without it no government can operate.

In earlier and less complex times, public finance was a fairly simple thing; comparatively little money was spent, and what was needed was obtained with no great difficulty. But those days are gone forever. More and more, people demand from their governments services and institutions such as schools, police and fire protection, parks, public health, welfare, roads, bridges, and the like. Since it would be difficult or impossible for the individual to obtain these on his own, he must divert a portion of his income from individual spending to a fund for public expenditure. In other words, he helps finance collective consumption through governmental activity.

Funds for collective consumption are produced through taxes, which are simply charges levied by government to raise money or revenue. Taxation takes many forms, each having a different effect. Some people feel that certain types of taxes are more desirable, fairer, and more effective; others feel differently. Most people seem to feel that they would rather not pay taxes at all. But they would not be willing to give up things that are purchased with them. As the great Supreme Court justice Oliver Wendell Holmes expressed it: "I like to pay taxes. It is purchasing civilization." To receive a service from government, it is unavoidable and essential that one understand its

151

full cost and pay for it. But at the same time it must be assured that the service is provided by the most appropriate and efficient means known to society. This is why public finance is such a difficult but fascinating subject.

State Finance

The fiscal, or financial, operations of the state* are carried on by the Department of the Treasury, one of the executive departments of government under the governor. It is responsible for the collection, custody, and disbursement (spending) of state revenue, the preparation of the budget, and the maintenance of a centralized accounting system. At the head of the department is the state treasurer, who is appointed by the governor with the advice and consent of the Senate. His chief assistant is the director of the Division of Budget and Accounting. In addition to formulating the annual budget, he serves as comptroller, or chief accounting officer, for all state agencies.

The Budget.   The budget is a comprehensive yearly statement, drawn up under the authority of the governor, of the financial operations of the state. Included in it are recommendations for appropriations (1) to pay the cost of operating the state's departments, (2) to make capital improvements, such as new buildings, and (3) to provide state aid to counties and municipalities. These recommendations are based upon item-by-item requests from all the agencies of the state and are for the fiscal year, which runs from July 1 to June 30. In addition, the annual budget includes a broad outline by the governor of his financial program for the coming year and his recommendations to the legislature of the taxes to produce the needed revenue.

The budget is the only public document that reveals all the functions and services of the state and how much money may be spent on each. It is designed to eliminate or reduce inefficiency, extravagance, and fraud in the state's fiscal operations. A recent issue of the printed budget ran to 876 pages. It, like its predecessors, represented long hours of painstaking effort, soul searching, and dollar stretching. The process begins more than a year in advance. Each agency assembles data on the costs of its services and then draws up an individual budget, which includes the purposes and amounts of the appropriations requested. The requests from all agencies within a department are combined together into the budget for that department. Each depart-

*For a description of finance on the county and municipal levels, see Chapter 6.

mental budget is then submitted to the budget director and his staff, who scrutinize every item and actually visit the institutions and establishments, where hearings open to the public are held.

The budget director is required to submit the total tentative budget to the governor prior to the end of the year, so that the latter may prepare his budget message to the legislature, which is presented in mid-January. The constitution requires that the budget be balanced; that is, the governor cannot recommend expenditures that exceed anticipated resources or revenue. A pictorial representation of a recent budget appears on the next page.

After the chief executive delivers his message, the bipartisan joint appropriations committee, made up of an equal number of senators and assemblymen, takes over. Months of study, public hearings, and analysis follow, but the governor's proposals are usually accepted with only minor revisions. The committee's appropriation bill is then considered by both houses of the legislature, which have the power to make further changes but rarely do. The annual budget is finally adopted by the passage of the appropriations act, usually in May, and becomes effective on July 1.

A brief examination of the illustration on page 154 shows how the state spends its money. Budgetary recommendations are divided into three major parts: $268.8 million, or 46 per cent of the total, for general state operations; $65.1 million, or 11 per cent of the total, for capital construction; and $256 million, or 43 per cent of the total, for state aid to counties, municipalities, and school districts.

Of the specific allocations, the outlay for education is by far the largest. It accounts for $245,327,364, or 42 per cent of the total expenditure. Among the major items, almost half of this sum, or $119 million, goes for state aid to local school districts; $57 million is for Rutgers University, the six state colleges, the Newark College of Engineering, and general operations; and $59.5 million is for the teachers' pension fund. Ranking second are the expenditures made by the Department of Institutions and Agencies for care of the handicapped, the sick, the needy and the criminal. Over $140 million, or 24 per cent of the budget, is allocated to hospitals, welfare services, and correctional institutions and programs. The next largest category is for highways, which requires $93,974,627, or 16 per cent of the budget. The major allotments are $30.8 million for operations of the highway department and $36.3 million for highway construction.

Thus it can be seen that more than four-fifths of the total expenditure of the state goes for three major areas: education, institutional services, and highways. The remaining 18 per cent is divided among

NEW JERSEY'S BUDGET
FISCAL YEAR 1964-65

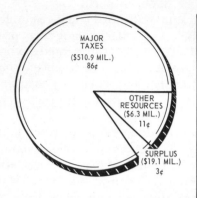

MAJOR
TAXES
($510.9 MIL.)
86¢

OTHER
RESOURCES
($6.3 MIL.)
11¢

SURPLUS
($19.1 MIL.)
3¢

STATE AID
($256.0 MIL.)
43¢

CAPITAL
($65.1 MIL.)
11¢

STATE
OPERATIONS
($268.8 MIL.)
46¢

MOTOR FUELS	$ 134,000,000	EDUCATION	$ 245,327,364
CORPORATION	92,900,000	HIGHWAYS	93,974,627
MOTOR VEHICLE	91,755,265	HOSPITALS	75,400,592
CIGARETTE	69,200,000	WELFARE	46,600,480
INHERITANCE	45,000,000	GENERAL CONTROL	31,222,367
BEVERAGE	30,500,000	POLICE	21,854,021
RACING	27,000,000	NATURAL RESOURCES	20,860,674
PUBLIC UTILITY	14,000,000	CORRECTION	18,664,555
EMERGENCY TRANSPORTATION	6,500,000	REGULATORY	10,826,715
		HEALTH	5,599,894
WELFARE & EDUCATION	30,993,270	OTHER	12,280,626
SPECIAL RECEIPTS	9,995,395	GENERAL CONTROL- LEGISLATIVE	2,253,855
ALL OTHER RESOURCES	22,162,607		
SURPLUS, JULY 1, 1964	19,857,242	GENERAL CONTROL- JUDICAL	5,060,250

MAJOR (bracket spanning MOTOR FUELS through EMERGENCY TRANSPORTATION)

OTHER (bracket spanning WELFARE & EDUCATION through ALL OTHER RESOURCES)

all the other agencies and programs. Herein may be found the basic reason why the state budget has almost trebled in the last dozen years. To provide the improved services desired by the citizens of New Jersey in the areas of education, institutions, and highways alone has re-

quired the expenditure of an additional $300 million, a sum far great-
er than the total annual budgets of the early 1950's.

Still more significant is the fact that more than half this increase has
gone into state aid to counties, municipalities, and school districts.
In addition, the proportion of the budget devoted to state aid has also
increased, from about 35 per cent to the present 43 per cent. In other
words, the state has had to devote greater amounts as well as an increasing proportion of its financial resources to aid local governments
in meeting their obligations to their residents. This trend began after
World War I, but has been accelerated in recent years. An explanation for it can be established by an examination of the revenue-raising
resources to be found in New Jersey.

Sources of Revenue

With a state budget of over a half-billion dollars, with municipalities
well past the three-quarters-of-a-billion mark, and with counties
spending more than $200 million each year, where does the money
come from to support these tremendous expenditures?

It comes from the taxes and fees paid to the different levels of
government in New Jersey. All told, there are well over two dozen
different types of revenue-raising devices, some of major importance
and others quite minor. A recent study found that every man, woman,
and child in the state paid an average of $226 in state and local taxes, an
amount consistent with those of surrounding states. However, on the
basis of the burden of taxes in relation to personal income (ability to
pay), New Jersey ranked forty-third. Furthermore, when local taxes
were excluded and only those on the state level considered, New
Jersey ranked fiftieth. In other words, it was the lowest in the nation
in state taxes collected per capita (per person).

Several conclusions may be drawn from these facts. The operations
of government, especially on the state level, have been efficient and
economical. The services rendered to the people, particularly by the
state, are not as complete as those performed for the people of other
states. Finally, it is apparent that the burden of all the services performed in New Jersey falls most heavily upon local government.

Property Tax. The principal source of revenue in the state is—and
has been since colonial times—the general property tax. It is a tax
levied on real estate, or land and improvements to it, and on tangible
personal property such as household furniture, factory equipment,
and farm stock. Two-thirds of all revenue collected in New Jersey for

local and state purposes is derived from the property tax. Almost all of it goes to local government, constituting 90 per cent of its revenue. Although the municipality in which the property is located levies the tax, it does not keep it all. It must share the revenue with the school district and the county. An average of 50 per cent is allocated to the school district. The county's share is determined by the county tax board, which sets each municipality's quota on a proportional basis. What remains is referred to as the local-purpose levy and goes toward the municipal budget.

In most communities a nominal value is placed on personal property, so that almost all the revenue comes from real estate. Over the course of time there has developed a large list of exemptions (for example, public property; religious, educational, and charitable property; and veterans' allowance), a number of injustices, and an utter lack of uniformity throughout the state. That is why the Commission on State Tax Policy some years ago was justified, when it issued its report on *The General Property Tax in New Jersey,* to subtitle it "A Century of Inequities."

Property taxes are levied by the municipality in which the property is located. The amount of the tax on a piece of property depends upon its assessment, or valuation, by the local assessors. This is usually some percentage of its true value, or the price it would sell for on the open market. If a piece of property has a market value of $20,000 and the assessment rate is 40 per cent, it will be assessed for $8,000. The sum total of the assessed valuations of all the taxable property in the municipality is called its "ratables." After a determination is made of the total expenditures for the year, the tax rate is then set to yield the necessary revenue. Thus, if the local budget is set at $1 million and there are ratables of $20 million, the tax rate would be 5 per cent, or $5 per $100 of assessed valuation. The owner of the property assessed at $8,000 would be subject to a tax of $400.

Although some improvements have been made in assessment procedures, the property tax remains poorly administered and grossly inequitable. There is a lack of uniformity regarding assessment practices between counties and within counties. Inequalities are widespread within municipalities themselves. Too many of them fail to reassess property often enough and, when they do so, make across-the-board adjustments. Generally only the larger communities have trained, professional assessors. To make matters worse, land is generally assessed at a higher ratio than improvements, and the cheaper parcels of real estate are generally assessed closer to true value than the dearer ones. Assessment ratios are higher in densely populated cities than in those of less density; higher in poorer, older neighborhoods than in good, new neighborhoods; and higher in tenant-occupied areas than in single-family zones.

It can thus be seen that the property tax as actually administered is one of the worst types of tax. Not only is it not applied uniformly, it also tends to be regressive. That is, the rate decreases as the value of the property increases. The heavy burden of the tax itself encourages underevaluation and exemption. Furthermore, the property tax cannot be justified on the ability-to-pay principle. This holds that a person's contribution to the support of government should reflect his ability to do so; that is, his taxes should be in proportion to his wealth. Ownership of property is not a good indicator of ability to pay. An elderly, retired couple with limited income, preferring to live in a home fully paid for years earlier rather than incur the expense of rental accommodations, would have much more difficulty in meeting rising taxes than would a family whose breadwinner was at the height of his earning power. Despite all this, New Jersey has the doubtful distinction of levying the highest per-capita property taxes of any state in the nation.

Railroad taxes are a variety of property tax. Because of the special nature of railroad property, it has been dealt with in a unique fashion for almost a century. Starting in 1873, laws were passed by the state legislature subjecting the railroads to taxation by both the state and the municipalities in which their property was situated. In 1884 a system of classification was established that divided railroad property into four categories:

Class I — the main stem or the roadbed not exceeding 100 feet in width.

Class II — other real estate used for railroad purposes, such as roadbeds of branches, passenger and freight stations, docks, and yards.

Class III — locomotives, cars, ferry boats, machinery, and the like.

Class IV — the remainder of the property, including the franchise.

The state collected taxes on Class I, III, and IV property, and municipalities on Class II. Over the course of time many changes were made in the rates charged and in the distribution of the revenue. In recent years, because of the rapid drop in railroad services and resultant decline in revenue, the state has turned over an increasing share to the municipalities to compensate them for their losses. At the present time railroad taxes have become a relatively insignificant source of revenue—except for Jersey City, which collects half the Class II tax in New Jersey—contributing a little over $17 million per year to both the state and municipalities. A proposal now under consideration is for the state to take over all railroad taxation, compensating individual municipalities for their losses. Then the tax load on the railroads could be reduced as a means of encouraging improvement of commuter transportation.

Other Taxes. In addition to property taxes, other taxes collected in New Jersey may be grouped into four categories: excise taxes, motor vehicle registration and licenses, corporation taxes, and inheritance taxes. Excises are taxes on the manufacture, sale, or consumption of particular commodities. They are generally levied on widely used items and provide a steady source of revenue. The commodities subject to an excise tax in New Jersey are gasoline, cigarettes, alcoholic beverages, and pari-mutuel betting at race tracks. The tax on gasoline alone has in recent years provided over one-quarter of the state's resources. The other three items have brought in an additional one-quarter.

Another major source of revenue, providing approximately 20 per cent, is the fees collected from driver's licenses and motor vehicle registrations. The fee on a passenger car is based on manufacturer's shipping weight; for trucks it is gross weight; buses are taxed according to capacity.

There is a wide variety of corporation or business taxes, which bring in another 20 per cent of the state's resources. Corporations pay a state francise tax, based upon their net worth, for the privilege of doing business in the state. Insurance companies are taxed on gross premiums, but are permitted to deduct sums paid for municipal taxes. Public utilities other than railroads, such as water, telephone, gas, and electric companies, are required to pay both a franchise tax and a gross-receipts tax. Although assessments are made by the state, municipalities collect and retain the revenue in lieu of a personal property levy.

The inheritance tax is a tax on individual beneficiaries, or heirs of the estate of a deceased person. The rate varies from 1 to 16 per cent, depending upon the amount received and the relationship of the beneficiary. The revenue from this source varies from year to year, but in recent times has provided about 5 per cent of the state's resources. There is also an estate tax levied on the entire estate of a deceased person no matter how it is divided among the heirs. Its yield is very small. Counties are allocated 5 per cent of the inheritance and estate tax revenue.

Problems and Controversies

As has just been shown, New Jersey collects most of its revenue from taxes on gasoline, motor vehicles, cigarettes, liquor, and racetrack gambling. Thus, although New Jersey is a "property tax state" at the local level, it is a "special tax state" at the state level. This caused the Commission on State Tax Policy some years ago to contend that "individuals pay taxes in New Jersey only when they own property, die, drink, smoke cigarettes, bet on horses or drive an automobile." This statement is somewhat exaggerated—a family that lives in an apartment indirectly contributes to the property tax through payment of rent—but it dramatizes the inequality of the tax burden as it affects different people.

Not only does the tax structure ignore the ability-to-pay principle, but it reflects a policy of temporary, patchwork efforts rather than a long-range financial program. Each time the state needs additional revenue, the excise on cigarettes or gasoline is raised a penny or another stop-gap device is introduced. No industrial, urbanized state has done so little to bring its tax structure up to date as has New Jersey. There is no tax base of significance to all citizens. New Jersey is one of the two states in the nation that does not have a broad-based tax.

The Issue of a Broad-Based Tax. Those who support the introduction of a broad-based tax, such as an income tax or sales tax, assert that the state has been in financial trouble for a number of years. It has actually spent more than it has taken in, by using treasury surpluses to provide the balance or by resorting to expensive bond issues, which means borrowing on the future. Furthermore, to maintain even a precariously balanced budget each year has meant starving existing services and doing without others.

Although for years the cry in the state has been "no new taxes," property taxes in the decade 1954-1963 increased a total of over one-half billion dollars and other taxes increased almost $300 million. The rate of increase was greater in the five years 1959-1963 than it was just before. In other words, the revenue system is now more heavily dependent upon property taxes than it ever was. As the Tax Policy Commission stated in its *Tenth Report,* published in 1963, "New Jersey has long been proud of the taxes it does not have; but the price it has paid

is a growing burden on real and personal property for the support of
. . . governments within the State."

As the demands for services placed upon municipalities, counties,
and the state outstrip revenue from existing taxes, the state must find
new resources to meet its expanding budgets and provide the state
aid needed by the localities. Otherwise, property taxes must continue
to rise, fixing a crushing burden on the homeowner and driving industry out of the state. The realistic advocates of broad-based taxes
recognize that their proposals might not reduce already-high property taxes, for the added revenue would be needed to meet rising
costs and new services. But since most of these additional obligations
will be incurred in any event, keeping property taxes at their present
level requires an extension of the tax base.

The Tax Policy Commission Report. For many years both major political parties in the state were pledged to oppose the introduction of any
new taxes. This prevented any effective support in the legislature or
the governor's office for a broad-based tax. In 1961 both parties
overcame their fear of voter reprisal and removed the "no new tax"
planks from their platforms. Following his election, Governor
Richard J. Hughes dropped several strong hints that a broad-based
tax was inevitable. The Tax Policy Commission was charged with
making a comprehensive re-examination of the tax structure of the
state to determine what changes should be made. Finally, its long-
awaited report was issued in January, 1963.

The commission, headed by Archibald S. Alexander, in its *Tenth
Report* recommended the adoption of a broad-based tax as the only
means of raising the additional $150 million per year needed to
finance necessary services, provide increased state aid to local governments, and effect tax reforms. A sizable increase in annual state
aid to education would improve the ratio between state and local
taxes and relieve the property tax burden. It would help to bring up
to standard the large number of districts where the increase in the
number of pupils has outstripped the increase of ratables, where the
school population remains high although the neighborhood is run
down, or where rural property is unable to maintain adequate school
support.

Among the tax reforms recommended by the commission were revisions in the railroad property tax and in the personal property tax
as it affects business. It proposed that the state take over all railroad
taxes and guarantee to the municipalities the revenue that they derived from this source. The state could then reduce the tax load on
the railroads without hurting the localities.

The recommendations involving business taxes were designed to eliminate a long-standing danger to businesses in the state, that of "tax lightning." Tax lightning refers to the possibility that a municipality may at any time suddenly increase to the legal limit the assessment of the tangible personal property of a business located in the community. This hazard has kept several large corporations from coming into the state, since they feared that although the taxes on business property were low at the moment, they could shoot sky-high without warning. To do away with this possibility in the future, the commission proposed the repeal of certain personal property taxes and the standardization of others. Municipalities would be compensated for their losses, and the state would raise the needed revenue by a corporate income tax of 5 per cent.

After carefully analyzing the tax structure and fiscal needs of the state, the commission recommended the adoption of a broad-based tax. In weighing the choice between a personal income tax and a sales tax, the commission studied the merits and demerits of each and concluded that the later was the better alternative. A 3 per cent sales tax, with food and prescription medicines exempt, would be easier to pay and a little more regressive as compared with an income tax.

Reaction to the commission's report varied greatly. Some supported it; others rejected completely any proposals for broad-based taxes. Some felt that a new tax was necessary, but that its adoption could be delayed a year or two longer. Still others were pleased with the commission's stand on a broad-based tax, but felt that an income tax rather than a sales tax would be better. They contended that an income tax was more closely related to ability-to-pay and gave the individual a sense of responsibility in directly contributing to the maintenance of his government.

Hughes and Revenue Raising. The most interesting reaction came from Governor Hughes himself. Several weeks after the issuance of the *Tenth Report,* late in January, 1963, he dropped a bombshell in a special message delivered to the legislature. Instead of supporting the commission's recommendation for a broad-based tax, he proposed an alternative solution. He asked for legislative authorization of a referendum by the voters to approve a $750 million bond issue. The state would borrow $150 million a year for the next five years, and the money would be spent for expanded construction of highways, institutions and agencies, and colleges. In addition, there would be freed from the regular budget $50 million a year that could be alloted to increased state aid for schools. The bond issue would be paid for by $42 million a year in surplus toll revenue from the New

Jersey Turnpike, which would become available to the state beginning in 1972, after the present turnpike bonds had been paid off.

Governor Hughes defended his proposal by the assertion that if it was turned down, a broad-based tax would be inevitable, but that it would take several years to get one through the legislature. Any further delay of even a year or two in expanding the financial resources of the state could, he warned, prove critical and dangerous.

Both support for and opposition to the proposal were immediate, divided generally on party lines. Some opposed it on the same grounds that they opposed the sales tax proposal: that additional money was not really necessary and that the state should "hold the line." Others opposed it on the grounds that the continued policy of borrowing and borrowing through bond issues was too costly and not as desirable as a pay-as-you-go approach. Still others held that the bond issue would raise less than the $750 million the Governor estimated and that a broad-based tax would have to be introduced in any event five years hence.

After some bitter wrangling both houses of the legislature adopted the bond issue proposal, which was placed upon the ballot in the November, 1963 general election in the form of two referenda. Despite an intensive campaign by Governor Hughes to rally popular support, both referenda were decisively defeated. Following this rejection of his program, Hughes indicated that he would have to go before the new session of the legislature and ask it to adopt some form of broad-based tax.

Thus, on February 3, 1964, the Governor included in his budget message a request for the enactment of a graduated income tax that would produce $150 million a year for state capital construction programs and aid to schools. The regular budgetary requests were to be met by existing taxes; the recommended income tax was to provide the additional funds needed by the state. The request for an income tax made Hughes the first governor since 1935 to propose a broad-based tax. In that year Harold Hoffman requested one, and the legislature adopted a sales tax, but then soon revoked it. Hughes stated that he did not propose a sales tax because it would have the greatest impact on those least able to pay.

Hughes' request was hailed as courageous, but little hope, at the time of this writing, was held for its enactment. Some of the leaders in the Republican-controlled legislature were favoring a series of small bond issues, others were inclined towards a sales tax, while still others felt, as they had all along, that no new revenue measures were necessary.

Thus it can be seen that New Jersey is at a major crossroads as far as its finances are concerned. The demand by the citizens for increased services from state, county, municipality, and school district must of necessity involve a tremendous increase in public expenditures. Increased expenditures require an expanded revenue, and no combination of increases in present taxes and miscellaneous new taxes can be adequate. In what direction the state moves will depend upon the enlightenment of its people and the statesmanship of its leaders. As Governor Hughes expressed it in an earlier budget message, New Jersey is in transition — "transition between a state striving merely to keep its head above water in meeting the year-to-year demands of its development, and a state that is preparing boldly to come to grips with its future."

DO/DISCUSS

1. Defend or contradict Holmes' statement about taxes. Do higher taxes assure greater civilization? Explain.
2. Many people in New Jersey feel that a broad-based tax is inevitable. Which of the following taxes would you agree to as being most equitable: (a) sales tax, (b) income tax, or (c) combination sales and income tax? Do you have any other suggestions?
3. Some people in New Jersey speak of instituting off-track betting or a state lottery as a means of increasing the state's revenue. Would you favor or oppose such a plan? List your reasons.

SECTION IV
Sociology

Towering high above the Palisades, the "Cyclone" provides thrills for its passengers.

CHAPTER 9

The People of New Jersey

Who are the people of New Jersey? How does the ethnic composition of the state's present-day population compare with that of the population at the beginning of the twentieth century, or with that of the people who lived here at any previous time?

To consider these questions is to approach the challenge of moving populations in any age. Sociologists call it the problem of population mobility. For New Jersey this term serves well, for even the Indian aborigines are believed to have ended their long trek eastward from the Pacific coast in the forested hills and sandy coastal plains of New Jersey.

The Lenni-Lenape

Where the Lenni-Lenape came from is uncertain. Samuel Smith, the writer of a history of New Jersey in 1765, concluded that the Indians of the area were originally Orientals, "descended from the Tartars, Siberians, and people of Kamtschatka." While modern scholars are not so certain of the Indians' precise ancestry, most writers hold to the theory that their origin was indeed Asiatic.

According to their own legend, recorded in picture writing on strips of bark and called the *Walum Olum*, or "Red Score," the Lenni-Lenape originated in northeastern Asia. From there they crossed the Bering Straits into North America, journeyed south and eastward through Canada, were forced by war and famine into what is now the

165

United States, and eventually reached the shores of the "salt sea," or Atlantic Ocean, in New Jersey.

These Indians so impressed the early English settlers with their desire for independence that Smith concluded that "liberty, in its fullest extent, was their ruling passion." True to this ideal, they considered death to be preferred to enslavement by the white man. Consequently a land-purchase policy served to keep peace with the rapidly increasing numbers of European settlers.

The total number of Indians in the Jerseys, East and West, cannot be accurately judged, but while Smith estimates that only 500 permanent dwellers occupied the tribal settlements in East Jersey in 1669, West Jersey was populated with a tribe "every ten or twenty miles." A major difficulty in counting the aborigines was created by the good hunting lands in the northern hills, which drew parties of hunters belonging to Five Nations tribes of Senecas, as well as Mohicans, from what is now New York. In addition, the attractive sandy shore line brought annual treks of Pennsylvania dwellers through the land of the "Unalachtigo," the "People who live near the ocean."

Officially, the estimate accepted by the New Jersey Census Bureau (in 1906) was 3,000 Indians for the entire area at the time America was discovered, with but 2,000 remaining in 1664, when the English established their first settlement at Elizabeth-Town.

Buying Indian Land.   Although Berkeley and Carteret, in 1672, directed that all Indian claims to land should be honored by paying agreed sums directly to the owners, the Lenni-Lenape diminished rapidly in numbers. In the noted "Concessions and Agreements" of the West Jersey Proprietors in 1676, provision was made for commissioners to meet with Indians to determine the price of land before any sale would be recognized by the government. In 1682 the East Jersey legislature again recognized the legality of Indian claims to land. Nevertheless, within a century (1758), less than 200 Lenni-Lenape remained to be settled in Burlington County on the first Indian reservation to be created in what is now the United States.

In most cases the land was purchased fairly, to "extinguish title" of the Indian. Governor Francis Bernard conducted three conferences with the assembled tribes of the Delawares in 1758 to conclude the final land sales to the English. These meetings ended at the sacred meeting place between the two rivers, the Lehigh and the Delaware, now Easton. Here the great chief of the Delawares, Teedyescung, brought representatives of the Munseys, Senecas, and Cayugas to confer with the Royal Governor concerning the purchase of the final Indian claims. With dignity the two races met about the council fire to follow the admonition of Teedyuscung: "Brethren . . . you must sit and talk together." From October 11 to October 26, 1758, the great council deliberated, ending with the exchange of many strings of black wampum, white wampum, and belts of black and white wampum, to signify complete agreement between the two parties. Nevertheless, within a century nearly every Indian had left the state for the final reservation in Oklahoma.

European Migrants of the Seventeenth Century

Between 1613 and 1618 the Dutch established their permanent settlements in Bergen, Passaic, and Hudson counties. By 1643 the Dutch had moved overland to the upper Delaware River, where they started the Pahaquarry copper mines. Despite the fame of the "Old Mine Road," which ended at Esopus (now Kingston) on the Hudson, the number of Dutch families in what is now Warren County was relatively small.

Jersey Draws Many Nationalities. By 1675 the great variety of nationalities that were to be the heritage of New Jersey had already made themselves known. In the settlements of the Dutch along the Hudson could also be found some Danes and Norwegians, and French Hugenots. From the Tinicum Island settlement in the Delaware River the Swedes were beginning to spread toward Swedesboro and other streamside farming or fishing locations in southwestern Jersey. Together with the English, in the Essex and Middlesex County areas after 1664, came the Scots and the Irish. The Dutch had continued their attempts to make permanent settlements in West New Jersey even after they had been unsuccessful at Fort Nassau, in 1623 and 1630. Otherwise, Swedes might have been more numerous in the lower Delaware Valley.

English settlements developed quite noticeable differences, due largely to the "Quintipartite Deed," which divided the province into East and West Jersey. East Jersey received migrants, beginning in 1664, who came in large part from other colonies. Many of the English who founded the towns of Elizabeth-Town, Newark, Woodbridge, Middletown, and Shrewsbury came from the Puritan colony of Massachusetts. Large numbers had made a stopover of a few years at Southampton, Long Island, on their way from Massachusetts to New Jersey. A group such as this would be expected to have a strong Puritan leaning. With the English came a number of French Huguenots scattered through the East Jersey towns, many of whom were artisans and skilled craftsmen. Energetic German farmers settled in Warren, Somerset, Hunterdon, and northern Bergen counties early in the eighteenth century. It is believed that famine in the Palatinate on the Rhine caused a majority of these Germans to migrate to some of the richest farmlands in New Jersey.

The Quakers. West Jersey became the first portion of the New World to receive a Quaker community. When the Quaker proprietors, led by William Penn, organized the colony of West Jersey in 1676, with Burlington as the capital, a new spirit of toleration became official policy. The "Original Grants and Concessions" of the proprietors, antedating the Declaration of Independence by a full century, spelled out the determination of the Society of Friends to secure complete religious liberty in the colony. Support for this policy of tolerance carried with it plans for a new form of social justice, under which orphans would be cared for or educated by the Yearly Meetings of the Friends. The strong schools essential to the program of the Friends were maintained in strength until the emergence of the common school system in the 1840's, and in part until the present. Reports of schools run by Quakers before the Revolution mention the towns of Salem, Greenwich, Alloway's Creek, Woodbury, Haddonfield, Evesham, Burlington, Mansfield, Upper Springfield, Chesterfield, and Vincentown. Many of these schools formed the nuclei of local school districts, once the state assumed responsibility for teaching all its citizens—Friends and all others—without discrimination.

The Slavery Issue in New Jersey

The Society of Friends brought to the areas in which they settled another advanced social theory, namely that no man should hold any other man in a condition of slavery. Perhaps as early as 1696 the Quakers sought to curtail the purchase of slaves. Surely the strongest antislavery encouragement came in 1758 in the Philadelphia yearly meeting, which officially advocated that Friends set their slaves free, but also insisted that the former owners make "Christian provision for them."

Again the social philosophy of a distinct population group helped determine the political atmosphere of the state. During the Revolution, Governor Livingston, a non-Quaker, recommended that the House of Assembly arrange for the manumission, or freeing, of slaves. Although these first efforts were unsuccessful, the issue appeared again in 1785—this time in the form of a petition prepared by Quakers. Legislation forbidding the importation of slaves was passed the next year. By 1804 the Quaker influence secured the "gradual abolition" act, by which the children of slaves became free if they were born in New Jersey. Although New Jersey had a larger slave population in 1800 than any Northern state except New York, the Quaker influence kept down the number of slaves in counties in which Friends were numerous.

Slaveholding was naturally associated with large landed estates in the South, but in the North many slaves served as domestic servants, or as laborers in the mills and warehouses in the cities. The location of New Jersey as a midpoint between the North and the South is probably one factor in the large number of slaves to be found in the state during the eighteenth century. We may question the accuracy of the figure of 4,000 slaves in the province by 1737, as quoted by the New Jersey historian Francis Bazley Lee, but his estimate that the slaves made up nearly 8.5 per cent of the total population is reasonably acceptable. Although the total number of slaves in New Jersey increased from 4,000 in 1737 to 4,600 in 1745 and to 11,500 in the first national Census of 1790, the fraction of the total population that they represented continually decreased. This large number of unfree dwellers in New Jersey in 1790 composed but 6.2 per cent of the total. A similar drop is represented in the figure in 1800, when the slaves had increased to about 12,500—considerably less than 6 per cent of the whole.

Quaker Influence Combats Slavery. Influence of the Society of Friends evidently made the areas of Quaker settlement lowest in terms of slave population. Leading in this respect in 1790 were the counties of Burlington, Gloucester, and Cumberland. Counties with the largest percentage of slaves in 1790 were Bergen, Somerset, and Monmouth, indicating that the patterns of society set by the earliest settlers in both East Jersey and West Jersey persisted for many generations after the original division in 1676.

With the dawn of the nineteenth century, the total number of slaves in New Jersey began a steady decline. By 1810, the number was down to 10,900; by 1820, to 7,500; by 1830, to 2,200; by 1840, to 674; by 1850, to 236; and finally, in 1860, just eight remained. Although slaveholding in New Jersey caused the state to have more slaves in 1830 than all of New England, New York, Pennsylvania, and four other states combined, economic as well as social pressures reduced the number very rapidly during the three decades preceding the final emancipation in 1863. Thus the Negro population of New Jersey experienced freedom much earlier than slaves in Southern states. By 1960, the 515,000 Negroes constituted 97.5 per cent of the population that was other than white, and 8.5 per cent of the total population of the state. These figures suggest something of the responsible position of the people for whom the citizens in early New Jersey worked so hard.

New Jersey's Population 1776-1790

By the time New Jersey assumed statehood, during the Revolution, its population had developed the main characteristics it was to hold until the great migrations of the 1840's. The first Federal Census of 1790 showed the entire state to have 184,000 people, or about one and one-half times the number living in the city of Trenton alone in 1960. This first Census included the English as the dominant nationality, with Dutch, Germans, and some Swedes, but with other groups in a very small minority.

Religious Sects Abound.   Some idea of the complexity of the background of the citizenry in 1790 may be gained from noting the religious groups to which they gave allegiance: Presbyterian, Quaker, Dutch Reformed, Baptist, and Anglican. Smaller numbers adhered to German Reformed, Lutheran, Swedish Lutheran, Moravian, and Methodist churches, while a few German Catholics were found among the North Jersey iron miners and charcoal burners, and among South Jersey glass workers. The Swedes along the Delaware and its tributaries in southern and western portions of Burlington, Gloucester, and Salem counties merged with the dominant English to lose their national identity by the time of the Revolution; yet many family names and locations survived.

Population Distribution in 1900

By the turn of the twentieth century New Jersey reported a population of 1,883,000 — about ten times the number reported in 1790. In this rapid growth the state had retained its share of the total population of the entire nation surprisingly well. In 1790 New Jersey had 4.7 per cent of the population of the United States, which still had but the original thirteen states. By 1900, New Jersey dwellers constituted 2.48 per cent of the total; but by then the United States had forty-five states, so the share of such a small state was even more impressive.

County growth reveals something of the nature of the increase for the whole state. This fact is borne out by the 2.7 per cent decrease that Hunterdon County reported for the decade 1900-1910. Of all the twenty-one counties Hunterdon reported the only case of loss in numbers. The rural farm population of this county was leaving for more industrialized areas faster than in any other section of the state. All of the other twenty counties received varying shares of the extensive immigration from Southern and Eastern Europe, as well as from other states.

Industry Spurs Urbanization. The general picture of population in 1900 reveals the results of trends, begun in 1840, in which industrialization brought larger and larger numbers to the larger urban complex of the environs of New York, and to the second urban area composed of the suburbs of Philadelphia, which are located on the New Jersey side of the Delaware. These two districts are sometimes known as the "greater metropolitan area" (Bergen, Essex, Hudson, Passaic, and Union counties) and the "lesser metropolitan area" (Burlington, Camden, and Gloucester counties). Practically grown together by 1960, the two districts in 1900 were still separated by over seventy miles of open farmland.

Effects of the rapid growth of industry by 1900 brought the urban counties into the lead in population, with the rural areas growing at a much more leisurely pace. The rank order of the counties, starting with the largest in population for the year 1900, was as follows: Hudson and Essex, with over 300,000 each; Passaic and Camden, with over 100,000 each; Union, Mercer, Monmouth, Middlesex, and Bergen, with a range of from 100,000 down to 78,000; Morris, Burlington, and Cumberland, from 65,000 to 51,000; Atlantic, Warren, Hunterdon, Somerset, Gloucester, and Salem, from 46,000 to 25,000; and the remaining three, Sussex, Ocean and Cape May, from 24,000 down to 13,000. At the 300th birthday of the state it is hard to realize that as recently as the year 1900 the figures referred to above represented the total number of dwellers in whole counties, not merely in individual cities.

New Jersey's Population in 1960

The most recent Census credits New Jersey with a population of 6,066,782. This large figure gives the state a rank of number eight among the fifty states; only seven states have a larger population. In 1900 New Jersey stood sixteenth among the forty-five states, which means that since the beginning of the century the increase of 220 per cent in the population of the state raised its position among the sister states much faster than the national average of increase. In the single ten-year period between the Census of 1950 and that of 1960, the state had an increase of 25.5 per cent in population, which was by far the largest gain since the years of depression in the 1930's.

Sources of Migration.   A notable increase in population raises the question as to the source of the migration. It is also of interest to know the sections of the state selected by the new people for their homes. To round out the picture, a brief survey of the present composition of the population as a whole will serve to highlight the changes of the past three centuries. The remainder of the chapter, will, therefore, deal with these topics in turn.

With regard to the sources of migration to New Jersey, the Census of 1960 indicated a rather significant change. About half of the increase between 1950 and 1960 was migration from other parts of the United States, rather than from outside our national borders, as in the past. New Jersey's history shows that beginning in the Colonial Period, migration from Northern European countries brought settlers, slowly but regularly, until Europe's political and economic unrest of the 1830's and 1840's increased the stream to a flood. New Jersey's population of 320,000 in 1830 more than doubled to 670,000 by 1860.

Between the Civil War and World War I, the flood of Europeans increased rather than decreased and the total population as early as 1910 was two-and-a-half million, or more than three times the amount counted in 1860. But following the First World War, changes in the national policy regarding the acceptance of new populations almost halted the migrations. Within weeks after the passage of the "national origins" law in 1929, the financial crisis launched the depression, which still further reduced the number of persons who were willing or able to come to New Jersey. During the decade of 1930 to 1940 New Jersey showed the smallest gain in its history: 2.9 per cent. But still the growth continued, with a gain of slightly more than 16 per cent by 1950 and, by 1960, a rise that was again large: 25.5 per cent.

This gain came from three principal sources—the three basic origins of population growth. For a population to increase anywhere there must be present one or more of these three sources: first, more births than deaths; second, movement into the state from out-

PROJECTION OF
NEW JERSEY POPULATION-YEAR 2,000*

NEW JERSEY POPULATION GROWTH

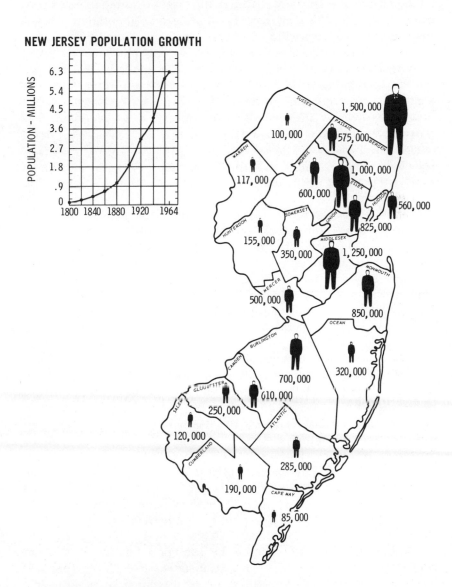

*BASED ON NJDCED STATISTICS – 11-59
FINAL USCB 1960 FIGURES

side the nation; third, movement into the state from other states. New Jersey can justly take pride that it has become so attractive to other states that migration from such areas alone equals the increase from favorable birth rates and from migration from foreign countries.

The source of migration may be discovered by noting the countries from which New Jerseyites of first- or second-generation foreign parentage came. It is well to remember, in this connection, that about one out of every three persons living in New Jersey in 1960 was either born in some foreign country or had parents who had migrated. This fact gives the state an unusually high number of residents who represent the cultures of other parts of the world. Despite this wide diversity in national backgrounds, only three countries sent to New Jersey more than 10 per cent of its total foreign stock. Out of the 2,100,000 who were of foreign stock, 24.9 per cent, or over half a million, called Italy their homeland. Germany came next with 11.9 per cent of the total and Poland was a very close third with 11.3 per cent.

With twenty-six countries represented by sizable groups of foreign stock, only three other nations could show as much as 5 per cent of the total. Of these the United Kingdom was easily first with 9.5 per cent, followed by Russia with 7.3 per cent and Ireland (Eire) with 6.4 per cent. Thus the six nations of Italy, Germany, Poland, the United Kingdom, Russia, and Ireland were represented in New Jersey by 46.4 per cent of all the foreign stock in the state. The original colonial groups of Dutch, Swedes, and Finns had given way to people from other portions of Europe. Only the United Kingdom, including England and Scotland, Wales, and Northern Ireland, still had a significant portion of the foreign stock of the state.

Smaller groups came from eleven countries whose share of the total ranged between 1 per cent and 5 per cent. These were Austria, Hungary, Czechoslovakia, Canada, the Netherlands, Asian countries, Latin-American countries, Sweden, France, Lithuania, and minor European countries. Tiny groups of people born in Norway, Denmark, Switzerland, Yugoslavia, Finland, Rumania, Greece, Portugal, and Mexico completed the picture. Each of these last nine nations had less than 1 per cent of the total foreign stock, but the total number of contributing foreign nations suggests the rich diversity of New Jersey's heritage of nationalities.

Of the 6,067,000 who made up the 1960 population, about 90 per cent of the total had been born in the state, while 10 per cent had been born elsewhere. But of this large group native to the state, only two-thirds had native parents, while about one-quarter came from foreign parents. Furthermore, the native parentage of the nonwhite population was much greater than that of the whites. Although 62.3 per cent of the whites did have New Jersey-born parents, 96.4 per cent of the nonwhite population had parents born within the state. Thus it seems that many more white people move to the area than nonwhites.

County Population Shifts. The rank order of counties in 1960 reveals something of the changes that have taken place since 1900. Four counties now have over a half-million people in each: Essex, Bergen, Hudson, and Union, in that order. Essex has pushed Hudson out of first place, while Bergen rose from ninth place to second.

Seven counties now have populations ranging from nearly half a million down to a quarter of a million. These counties, in order of their population, are: Middlesex, Passaic, Camden, Monmouth, Mercer, Morris, and Burlington. Of the first two, Middlesex moved up from eighth place in 1900 to fifth, but Passaic dropped from its former third to its present sixth place. Both Morris and Burlington counties held the same rank in the state in 1900 and in 1960, tenth and eleventh, respectively.

Five counties reported populations between a quarter of a million and 100,000: Atlantic, Somerset, Gloucester, Ocean, and Cumberland. All but Cumberland moved up in the rank of counties since 1900, with Ocean showing the most spectacular gain of all, rising from twentieth in 1900 to fifteenth in 1960.

The remaining five counties, in descending order of population, were Warren, Salem, Hunterdon, Sussex, and Cape May. Salem has maintained its eighteenth place, while Cape May has continued to be number twenty-one, enjoying its position as the least populated county in every Census since 1880, except those of 1930 and 1950. In those years Sussex was the most completely rural county in the state, but in 1960 Cape May again became the area in which solitude was most attainable.

Census studies reveal many significant changes or developments that are taking place within the state. Among the most noteworthy changes noted above may be the actual size of the population in the largest and smallest counties, the density of settlement, and the extent to which the state has become one of the most urban of all the fifty states.

Essex County leads all the twenty-one counties, as the rank order shows. With 923,500 people, Essex is crowded with nineteen times the 48,500 people living in Cape May County, still the most open and rural of the counties. This contrast is even greater in view of the

NEW JERSEY TOTAL POPULATION BY COUNTIES

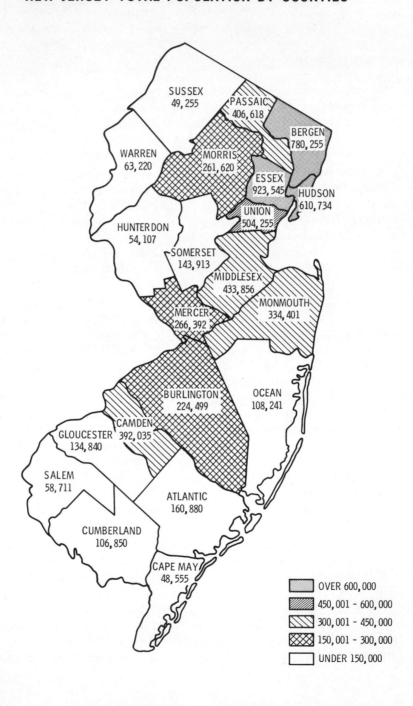

SUSSEX
49,255

PASSAIC
406,618

BERGEN
780,255

WARREN
63,220

MORRIS
261,620

ESSEX
923,545

HUDSON
610,734

UNION
504,255

HUNTERDON
54,107

SOMERSET
143,913

MIDDLESEX
433,856

MERCER
266,392

MONMOUTH
334,401

BURLINGTON
224,499

OCEAN
108,241

CAMDEN
392,035

GLOUCESTER
134,840

SALEM
58,711

ATLANTIC
160,880

CUMBERLAND
106,850

CAPE MAY
48,555

OVER 600,000

450,001 – 600,000

300,001 – 450,000

150,001 – 300,000

UNDER 150,000

areas covered by the two counties. Essex County with its 127 square miles is slightly less than half the size of 265-square mile Cape May County. Expressed another way, for the same amount of space available for one person in Cape May County, Essex has roughly thirty-eight persons! This situation highlights one of the most important elements in the wide diversity of conditions found in New Jersey.

Great differences in density of population in specific areas create even more striking contrasts than the figures for whole counties. For example, although the whole state has an average density of 807 persons per square mile, the most rural areas have as few as three per square mile, while the highest concentration in the cities is in West New York, with more than 39,000 persons living in one square mile! New Jersey has, therefore, examples of almost uninhabited areas as well as some of the most densely populated of cities.

In addition to the types of population already mentioned, the rural farm areas show decreasing density. Although New Jersey was predominantly agricultural as late as 1880, the agricultural areas now have but fourteen persons per square mile engaged in farming. The State Department of Conservation and Economic Development suggests that this low number is a reflection of how relatively few people have remained on farms in the face of the attractions of industry and urban life. Another factor is the great improvement in the amount of work each farmer is able to accomplish with modern farm equipment. Mechanization of the farm makes more production possible with fewer and fewer workers.

The 'Urban Fringe' Grows. Urban though the state may be, a trend away from the most densely settled areas has begun. The 1960 Census revealed New Jersey to be the most urban of all the United States, with 88.5 per cent of the people living in urban areas, yet nine of the twelve municipalities in Hudson County showed a decrease in population. At the same time, neighboring Bergen County showed no significant decrease in any of its seventy municipalities. Thus the movement away from the older city areas to the newer urban communities increases rapidly. Another example of the same trend may be noted in Essex County, where Newark lost over 7.5 per cent of its 438,000 citizens between 1950 and 1960, while Livingston Township and North Caldwell Boro each increased more than 130 per cent. In the same manner, Camden lost about 6 per cent of its population of 124,000 during the same time that Levittown in Burlington County gave evidence of the popularity of the newer type of urban living by growing a truly remarkable 1,292 per cent.

The rapid growth of the "urban fringe," which is located outside the older city areas, creates two serious questions that challenge state and local officials as well as all those interested in the future of New Jersey. Of first concern is the way in which the newer urban areas are growing. Can needed services be made available to the residents of these areas; will they soon become unpleasantly overcrowded slums, or will they develop into well-planned, vigorous, healthy communities of a new type? A related question demands the best efforts of officials and citizens alike in the older city areas: Can the most densely populated sections of the state replan, rebuild, renew themselves quickly enough to reinterest the fleeing population in the cities? For it is the city that has been and still is the heart of the economic life of the state. To these problems, much time, money, and attention are being devoted by state and local agencies responsible for the manner in which the future population of New Jersey will live.

DO/DISCUSS

1. Graphically illustrate New Jersey's county population totals by drawing twenty-one proportionally scaled pictograms (front view outline of a man). Place them on a base line according to size, one inch equaling 200,000 people. They need to be colored in sets of three for each color (seven colors will be used). On an accompanying desk outline map of New Jersey use the same color scheme to identify the corresponding counties. Draw some conclusions from your findings.
2. Today the New Jersey workingman frequently lives in a community other than where he is employed. Often he works outside the state. Point out some difficulties this situation may bring about for the man and for the state.

CHAPTER 10

Education

In the development of public education, the people of New Jersey learned to work together to secure a basic essential of free government. The story of how New Jersey citizens slowly awoke to their need for public education is an exciting one. From a group of people, merely transplanted Europeans, to a sturdy, complicated, densely populated state covers a span of more than three and a half centuries, yet each step of the way has brought new realizations, new needs, and new accomplishments in developing well-educated citizens.

A close look at the education given colonial New Jerseyans shows us a typical form of European church schooling. Then, as independence became a goal, with self-government the prize, more education appeared essential. Finally came the realization, between 1812 and 1850, that democratic self-government would require an entirely new kind of public education. This era saw the beginning of the schools New Jersey knows at present.

Education in Colonial New Jersey

Dutch and English Traditions. Colonial New Jersey quite naturally reflected the patterns of education that prevailed in the Dutch and English homelands during the seventeenth century. With the Dutch, the school as well as the church formed part of the necessary cultural equipment of any new colony. Education for citizenship included in-

179

struction in reading, writing, arithmetic, and religion. These subjects enabled one to become a practical businessman as well as a good Christian well versed in the catechism. Little thought was given to those of great wealth. Nor did Dutch officials seem to worry over the few who were plagued by poverty. Consequently the middle class received most of the attention. With the English, however, class distinction dictated private education for those who could afford it. For those too poor to secure even the fundamentals needed to read the Prayer Book, each town tried to provide so-called "pauper schools." In both Holland and England, literacy was considered necessary for all.

Systems of education seemingly adequate in Europe proved to have two handicaps in a new colony in which neither social aristocracy nor religious orthodoxy seemed desirable. One difficulty lay in the refusal of the colonials to develop a class of aristocratic rulers. Another problem was rooted in the presence of Dutch Calvinists, Anglicans, Puritan Separatists, Scottish Presbyterians, Friends, and other religious groups. To allow any one faith to set educational patterns would be to deny the religious ideals for which many had come to the New World. Nevertheless, a period of nearly two centuries was needed to secure independence from these dominating European ideas. An understanding of this long struggle is a vital part of the heritage of all who enjoy the benefits of the complex educational system of the present.

The town of Bergen, now Jersey City, had the distinction of possessing the first recorded school established by the Dutch in their colony. In 1662 Englebert Steenhuysen agreed to teach the school in Bergen under contract to the local magistrates. Steenhuysen had a house and lot in town and a farm. Since the school he taught occupied the present site of Jersey City's School Number Eleven on Bergen Square, this area can be said to have been used for education for three full centuries.

Schoolmaster Steenhuysen soon found himself in difficulties over taxation. He had refused to contribute to the support of a soldier as part of his civic obligations. Persisting in his position, he attempted to resign, but the local authorities refused to allow him to escape his responsibilities so easily. To settle the dispute and calm the irate schoolmaster, the whole affair was taken before the Director General and Council in New Amsterdam. The teacher was ordered to fulfill the remainder of his contract, thus setting a precedent for civil control over a school related to a church. The decision also demonstrated the relationship of a local school to the central authorities of a colony or state, in its assertion that the civil government alone determined all legal matters regarding education.

The coming of the English in 1664 seems to have made little immediate difference in the manner in which the Dutch and English communities secured an education for their children. With Anglican Church members in English settlements and Dutch Reformed Church members in the Dutch areas, little hindrance to establishing schools arose. But agreement on such matters as starting and supporting schools seemed harder to reach as shelter was given to people of many political views and differing religions. So with New Englanders bringing in Separatist traditions, the followers of George Fox introducing Friends schools, the Scottish settlers trying out a Presbyterian form of school, and smaller groups hoping to set up still other types, some form of community action appeared necessary.

Community Action on Schools. This action took the form of a law, passed by the legislature of East Jersey in 1693 and amended in 1695 and 1698. (Indeed, so wisely did the lawmakers plan that no major change occurred in New Jersey's system of schools until 1829.) According to the law, provision for the education of the children in any community, regardless of their cultural background, was dependent upon three steps being taken by the community wishing to start a school.

First, the supporters of the school secured a warrant from the justice of the peace (who was frequently a church official as well) calling for a town meeting. Second, the townspeople met to select a school committee of three men to set the salary and hire a schoolteacher. Third, the legislature instructed the town to levy sufficient taxes upon the citizens to support the school. The lawmakers went so far as to threaten any who failed to support the school with the sale of their property. Thus the towns could set up what amounted to a type of district school, quite similar to that used in the New England colonies. But what is most significant is the clear demonstration of the power of the community to provide schools supported by taxes levied on all the citizens equally.

Although the law of 1693 seems to be generous, adequate, and, above all, reasonably fair to each group of citizens, several important objectives remained to be achieved. These goals included the removal of the stigma of "pauper school" from the tax-supported institution, a state rather than a local tax for schools, removal of the remainder of sectarian control from the schools, making the schools free to all citizens by removing the tuition fees, and finally the setting up of a system of higher education, first in high school and then in college.

Two full centuries passed during the time New Jersey leaders were occupied in realizing these objectives.

Toward a State School System

How could a colony and state take so long to achieve its aims? One answer may be the fact that not until the 1820's did the new nation gain a clear idea of the kind of political democracy it really wanted. Washington, Adams, Jay, and Hancock professed their sincere desire to support an enlightened public opinion, while Madison said explicitly: "Knowledge will forever govern ignorance; and a people who mean to be their own governors must arm themselves with a power which knowledge gives." But it was Jefferson who saw the potential worth of each child, who should be educated by a system "that was divorced from ecclesiastical control and that was universal and free at the elementary level." The new idea, therefore, was that a system of free schools, not merely "knowledge" or enlightenment." This innovation in education progressed slowly, as did the equally new idea that all citizens should participate in all phases of government.

A State School Fund Is Established. Thomas Jefferson took an unexpected part in improving educational opportunities in New Jersey when he had his observations concerning schools printed in a small booklet. A copy of this document came to the hands of James Parker of Perth Amboy in 1803. Parker, wealthy landowner, political leader, and member of the New Jersey Assembly, immediately began a long campaign to get the state to accept its proper responsibility of supporting and directing educational endeavors. A first step, as he saw it, was the establishment of the New Jersey State School Fund—a combination of state-owned bank stock, stock in the Delaware and Raritan Canal, and income from waterfront land (riparian rights). Income from this money would be used to aid the communities of the state in founding or supporting elementary schools, just as Jefferson suggested.

The painfully slow progress of educational change kept Parker working to get his ideas accepted until 1813, when a committee studied the need for "free schools." The resulting report, published in February, 1814, was studied, but two years passed before the school fund was created by action of the legislature (on February 9, 1816), with an initial amount of $50,000 secured in 1817. Since only the income could be used for schools, more money was added each year, but not until a number of years had passed was the fund large enough to provide an income worth dividing. Later on, in 1838, the $30,000 divided gave only thirty-one cents to each of the 97,000 children in the schools.

Education and Business. Far more important than the amount of money supplied by the state was the new basis for close relations between business and education. No longer would schools be confined to religious instruction, reading of the Bible, or reciting the catechism. After the establishment of the school fund in 1817, the support for education by the state was closely linked to the industrial and commercial condition of New Jersey. The state's contribution to a system of schools could increase only in proportion to its willingness and financial ability to set aside substantial portions of profit. Thus education became part of the business of the state, with the obvious need for some kind of businesslike management.

Sound Management Is Obtained. The first step in making education an effective function of the state was to secure a body of officials to manage the school funds. Who should take the responsibility? During colonial times the legislatures had used their charter-granting powers to enable local school trustees to operate in individual communities. There had been no supervision or control by the state, for the town or township had paid the entire expense of the school. After 1817 the state needed officials to make certain the relatively large sums placed in the school fund would be safely invested. By 1829 these officials would also be responsible for ensuring an equal distribution of the income to local schools. To meet these needs the legislature in 1818 designated as "Trustees for the Support of Free Schools" the vice-president of the Council (the upper house of the state legislature until 1844), the Speaker of the Assembly, the secretary of state, and the attorney general. At last the state was in the business of education.

The next important change brought public support for the "common school" and finally secured trained professional educators as state officials to superintend the work. James Parker found others who agreed with his ideas. Judge Richard Stockton Field of Princeton, Chief Justice Joseph C. Hornblower of Belleville, E. C. Wines of Princeton, Bishop George W. Doane of Burlington, and others led what amounted to a crusade for the "common school" during the 1820's and 1830's.

'Friends of Education.' Popular education in New Jersey grew out of the demands of people who organized themselves to attain their goals. During 1828, groups of these citizens met throughout the state to discuss various means of providing a better school system. The practical name of "Friends of Education" served to identify their aims as well. In the more or less informal branches of the "Friends" met teachers, lawyers, clergymen, and legislators—all persons of influence who knew the value of the good education they felt was lacking. From their various meetings they chose delegates to hold a state convention in Trenton in November, 1828.

Public opinion depends on the activity of vocal citizens. This the "Friends" demonstrated by carefully marshalling their facts, before and after their state convention. The county groups had appointed investigating committees to inspect the schools in the various communities represented. In Trenton the "Central Committee to gather and disseminate information regarding the common schools of the state" reviewed the reports and distributed their summary throughout the state, giving New Jersey voters a comprehensive picture of the poor state of existing schools. The summary indicated that one-third of New Jersey's children had received no education in any school. But the report was encouraging in its evidence that the leading men in the state thoroughly understood the nature of the public school system for which they were developing increasing public enthusiasm.

MacLean's Recommendations. Princeton College provided a somewhat surprising source of aid for the cause of a state system of free public education. In January, 1828, Princeton's vice-president, John MacLean, addressed the Literary and Philosophical Society of New Jersey with "A Lecture on a School System for New Jersey." To meet the urgent needs of the state he advocated local and state school taxation, school boards chosen by popular election, the establishment of a normal school to train teachers, a state board of education, and a professional educator to serve as administrator of the state system. So accurate was MacLean's analysis of the situation that his recommendations were practically identical with the state system as it was finally set up in 1867, nearly forty years later.

MacLean carefully outlined one problem that has continued to exist to the present day: the setting of educational policy in the state. Should the state legislature delegate responsibility for the state school system to a single individual (state superintendent of schools or commissioner), or to a board of school directors (state board of education)? The former would be connected with the state government and might come under the political control of a particular party, while the latter would presumably represent the people of the state as a whole. Neither answer has satisfied the people of New Jersey completely, but a combination of the two has worked reasonably well.

First State School System Is Established (1829). New Jersey's first state school system demonstrated the effectiveness of the personal leadership of MacLean and the "Friends of Education," for the legislature passed the necessary law in 1829, the year following the lecture at Princeton College. In this course of action New Jersey was following the national trend toward the ideas of President Jackson—social reform, extension of the suffrage, increased care and education for all Americans. Political considerations, however, awarded a share in the control of the school system to each township committee in the state. Thus the school became another responsibility for the local officials—one for which they had no special preparation. Despite the hopeful gesture on the part of the legislature in passing the law, the weakness of the system brought it to an end within a year, returning state support to educate only the "paupers."

Lack of a state official responsible for securing support for state schools left the entire burden on the unofficial groups of "Friends of Education." These reformers again worked hard to gain acceptance for their program of a centralized system. From 1830 to 1838 they held local meetings, used newspaper columns, and wielded whatever political influence they had to secure new legislation favorable to a system of free public schools.

Unexpected help for the cause of state-controlled education lay in the disturbing misuse of the $746,000 given to New Jersey by the Federal Treasury in its distribution of excess funds in 1837. Although this money was to be used for "public institutions," so much of it found its way into county treasuries—and disappeared—that the people of New Jersey were alerted to the need for a responsible state agency.

Second State School System Is Established (1838). An even more effective means of arousing public interest was that employed by Chief Justice Hornblower, who exerted his great influence to call a state convention of the "Friends of Education" on January 16, 1838. Again these devoted leaders called for "normal schools, legal compulsion of parents to educate their children, special school taxation, distribution of funds according to enrollment, state superintendence, certification of teachers by state authority, and free tuition." Henry Barnard reported in his *American Journal of Education* that New Jersey was convinced that a reform in education was essential for the "preservation of free institutions." The chairman of the committee presenting the findings of the convention was Episcopal Bishop George W. Doane, who must have been an effective orator in his denunciation of the idea of free public schools for paupers only. Again the group passed a resolution demanding a state superintendent of public schools, indicating a growing realization of the futility of relying on a decentralized school organization. Again they were doomed to disappointment in this respect, for the limited state system established by the legislature in the same year (1838) omitted the most important feature—a professional educator to direct the schools.

This time there was slow but sure progress toward a unified state system, from 1838 to 1845. Friendly newspapers gave of their space to publicize the poor condition of the schools under town government and with no direction by state officials. The Newark *Sentinel of Freedom* led such papers in its devotion to the cause of free public education, both in space on its pages and in telling arguments. The *Sentinel* voiced the sentiments of its Whig Party owners in Essex County, long a center of Whig political power. An example of the paper's appeal for a state superintendent of schools appeared in January, 1841: "The system is without a head . . . There is scarcely a State in the Union, having a system of Public Schools, that has not found it absolutely indispensable to provide a suitable officer, charged with the duty of superintending them."

Four years later, in 1845, a year of great achievement in New Jersey's educational history, the *Sentinel* published the most completely documented defense of school reform. Four issues of the paper stressed the prevailing concept of civic duty in relation to public education. The state should meet its obligation to all the children, said the *Sentinel,* by: permitting increased taxes, adequate to the support of free public schools; requiring townships to increase their school taxes; making the certification of teachers mandatory, penalizing any local school trustee for the nonperformance of his duty; ensuring that local school funds are used for their proper purpose. Again, as in 1841, the *Sentinel* concluded that the laxity in the running of schools could be corrected only by the appointment of a superintendent for the entire state who should be a "man of cultivated mind, and enlarged views, possessing energy and decision of character, and above all a practical Teacher."

The governors of New Jersey were practically unanimous in their co-operation with the "Friends of Education," for indeed most of them belonged to the organization. As early as 1830 Governor Peter D. Vroom officially declared that in education alone lay safety for state as well as local government. In 1839 Governor William Pennington expressed hope that improved educational facilities in the state would protect social institutions. By 1844, the year in which the state wrote its second constitution, Governor Daniel Haines used his increased power under the new constitution to request co-ordinated action to secure the appointment of a state superintendent of education. The following year, 1845, the legislature took the long-awaited step, but not before the "Friends of Education" gave the impetus with a final state convention.

A State School Superintendent Is Appointed (1845). The climactic meeting in Trenton in February, 1845 demonstrated the great power of a determined public to improve educational conditions. "Friends of Education" began their preparation for this meeting with large local meetings such as the one in New Brunswick City Hall in September, 1843. A large proportion of the teachers in the city were present, for a committee of fifteen was selected from among them to examine and select textbooks for use in the primary schools. Most of 1844 was taken up with the preparation of the new state constitution, but early in January of 1845 the active Essex county group met in the courthouse to prepare for the state meeting in Trenton in February. Similar meetings throughout the entire state prepared delegates to represent each of the nineteen counties then in existence. Every part of the state, aroused to action, participated in this mass effort to improve education. Had not the legislature provided the beginnings of care for the mentally ill in 1844? Now it was time to provide a unified system of education for the mentally sound.

Respect for the general state meeting arose from two factors: first, the delegates included leaders from political groups, doctors, clergymen, and teachers; second, the geographical areas represented all parts of the state. Chief Justice Hornblower led the Essex County delegation of seventy-seven. William P. Roveson of Warren County was selected president, with a vice-president selected from each of the nineteen counties. Judge Richard S. Field of Mercer County was a leading speaker. Thus the convention, although unofficial, took on the semblance of a carefully selected constitutional body. So significant were its membership and its deliberations that during the second session (February 25 and 26) the New Jersey Assembly ruled a suspension of its own meetings in order to permit all its members to attend the "Educational Convention."

In constructing a simple agenda of two parts the delegates got to the heart of the needed balance of state and local powers in educational matters. First, they emphasized the want of a state official, a "general agent," as the great defect of the common school system. Second, they placed definite limits on the idea of centralization to ensure that purely local matters would be governed by each local school unit. After debating the issues involved, the delegates stated their agreement on the questions in the agenda and presented their findings in a recommendation to the legislature for action. With apparent agreement by governor, legislature, and leading professional men, the school law of 1845 finally provided for a superintendent of schools for New Jersey, to the satisfaction and joy of all friends of education.

State Superintendents 1845-1865. The twenty-year period following the establishment of a centralized state system of education saw four men hold the office of State Superintendent of Public Schools: Theodore F. King, 1845-52; John H. Phillips, 1852-60; Frederick W. Ricord, 1860-64; and Caleb M. Harrison, 1864-65. During this period New Jersey experimented with a system of state control of education in which the state official attempted to advise and direct the schools controlled by the local towns and townships. Inasmuch as these local units had built schools, hired teachers, chosen textbooks, given or neglected to give examinations since colonial days with no outside interference, the new experiment in state control often found a cool welcome. In August, 1845, Superintendent King called a school meeting in Essex County to which only six teachers and school committeemen came. In September of the same year the town of Paterson sent not a single person to attend either of two announced meetings with the state superintendent. Revisions of the law in 1846 gave the official more power, but during the entire twenty-year period the local school committeemen guarded their own power jealously.

State control meant statistical reports. At first these were simple tabulations of the number of schools, the amounts received by each from the School Fund, the number of pupils residing in the districts, and the number of these who attended school during the year. Local prejudices were not disturbed nor local autonomy reduced by this type of reporting. The figures compiled merely served to inform the state how its funds had been used; there was no way of imposing any pressure on the local school authorities.

As early as 1848, Superintendent King called attention to the fact that New Jersey had nineteen counties, 174 townships, and 1,640 school districts. This large number of districts was the result of the law of 1693 that allowed towns to start as many districts—each with its own school—as the population warranted or demanded. The trustees of each school were responsible to the annual town meeting, and heretofore had had no direct contact with the state government. Under the state superintendent's ruling, each district was required to report annually; but many stubbornly refused to do this, thus emphasizing the need for authority to enforce regulations set by the state.

Civil War Period Brings Educational Problems

Increased migration from Europe in the 1840's and 1850's added to New Jersey's population a source of labor that enabled a rapid growth of industry to center in such towns as Newark, New Brunswick, Paterson, and Jersey City. In Newark, thread and cotton goods manufacture created close ties with the cotton-producing South. With South Jersey adjacent to slaveholding Maryland and Delaware, other ties with the South fostered sentiments hardly in keeping with a Northern state. New immigrants could be expected to look with disfavor on the competition of slave labor, so there appeared to be a wide difference in economic viewpoints. Such variations would slow the assimilation of the new citizens unless a common education could bring a more common enlightenment. Hence industrial leaders added their voices to the demand for a more businesslike state school system.

Reforms Are Delayed. Civil War tensions temporarily prevented the major changes in education that accompanied the transition in industry from small factories to large corporations. War service did reduce the number of men teachers, bringing in women replacements. The ladies, who formerly were considered suitable for dame-school teaching only, held their new positions as the war ended. Men, thus challenged, turned more and more to administrative positions as principals or superintendents. Changes of this nature gave the state officials trained men able to unify the organization of the whole system. Superintendent Harrison and the Trustees of the School Fund spent much of their time in 1865 preparing for the type of administration that would make use of war-learned skills of managing large numbers of people and managing centralized corporation-type organizations. The year 1866, therefore, was another milestone in educational progress.

The School System Is Run on Corporate Lines (1866-1911)

As Union Army veterans reached their homes at the close of hostilities, state educational leaders began their plans for patterning the school system in the form of a great corporation—that type of consolidated business organization which had proved so crucial in securing victory in 1865. Population, like business, grew to new proportions, providing more and more children needing schooling. In 1860, New Jersey had 672,000 people, an increase of 38 per cent over the previous Census. Such growth demanded new plans for schools.

Industrial employees multiplied with equal rapidity during the same period. In 1860, these workers numbered 56,027, an increase of 47 per cent since 1850. After the war the speed of growth continued, with a 36 per cent rise by 1870 and an immense jump of 66 per cent by 1880. Surely New Jersey was a full-fledged industrial state, no longer based on quiet rural agriculture. How could the state give its citizens educational opportunities appropriate to its new status?

The Plan of 1866 Reorganizes the System. To answer this question the legislature enacted into law the recommendations of the state superintendent: first, a state board of education should be created; second, the state board should hire a state superintendent of public instruction; third, county superintendents of schools should serve as state officials located in each of the county seats.

This plan of 1866 brought to the school system the chief advantages of the corporation-type organization, for it set up a state board equivalent to the board of directors of a great industrial concern. These men would determine the policies the state schools should follow. As directors they would engage the services of a qualified executive to manage the system. Added dignity to the office called for a new title, "State Superintendent of Public Instruction." Such an official, with the backing of the state board, should command the respect of the legislature in his requests for new funds, facilities, or organizational changes. Finally, the county superintendents resembled assistant or branch managers, supporting the central administration's policies by ensuring the application of state authority equally to each county. A system of this sort could operate for the benefit of the state's children as effectively as the Camden and Amboy Railroad could operate for its own profit. And so it did until 1911.

The years 1866-1911 demonstrated an important principle of New Jersey educational history, namely that as long as the people of the state are convinced that the system is suited to the times, they support it, but when major revision is needed, they withhold their approval until the system is changed. From 1866, when State Superintendent Ellis A. Apgar began his work by practically rewriting the school laws to agree with the new system, until 1911, when the fifth state superintendent, Charles J. Baxter, ended his term, little change took place in the manner of running the state school system. Nevertheless, the satisfaction evinced in 1866 with the corporate form of organization gave way to almost complete lack of respect for the state system as New Jersey moved into the twentieth century. By then, business methods included use of research, specialized training, and subdividing of services into many new fields of work. To keep in step, the state had once again to remodel its educational system — from the state down to the local district. Thus the year 1911 became another milestone in New Jersey's continuing effort to keep education abreast of changes in social conditions.

Teacher Training Is Improved.   But what of the additional services added to the state system between the Civil War and 1911? Provision for securing well-trained professional teachers and the inclusion of the new high schools into the state school system are the major achievements. Less widely acclaimed were the additions of a larger staff to the state superintendent's office, adoption in 1889 of a new method of appointing the state official (by the governor, instead of the state board), and the clarification of the legal power of the state school official whereby his decisions gained the binding force of court decisions.

Efficiency became a goal in education after the Civil War, paralleling similar goals for well-trained workers in industry. The first steps in securing well-prepared teachers date back to the founding of the State Teachers Association in New Brunswick in 1853 and to the founding of the Trenton Normal School in 1855. One town superintendent noted the need for acceptable teachers during the 1850's by including in his annual report: "I have licensed only about one quarter of those who have applied; objections, either in qualifications as teachers, or in character as regards morals, having been too numerous to pass over."

Teachers themselves had taken up the challenge to improve the quality of the profession by using the enthusiasm generated by the "Friends of Education" to call a state meeting in the Bayard Street School, New Brunswick, on December 28, 1853. Led by a revered teacher, Nathan Hedges of Newark, the fifty who were present started the New Jersey State Teachers Association. Purposes of the organization included the support of county (and later state) teachers' institutes to improve methods of instruction, and the securing of even more effective education for teachers through a normal school.

Organized efforts by the teachers aided the strong tide running toward state-controlled teacher education. The leader in the normal-school movement was Judge Richard Stockton Field, who seemed to work as devotedly for educational causes as he did for his own legal practice. These efforts brought legislative action in February, 1855, providing a normal school and a model school of 250 pupils in which the young teachers could practice their profession. Judge Field, selected as President of the Trustees of the State Normal School, found inadequate funds supplied by the state to run the school, so he frequently contributed of his own wealth. Thus supplied, Professor William F. Phelps, the first principal, gained state-wide support for the effective education of the teachers in New Jersey.

State Board and Normal School Trustees Are Consolidated. These two strong agencies, the Teachers Association and the Normal School, prospered in their work but remained outside the state-controlled school system. The objective of increasing efficiency demanded that there be a consolidation of the State Board of Education and the Trustees of the Normal School. Despite the trend in this direction under the leadership of State Superintendents Ellis Apgar and Edwin O. Chapman, it was only after Governor Leon Abbett stated that "Every college and school supported by the state should be under the management of the State Board of Education" that the union was finally effected in 1891.

The same desire for increasing efficiency through consolidation of small units into larger ones led to the adoption, in 1894, of the town as the smallest educational unit. Heretofore the large number of small school districts made it necessary to have separate boards of trustees for each school building. Hereafter an elected board of education for each town directed the work of all the schools in the unified district. By this time, however, all the larger cities had their own school organizations, directed by one school board and a superintendent.

Further steps in making the school buildings themselves more healthy and safe gave the state board responsibility for approving all specifications for the heating, lighting, and ventilation, as well as for hygienic conditions, after 1898. At last the state had brought under unified direction schools through the elementary grades, the curriculum, the teachers, and now even the buildings. The correspondence to the corporations was almost complete.

School System Absorbs High Schools. The large towns and cities completely controlled their own high schools until 1895, when state funds became available to add this badly needed service to the school system. New Jersey education moved slowly to catch up with an industrialized state that needed high school graduates as employees. In 1904 the state superintendent employed Professor Louis Bevier of Rutgers College to undertake a survey of conditions in the high schools. All the authority Bevier had was that of an inspector, but he could and did report at intervals over a period of five years. These detailed reports on curriculum, daily work programs, equipment, training of the teachers, school buildings, libraries, and laboratories pointed out many of the kinds of research the state office of education should have been making to keep up with current conditions. Slowness of the legislature to make the changes necessary brought on a flood of criticism from public and educators alike. Lack of careful control of health conditions for both pupils and teachers seemed to bear the brunt of the derogatory statements as reported in the state board records. Finally, modernization came in 1911 with a completely new idea of the state educational organization.

Modernization Is Achieved in 1911

The New Jersey legislature made a second major alteration in the form and function of the state educational office in May, 1911. Woodrow Wilson, former president of Princeton University, took office as governor of New Jersey the same year and included the needed changes in education as part of his sweeping program of social and political reform. The new governor was a crusader, eager to usher in a new era of "political efficiency and morality." Ready-made to fit into his program, the infinitely detailed study by state Senator Joseph S. Frelinghuysen and his committee on education gave the governor the benefit of two and a half years' investigation into means by which the central office of education could be reconstructed.

A Commissioner of Education Is Named. The law of 1911 therefore created a new pattern for the state office, for it abolished the title "Superintendent of Public Instruction" and replaced it with "Commissioner of Education." Although many citizens believed the new title to be but a change in wording, Governor Wilson used his power of appointment to make the office of commissioner the greatest single source of power in education in the state. Beginning with the tenure of Calvin N. Kendall (1911-1921), the commissioner's responsibilities grew consistently with the assumption of new duties and the addition of many subsidiary employees who were specialized in various aspects of education. Even two world wars served to check only temporarily the steady growth of the central office.

High standards of administrative competence demanded that not only should the commissioner have long experience in his field but that each of the four assistant commissioners have equally outstanding records. A supervisor of secondary education, a supervisor of elementary education, a supervisor of industrial education (including agriculture), and an officer to hear all controversies and legal disputes arising under school laws assisted the commissioner in New Jersey's first professionally trained state school administration.

Policy-Making Board Is Set Up. Following the democratic principle of citizen control over the actions of government, the school law of 1911 set up a State Board of Education, with eight members, to formulate the policies that would be carried out by the commissioner and his staff. Newspapers of the time hailed this step as evidence that New Jersey had at last met the requirements of a rapidly growing industrial area by organizing the schools on a scientific basis. When the former state board decided the kind of education needed it acted neither as a group of educational experts nor as trained educational administrators. The new state commissioner, and his staff of professional educators, at last could have direct control of administering the entire state school system.

State-Local Balance Is Sought. Desirable and effective as the increase in state control of education was, such a trend involved danger for the cherished right of each local community to decide what its own children needed in the way of education. By 1912 the state commissioner was warning local school districts that although his office would give the best possible advice and counsel on school affairs, too much uniformity in the state would play havoc with the initiative of individual teachers or superintendents. In pursuance of this liberal policy, the state school office continued to research carefully, and then publish, subject matter tests for elementary grades, curriculum monographs or guides, qualifications for teachers, plans and specifications for adequate school construction, suggestions for beginning the transportation of pupils, and varied documents on insurance, health, safety, and physical education. The recognized objective of this type of scientific professional advice to educators and local school officials was to secure a balance between the encroachment of state government and the localized community control of schools. While the state authorities advised, the local officials made final decisions. This arrangement continued until two world wars brought extensive changes.

Toward Consolidation (1911-1945)

Special Problems Arise. In the time between 1911 and the end of World War II, in 1945, the rapid increase in the kinds of educational services demanded by the people of New Jersey frequently upset the balance between state and local governments. For example, the rapid mechanization of the armed forces during World War I pointed up the inadequacy of rural schools to train citizens for a scientific world.

To meet this need, many districts consolidated one- and two-room rural schools into larger, more adequately staffed and equipped schools. On the other hand, some rural districts challenged the state authorities in order to retain for a time their small schools.

A related problem arose over the establishment of schools devoted to vocational training. Determination of the nature or even the location of a school serving many districts might raise serious controversy. This argument was avoided by making the county school officials responsible for vocational education through the "Vocational School Act" of 1913, the basis for subsequent development of this type of training, supplemented later by the Federal Smith-Hughes Act of 1917.

Rural communities recognized their need for improving their local schools, even though they were often too small to warrant the appointment of a trained supervisor. Again the problem of state control was met by creating, in 1916, the office of "helping teacher," to become part of the county superintendent's staff in those counties with large numbers of country school districts. Expanded in 1920, this system gave less densely populated areas some of the professional assistance available previously only in wealthier school systems.

At the same time that vocational schools were beginning, and helping teachers started their work of improving methods of teaching, other problems engaged the attention of the commissioner of education, highlighting the fact that New Jersey's state school system was growing in several directions at once. Among these diverse developments may be noted the transfer of direct control of the state normal schools from the State Board of Education to the commissioner in 1926, the beginnings of inspection of school buildings for safety and health conditions, the inspection of school accounts, and many special services in both world wars, such as scrap drives, bond drives, issuance of ration books, and the like. Other duties related to standardizing requirements for teachers' licenses and co-operating with the reorganized State Library and later with the State Museum. In the field of teacher training, summer normal schools, beginning in Newton, Collingswood, and Ocean City, had developed rapidly after 1918.

Reorganization of School Administration Is Studied. Evidently the diversity of the state commissioner's duties called for reappraisal and rearrangement, for the idea of professional state school administration that Governor Wilson promoted in 1911 needed rethinking long before 1945. But revision of methods in administering state government is hard to achieve. Evidence of this fact is seen in the span of seventeen years that elapsed between the appointment of the first

"Commission to Survey Public Education" by the legislature in 1928 and the final achievement of a change in the nature of the state school administration in 1945.

The first commission worked from 1928 to 1930 with a staff of fifteen educational specialists, directed by Dr. Harlan Updegraff. Unfortunately, publication of the commission's recommendations coincided with the intensification of depression conditions, which naturally postponed any major changes. World War II again deferred plans for modernizing the structure of New Jersey's state educational system, but by 1945 a larger movement for reform included all phases of state government.

A bewildering combination of 102 state government agencies, departments, bureaus, and commissions had become so overlapping or duplicating, or so unmanageable, that Governors Moore, Edison, and Edge had all recommended dramatic reorganization. Conditions contributing to friction between governors, the agencies themselves, and the legislature could surely prevent improvement in education as well.

In order to initiate a thorough reform in the state government the 1944 legislature created the "Commission on State Administrative Re-organization," to effectively consolidate, co-ordinate, rearrange, and simplify the operation of the state government.

A Department of Education Is Created. The work of this commission resulted in legislation that made a new Department of Education out of eight agencies formerly operated separately:

1. The State Board of Education.
2. The Office of the State Commissioner of Education.
3. The State Board of Regents, charged with determining the needs of the state for higher education.
4. The Board of Visitors, charged with the supervision of the State Agricultural College.
5. The Board of Managers, charged with the direction and management of the New Jersey Agricultural Experiment Station.
6. The State Library Commission, which operated the law library and a general reference library in the State House Annex.
7. The Public Library Commission, which conducted the extension and loan service to county and municipal libraries.
8. The State Museum, formerly in the State Department of Conservation and Development.

In presenting the necessary bills to the legislature for passage, the Reorganization Commission emphasized the principle that educational matters were a direct concern of all the people of the state. To implement this principle, public and organizational meetings were held in all areas of the state to discuss the nature and/or merits of the proposed changes. This democratic procedure was so successful that to the final report of the commission was attached a list of eighty-two New Jersey organizations that approved the principles embodied in the bill, which was finally enacted into law in the spring of 1945. Thus the current form of New Jersey's central school administration took shape.

Responsibilities and Duties of State Educational Officials

The State Board of Education. As more citizens of New Jersey come into direct contact with the work of the state board, the many-sided nature of its work becomes more apparent. So few people meet the whole scope of its powers, however, that it will be helpful to enumerate the more important functions that the legislature has assigned to the twelve lay members of the State Board of Education:

1. Prescribe and enforce rules and regulations necessary to carry into effect the school laws of the state.
2. Prescribe rules and regulations for granting certificates or licenses to teach or administer schools.
3. Prescribe a uniform and simple system of bookkeeping for use in all school districts.
4. Give approval to all public secondary schools.
5. Hear and give decisions on appeals from rulings made by the commissioner of education in controversies and disputes arising under the school laws.
6. Establish standards for higher education.
7. License institutions of higher education.
8. Approve the basis or conditions for conferring degrees on graduates of approved colleges.
9. Survey the needs for higher education, and recommend to the legislature procedures and facilities to meet such needs.
10. Advise with the State University of New Jersey regarding its annual budget for services, lands, buildings, and equipment, and jointly with the State University make recommendations to the governor and to the legislature in support of the budget; also, make contracts with the State University in behalf of the state.
11. Recommend to the governor and the legislature appropriations necessary for services, lands, buildings and equipment

to be used in institutions of higher education, other than
the State University of New Jersey, and make contracts with
such institutions.

12. Exercise policy-making powers of control over such institutions of higher education that may be used by the state.

13. Approve all plans and specifications before any contract for
the erection of any public school building may be made.

14. Approve courses of study in industrial or manual training.

15. Prescribe, with the Board of Control, regulations for the
approval of psychological and psychiatric examiners of
handicapped children and prescribe rules for the approval
of classes for the physically and mentally handicapped.

Acting under the 1947 Constitution of New Jersey, the State Board
of Education serves as the head of the Department of Education. In
this capacity, the state board's decisions in most of the areas outlined
above have the force of law. The state courts will, however, accept
appeals from these decisions if it appears that existing state law is involved. Even though the law gives the commissioner of education
power to decide on many legal matters, such decisions are subject to
appeal to the state board, so that the final policy-making responsibility in education lies with the board itself. The twelve lay members,
serving six-year-terms without remuneration after appointment by
the governor and confirmation by the Senate, have established a firm
tradition of nonpartisan control over the schools of the state.

The Commissioner of Education.   As the chief state school officer in
New Jersey, the commissioner of education carries out the policies
determined by the State Board of Education. He is appointed by the
governor, by and with the advice and consent of the Senate, for a
term of five years. As chief executive and administrative officer of the
Department of Education, he is also the Secretary of the State Board,
and is official agent for all purposes. He directs the work of the professional staff of state school officials, each division of which is headed
by an Assistant Commissioner of Education. In considering some of
the most important duties of the commissioner, their professional
nature may be noted in contrast to the policy-making functions of the
state board:

1. Decide controversies and disputes arising under the school
laws, or under the rules and regulations of the state board.

2. Hold meetings with city and county superintendents to discuss school affairs and ways and means of promoting a
thorough and efficient system of education in New Jersey.

3. Investigate the advisability of creating regional school districts.
4. Apportion state school aid equally to all public schools.
5. Approve the location, rules of management, and courses of study of vocational schools, subject to the approval of the state board.
6. Manage and control the six State Colleges (Trenton, Montclair, Newark, Glassboro, Paterson, and Jersey City) and the New Jersey School for the Deaf, in Trenton.
7. License nonsectarian private boarding schools, private trade schools, and child-care centers.
8. Issue qualifying academic certificates.
9. Present annually to the state board a report containing statistical tables and suggestions and recommendations for the improvement of the schools.
10. Conduct state-wide tests of school pupils whenever he deems it advisable.
11. Prescribe a minimum course of study for high schools and for elementary schools if he deems it advisable.
12. Exercise over such institutions of higher education policy-making powers of control that may be used by the state.

Summary

From the colonial legislature's permission to allow a school in whatever community requested one, to the present highly centralized state school system, citizens of New Jersey have made their educational aspirations come true. From education for "paupers" the state has accepted responsibility for all its children including those with all types of physical or mental handicaps. Ever-widening services of an educational nature have accompanied the increasing centralization of responsibility for such services in the State Department of Education. But should this steady concentration of authority and duty continue unabated?

Current problems also include rising school construction costs, vetoed local school budgets, school curricular offerings, population expansion and new areas of concentration, vocational education, teacher preparation, higher education including junior colleges, and one of the most urgent of all, civil rights. These are but a few of the challenges awaiting the well-informed, well-educated New Jersey citizen, as he accepts his share of responsibility for a truly superior school system. Meanwhile he strives to achieve an adequate balance between the authority delegated to the local school officials and that retained by the state itself.

DO/DISCUSS

1. Did New Jersey's schools of the past reflect the times or did they play a special role in shaping society? Might the school of tomorrow have a different function?
2. Identify some characteristics of present-day schools that were implanted by practices of yesteryear. Which need revisions? Which need to be retained?
3. List the five most pressing problems confronting New Jersey's schools today. Do the same for the state's schools of the past. Has the nature of the problems changed? Explain.
4. Elaborate on each of the following remarks on education credited to John Fitzgerald Kennedy:
   a. "Excellence in education must begin at the elementary level. We cannot afford to wait for another year, or for another approach, or for the day when these problems vanish."
   b. "A child miseducated is a child lost. The damage cannot be repaired."
   c. "Civilization, ran an old saying, is a race between education and catastrophe. It is up to you to determine the winner of that race."

CHAPTER 11

Caring For Those in Need

One of the gravest responsibilities of a state is the welfare of the human beings who live within its borders. People anywhere may be expected to progress, produce, and prosper if the normal needs of life are met and they are well, physically as well as mentally. But what reasonable person could expect six million people to meet all the criteria for happy, well-adjusted citizens? Obviously, many in New Jersey, as elsewhere, need some type of advice, care, direction, punishment, support, or other kinds of assistance for shorter or longer periods of time. Therefore, the perplexing question, as to what kind of care is needed by what citizens, is present in any state, but develops with uncommon intensity in the urban state of New Jersey.

In the government of New Jersey, the Department of Institutions and Agencies bears the responsibility for searching out answers to the questions noted above. This portion of the state's executive branch involves the administration of mental health, welfare, and correctional activities. The same department also has responsibility for supervising all the institutions and welfare services offered by the state. Attached to this branch are the State Parole Board and the Bureau of Legal Affairs. Any study of the achievements of New Jersey would, therefore, include consideration of the history, extent, and quality of the concern exhibited by the state for each of its citizens. Thus the objective of this chapter is to consider the treatment accorded representative groups of citizens whose needs are of importance to the state as a whole.

201

Welfare in New Jersey Before 1830

The Dutch View. Public welfare in the colonial Jerseys (East Jersey and West Jersey) closely reflected the thinking of the homelands of the settlers. The New Netherland settlements along both shores of the Hudson River soon gave evidence of the Dutch heritage of concern for the individual. The Reformed Church, as a state church supported by taxation, had the responsibility of caring for the sick and the poor of all faiths. This liberal policy was carried out by a "Sieckentrooster," who found the sick and needy of each town and notified the clergyman responsible for dispensing aid. Church collections for aiding the poor seem to have been the chief source of funds for this work.

Another form of aid to the Dutch settlers came from the services of the "Orphanmaster." This official cared for orphans by "binding" them out to citizens who gave the children food, shelter, clothing, and religious instruction. In return the orphan was expected to work in the home or farm to which he was "bound." The practice was probably much more humane than establishing institutions for orphans, but the treatment was quite likely to be kind or harsh, depending on the nature of the home in which the child was placed. That the practice was widespread is attested to by the sending of several shiploads of orphans to New Netherland from the overseers of the poor in Amsterdam.

In addition to the "bound," or "indentured," children, New Amsterdam provided aid for the poor through work projects under the direction of Governor Stuyvesant. Thus the Dutch not only attempted to give systematic care to those in need but also tried to remove the causes of poverty through the same type of humane methods used in Holland. Peter Stuyvesant had these plans combined in his poor-relief ordinance of 1661, passed by the Governor and Council of the Dutch West India Company.

The English View. With the coming of the English in 1664 a new approach to welfare seems to have developed. Two influences centered in the Jerseys, one from the movement of the Puritan New Englanders to Elizabeth and Newark, and the other from the arrival of Puritans who had found the restoration of King Charles II displeasing to their strict religious tastes. Both groups seemed to consider that need for welfare indicated the presence of evil.

Early in the eighteenth century the English required the overseer of the poor, a local official in each community, to submit his decisions to the court. Failure to meet the social standards of adequate provision for all his family's needs seems to have made a man a sort of outcast, if not a criminal. Thus the courts participated in judging the appeals for community assistance for the ill, the indisposed, and the indigent. And when such care was approved, the recipients were stigmatized in some manner. Children were removed from the home unable to provide for their care, public auctions were held to find citizens willing to give the care needed, and the unfortunate ones were officially labelled paupers. The label of pauper persisted in schools for the poor until the middle of the nineteenth century, illustrating the distaste felt for those considered the social misfits.

Probably the lenience of the Dutch with regard to care for the poor prevented the English colony of New Jersey from following the harsh treatment of the poor in England. In the homeland the poor who could work, but who would not, were whipped publicly. This policy was supported by English law, which changed little from the Elizabethan Poor Law of 1601 until the statutes underwent a thorough revision in 1834. Nevertheless, the poor in New Jersey who were "bound" out as children, or who were placed in "almhouses" as adults, found little geniality or warmth in tax-supported aid to them as paupers.

Some Early Welfare Progress. The Quaker influence in the province of West Jersey led to extensive care for the poor, but with a distinct no-nonsense attitude. Provisions in the laws of the province to prepare workhouses, in which the poor could labor for the good of the community, were carried out by the middle of the eighteenth century. These institutions were useful in caring for those who might otherwise have found themselves in the debtors' jails—sad places indeed during the Colonial Period.

Both the American Revolution and the French Revolution brought changes in attitudes toward existing social conditions. These changes found expression in New Jersey in the establishment of a state prison to take the place of the former practices of inflicting pain as punishment for crimes. The state opened its first prison in 1799 in Trenton. This remained the only state institution where punishment of criminals took the form of an imposition of a sentence of "hard labor" for a period of time judged commensurate with the seriousness of the crime. By 1836 the old prison needed rebuilding as well as enlarging. The reconstructed prison remains in use despite serious protests from time to time.

The revolutionary changes in methods of punishing criminals also brought the construction of jails as well as workhouses in each of the counties. Thus the idea of local responsibility for the care or correction of the needy citizen grew at the same time that the leaders were exploring the idea of the state as a source of aid.

The 'Humanitarian Revolt' of the 1830's and 1840's

Despite these examples of enlightened attitudes, most citizens prior to 1840 felt little civic responsibility for the care or protection of the citizens who were ill, insane, indigent, or merely aged. Such persons could be cared for by relatives, churches, private charities, township or county governments, or not at all. But agitation for increased attention to the needy ones developed in New Jersey as it did in neighboring states at the time. Known as the "humanitarian revolt," this movement in the 1830's and 1840's produced great advances in the treatment of the poor, the insane, and others. Forerunners of these changes in other states turned attention to New York, where the "Society for the Prevention of Pauperism" continued the work it had begun in 1817.

Parker's Contribution. James Parker, a highly respected political leader and legislator from Perth Amboy, had secured a modest beginning in 1817 for a state educational system that would gain public acceptance only in the 1830's. In the earlier year Parker induced the New Jersey legislature to establish the State School Fund for the purpose of giving financial aid to state public schools. Parker advanced the optimistic view that a school for all the public would solve most of the problems of poverty and crime. While the school fund grew through additions of stock in the Camden and Amboy Railroad, money from the sale of waterfront lands, and stock in various banks, twenty-one years passed before the state government was ready to accept Parker's idea of a school system.

Distrust of the wisdom of local administration of welfare grew slowly during the first third of the nineteenth century. But with the increase in widely supported organizations like the "Friends of Education" in New Jersey and other states, the "New Jersey Lyceum," the "Society for the Prevention of Pauperism" in New York, and a similar society in Boston, many people felt that the time had come to use the resources of the whole state to meet problems that involved the whole state. Thus was the stage set for the introduction of new programs of welfare.

On April 9, 1838, the legislature appointed a committee to gather statistics about "lunacy and idiocy" in New Jersey, to determine if there existed a need for an insane asylum to care for such unfortunates. The committee named included leading doctors, judges, and political leaders. Selection of such a respected group indicated the importance attached to the work. With the discovery that 338 lunatics and 358 idiots existed in New Jersey, either at large or as inmates in the county jails, the investigating committee immediately decided that an asylum was essential. However, former customs were stronger than new ideas, with the result that mental cases continued to be tied or chained in cagelike cells in the county jails or poorhouses for another six years before anything was done.

The Work of Dorothea Dix. Surprisingly enough, it was a woman from New England, Miss Dorothea Lynde Dix (1802-1887), who invaded the male realm of politics to shame the legislature into providing the needed asylum. Born in Maine, she was running a school in Boston in 1841 when she became aware of the lack of care given mental patients. Going from state to state she studied hundreds of cases in which mentally ill persons were treated little better than caged animals.

Arriving in New Jersey in 1843, Miss Dix surveyed conditions with the help of local officials in all parts of the state. She noted cruel or inhumane detention of mental cases in counties from Sussex to Cape May. Using this method of careful reporting of individual cases, giving specific locations, names, and dates, she compiled a comprehensive as well as impressive document. It was undoubtedly the most objective report on the need for care of the mentally ill prepared in New Jersey up to that time. On January 23, 1845, the report of Miss Dix, called a "Memorial," was presented to the legislature in Trenton. Both the Senate and the General Assembly immediately ordered 500 copies of the thirty-nine-page report printed for distribution. Its contents so shocked the lawmakers, and the public in general, that a law for the care of mental patients was soon passed. Before the end of 1845 New Jersey's first asylum for the insane was under construction in Trenton.

The "Memorial" written by Miss Dix thus contributed to a profound social change, but it also has served as a memorial, in the usual meaning of the word, to the courage of one person who determined to gather evidence on social welfare conditions, using whatever means of travel she could find. Bumping along the dirt roads of rural New Jersey in an open horse-drawn carriage took stamina and devotion to a cause. As a tribute to Miss Dix, a grateful New Jersey built a private apartment as an annex to the State Hospital in Trenton, the institution she had been instrumental in founding. This home was for the use of Miss Dix in her years of retirement; there she died in 1887.

Beginning in such a modest way, New Jersey's citizens increased their demands for services rapidly throughout the ensuing century. Today, therefore, care is provided by state welfare agencies and officials for mental health problems, many types of direct welfare services, and extended correctional treatment, which includes parole and rehabilitation. Well-informed citizens know the nature of the services their state is capable of offering. Thus the modern organization of New Jersey's welfare activity deserves attention in some detail.

Problems of State Administration of Welfare

As was mentioned at the outset, the welfare activities of the state are directed by the Department of Institutions and Agencies. As in the case of education, the work of this department is guided by a group of citizens, rather than by a single executive. The State Board of Control serves as the head of the Department of Institutions and Agencies. Its nine members are appointed by the governor, "with the advice and consent of the Senate," for terms of eight years each. It is the duty of this board to appoint a Commissioner of Institutions and Agencies, who is the professional administrator of the state's largest department. The board also has the responsibility of determining policies as well as supervising all state institutions.

Some idea of the importance of the task assigned to the Board of Control by the legislature may be gained from the fact that on an average day over 150,000 persons are under the care of some agency or institution responsible to the board. Not only must these people be cared for, but the people of the state, through the legislature, expect the various institutions and agencies to be operated "efficiently, economically, humanely, and scientifically."

Establishing Community Relations. One of the most perplexingly persistent problems of welfare administration in New Jersey is that of relationships with local or home communities. State agencies frequently suffer from their identification with the state rather than with the local community. The idea of "State" seems cold, impersonal, even partially or completely removed from the community to which the individual belongs. When in the past a child, under the care of the State Board of Child Welfare, came to be known as a "state child," this problem appeared most clearly. The "state child" seemed to belong to everyone; which of course meant no one. But when successful welfare work is able to engender a sense of belonging to someone or some place, real progress toward solution of this kind of problem may be reported.

The Commissioner of Institutions and Agencies is the official responsible for all the activities in relation to welfare. He is appointed by the State Board of Control, subject to the approval of the governor. Although he serves an indefinite term, he may be removed by either the board or the governor, after having been given notice and a hearing. This is one of the ways in which the state attempts to gain the long-term services of a qualified administrator, while retaining the power to make needed changes.

Extent of Welfare Work. The vast extent of the work carried on by the Department of Institutions and Agencies in New Jersey is suggested by a list of the institutions accountable to it:

State Hospitals for Mental Disease:

> Greystone Park
> Trenton
> Marlboro
> Ancora
> Neuro-Psychiatric Institute, Princeton

Other Mental Facilities:

> Diagnostic Center, Menlo Park
> Arthur Brisbane Child Treatment Center, Allaire

Tuberculosis Hospital:

> New Jersey Sanatorium for Chest Diseases, Glen Gardner

Mental Deficiency Institutions:

> Vineland State School, Vineland
> North Jersey Training School, Totowa
> State Colony, Woodbine
> State Colony, New Lisbon
> Edward R. Johnstone Training and Research Center,
>   Bordentown

Correctional Institutions:

> New Jersey State Home for Boys, Jamesburg
> New Jersey Reformatory, Annandale
> New Jersey Reformatory for Women, Clinton
> New Jersey State Home for Girls, Trenton

Penal Institutions:

New Jersey State Prison, Trenton
New Jersey State Prison, Rahway
New Jersey State Prison, Leesburg
New Jersey Reformatory, Bordentown

Other Institutions:

Highfields Treatment Center, Hopewell
Warren Group Center
Turrel Group Center

Homes:

New Jersey Home for Disabled Soldiers, Menlo Park
New Jersey Memorial Home for Disabled Soldiers,
    Sailors, Marines and Their Wives and Widows,
    Vineland
New Jersey's Firemen's Home, Boonton

In recognizing its responsibilities for welfare, the State of New Jersey provides assistance for all age groups of the population. Two of these groups usually need the greatest amount of care: the very young and the very old.

All types of assistance are provided by the Division of Welfare of the Department of Institutions and Agencies. The work of this division includes jurisdiction over the Bureau of Assistance, the State Board of Child Welfare, and the State Commission for the Blind. The division also carries out related welfare activities, which include civil defense welfare services.

Four programs spread the work of the division to special classes of those in need. Old-age assistance, assistance for the permanently and totally disabled, general assistance, and assistance for dependent children all claim large portions of the time and money allotted to welfare work.

Suggested Reforms.   Complex though the work of the department may be, the varied types of personal care for the citizens of the state may become more closely related in the future than they have been in the past. In 1958, Governor Robert B. Meyner appointed a committee to study the Department of Institutions and Agencies to recommend how social welfare work in New Jersey might best be carried out. Underlying the extensive changes recommended by the study committee is the conviction that all aspects of social welfare are part of a single picture—a picture whose parts must be considered in relation to each other.

No longer may the troubles of an individual be considered the problems of that person alone; they are the concern of every person in New Jersey. No longer may the act of one person—an act of stealing, or the loss of one's income, or even a sudden mental breakdown—be thought of as an isolated symptom. Each of these situations is to be recognized as parts of the much larger problem of the individual in his relation to social conditions existing in the state as a whole. When anyone suffers, New Jersey society as a whole suffers.

In recognition of the current trend toward unification of social services, the study committee recommended that the state give full attention to bringing isolated services to an end. To do this, personal care will have to be treated as a web that stretches from the home to which trouble has come, out into the community, through the institutions and agencies of the state or the counties, then back to the home. Thus the home of the troubled individual would become the center of focus for welfare work, with each agency adding its particular contribution.

The vast and increasing number of cases that need treatment or aid in New Jersey makes such a program difficult. With a rising population, concentrated in urban areas, and with the lack of understanding of the various types of social services, only a fraction of those who need care by the state receive it. To increase understanding of the nature of the services rendered by the welfare divisions of the Department of Institutions and Agencies, further attention will now be given to them.

Bureau of Assistance. The Bureau of Assistance is the agency that has broad jurisdiction over the twenty-one county welfare boards and a somewhat more limited jurisdiction over the 375 municipal welfare departments. This bureau deals, therefore, with all types of personal and family need, whether it be an emergency—a natural disaster, an influx of Cuban refugees, some family loss due to accident or fire—or a long-time need, such as that caused by children without support, or aged folk in need of medical care. The activities of this bureau change rapidly in response to business conditions; for when the pace of industry slackens there is a corresponding increase in the problems brought on by unemployment. For example, in June, 1961, the 202,600 unemployed workers in New Jersey represented 8 per cent of the total labor force in the state. This large number of persons out of work was 59,000 more than in June, 1960, thereby increasing the demand on all levels of welfare for food, medicine, housing, child care, and similar types of aid. With improvement of business the load again eased on the Bureau of Assistance.

Of all the programs of this bureau, the newest is Assistance for Dependent Children, or ADC, as it is known by the welfare staff. The legislature assigned this program to the Bureau of Assistance, to begin January 1, 1960. Previously, care for children lacking normal means of support was the responsibility of the State Board of Child Welfare. No major change had been made in the allocation of this phase of child care for about fifty years. Under the new arrangement, ADC brought to the Bureau of Assistance an initial caseload of 23,858 situations, which involved a total of 33,585 children. By June, 1961, 50,611 children were receiving aid. Numbers of this size emphasize the problems attendant upon rapid growth of population in the state, especially in the youngest age group.

Amendments to the United States Social Security law immediately place additional administrative responsibilities upon state and county welfare officials. The changes in the national law in the fall of 1960 and the spring of 1961 necessitated prompt action on the part of the County Welfare Boards to enable New Jersey citizens to take advantage of the broadened eligibility and the increased benefits provided by the amended social insurance laws. Thus the state agencies serve as intermediaries between the national welfare plans and the county or municipal agencies that must carry out the new welfare arrangements.

If the state punishes a person for a crime by putting him in prison, what is the responsibility of the Bureau of Assistance to the prisoner's family? Does the state end its care of the children immediately upon the release of the prisoner? This age-old question is getting new answers as studies are made under the Assistance for Dependent Children program of means by which the family involved can be reunited and rehabilitated. This care is especially vital during the period of parole following the term in prison.

In addition to the types of care that have been discussed, the Division of Welfare provides Old Age Assistance to increasing numbers of the aged, whose lives are prolonged by the new drugs as well as by improved medical and nursing care. By June, 1961, about 19,000 aged persons in New Jersey counted on the state for part or all of their support. About $6.5 million is spent annually on improving the lot of the old.

For those who are neither too old nor too young, but are unable to support themselves due to some disability, the Division of Welfare provides nearly $2.5 million for Disability Assistance. About 7,500 disabled persons receive this aid.

State Board of Child Welfare. The State Board of Child Welfare is the chief agency responsible for management and direction of the various forms of child care needed in an urban state. During the year 1960 this board was freed from the program of assistance for dependent children, and the subsequent revision of organization concentrated on services for abandoned and neglected children.

One of the most serious problems met by the state is the placing of abandoned children in homes for adoption. The urban character of the state increases the difficulty, for many of the unwanted infants are of foreign parentage—especially from new groups of immigrants. State officials have found the International Social Service to be of help in working out new plans for adoption procedures in co-operation with the county governments. Thus the state serves to co-dinate care for children to insure that all who need assistance receive it. Seventeen adoption agencies within New Jersey are certified by the state, and twenty out-of-state adoption agencies are certified to work in New Jersey.

Largest of all groups of children for which the state is fully responsible is the foster-home group. With over 7,000 children to care for, the state shares with the counties expenses of nearly $5 million annually. In this way great progress has been made since 1899, when all children needing care were placed in "almshouses," or poorhouses. With the establishment, by state law, of the State Board of Children's Guardians, the state could remove every child in such an institution and place him in a family home. By 1913 widows with children under sixteen years of age could receive money to help them care for their children, so they could keep them in their own homes. In 1915 further provision was made for children who were determined by court action to be neglected.

"Home Life Department" action gave continuing attention to children without normal home life to ensure them the maximum opportunity to obtain the care children normally receive. By 1941 this attention was extended to investigation of homes seeking children for adoption. Then, in 1947, the scope and character of the work of the State Board of Children's Guardians led to the creation of the new title of State Board of Child Welfare, indicating more clearly the extensive responsibility the state accepts for all its children.

State Commission for the Blind. The New Jersey Commission for the Blind also devotes a large portion of its work to children. On June 30, 1961 there were 1,409 children registered with the Education Service of the commission for care. The commission is another component of the Department of Institutions and Agencies. The goals of this agency emphasize the prevention of blindness, with retraining and rehabilitating of individuals who lose their sight.

All ages of New Jersey citizens are included in the Eye Health Service program of preventing blindness and conserving vision. In 1961, 1,606 cases were referred for glaucoma treatment. To advance public information and increase public concern, the Motorized Eye Health unit visits schools throughout the state to examine the eyes of school-children.

Welfare of the blind involves other types of service aimed at making the visually handicapped self-sustaining. The Rehabilitation Training Center prepares the blind for earning a living, while the Home Industries Service directs the manufacture and sale of a variety of handicrafts produced by the blind in their own homes. This latter agency counts the information it imparts to the public as one of its major contributions to knowledge of the blind, their problems, and their potential capacities. Quite logically, many of the blind need financial assistance, which comes to them through the program of Aid to the Needy Blind. About $1 million annually is given in this form. form.

With 1,400 children listed as blind or near-blind, the educational program of the Commission for the Blind is a major item in the annual work for this type of handicapped citizen. Although the aim is to keep the near-blind and many of the totally blind in regular school situations, many have multiple disabilities. Other physical limitations are frequently present, as well as family or personality complications related to the fact of blindness. To determine the best care for each child the commission staff correlates its work with that of the Department of Education. Of the total 1,400 children, only slightly over 100 are given boarding school or other institutional treatment, thus keeping the majority in the home as well as attending the regular community schools.

Mental Health and Hospitals

The modern New Jersey mental hospital makes a happy contrast to the prisons Miss Dix found in use. With nearly 30,000 patients cared for in the seven state and six county mental hospitals, research and training of staff brings continuous improvement of methods of treating the mentally ill. The reduction of the number of patients remaining in the state hospitals, contemporaneous with a rise in the number of patients admitted, is just one achievement of the radically improved methods of treatment.

Rising figures of admissions to mental hospitals are, however, a certain warning of tragedy on our social horizon. As in most states, the number of persons admitted depends less upon how many people need treatment than it does on the space available in the institution. As sociologists agree that no one knows the number of those who have neurotic or psychotic tendencies, it is impossible to predict the actual relation of treatment to need. There is, however, more agreement as to the causes of mental ill health, either under temporary conditions of great mental stress or related to some condition of physical illness. Thus the need for adequately trained doctors, nurses, and other staff personnel increases more rapidly than does the need for space in the state institutions.

The New Jersey State Commission on Mental Health reported in 1961 that as progress in medicine had accelerated in recent years, new types of care had been developed. Modern treatment methods for persons suffering from convulsive disorders (epilepsy) have made it necessary for fewer and fewer of such cases to seek treatment in an institution. On the other hand, emotional disorders in young children are more easily identified with properly trained staff and equipment. With adequate care, many of these children will now be able to remain in society in their adult years, provided they receive institutional care as children. In this connection, many more places must be found for children in diagnostic centers and child-care institutions. Recognizing these changes in need, the legislature in recent years has discontinued the Skillman Village for Epileptics. In its place is the New Jersey Neuro-Psychiatric Institute at Princeton. For a similar reason the Arthur Brisbane Child Training Center was established at Allaire.

Conditions for Restricting a Person's Liberty. Liberty is restricted for any person, whatever his age, when he is given institutional care. This fact is one of the great problems of mental treatment. Who is responsible? Who should say when the individual should lose his liberty, if he has committed no crime? The Commission on Mental Health concluded that any mentally disordered person should be restricted, even though he had committed no crime, under certain conditions. The first condition would be that the individual demonstrate by his overt behavior that he would constitute a "probable peril to life, person or property" if unrestrained. The second condition would be that the state courts determine and verify the need to restrict the liberty of the person concerned. This conclusion would be reached by the courts only with the help of those who had adequate professional training. The third condition would be a court order authorizing detention. Again a qualified staff would take charge to make a thorough study of the individual and recommend and direct the program of rehabilitation. By these steps our society seeks to guarantee that the rights of the individual who may be ill, as well as the rights of the community, will be equally protected.

State-County Co-operation.   Sharing of state and county responsibilities for the care of the mentally ill creates another of the problems unique to New Jersey. With a long history of vigorous support of home rule, the counties have had the right to "erect, maintain and supervise" mental hospitals of their own since 1890. Where the county hospitals are unable to care for patients who are dependent on the county for support, the state institutions care for them. But since 1918 the counties have been responsible for one-half the cost of the care for such patients. The state, however, reimburses the county for its work in the county hospitals.

The interrelationships that exist between the counties and the state are rather unusual in New Jersey for only four of the fifty states have any county hospitals at all. In New Jersey one-third of all public mental hospital patients are cared for in the county hospitals, raising the importance of the county as a unit of government. In addition, the Community Mental Health Services Act of 1957 offered the counties "grants-in-aid" in setting up mental health services in local municipalities. For this type of aid the state will provide half the expense only when the remainder comes from local or county funds, either public or private. This is the legal side of the activity, but what of the social effect of such a division of responsibility between county and state?

Rehabilitation, as mentioned earlier, is the goal of mental health work of all kinds. Readjustment to normal life is nearly always related to a feeling on the part of the patient of belonging to someone or something. The individual can usually feel more closely identified with a familiar community than he can with an impersonal, faraway idea called the "State." The Commission for Mental Health therefore concludes that county mental health services have been an effective means of strengthening ties between the patients and the communities in which they feel they belong. Social competence as well as economic stability seems to be improved in released patients where the home county has been the agency giving the needed mental care. It is to be expected that the social importance of this state-local co-operation will suggest many more types of service to be jointly shared in the future.

Mental Retardation

Chronically handicapped persons have been recognized throughout history, but the development of scientific treatment as well as the passage of a whole body of specific law demanded that the term "mental retardation" be defined with precision. In New Jersey, the term means:

> . . . a state of significant subnormal intellectual development with reduction of social competence in a minor or adult person. This state of subnormal development shall have existed prior to adolescence and is presumed to be of life duration.*

Two main groups of the mentally retarded arise, at least among adults, for which society must make specific provision in the law. First is the group composed of those who are measurably subnormal in their intellectual development, but who may have the capacity for near-normal living and working in a competitive society. Second is that group which has impaired intelligence, coupled with continued inability to meet normal social situations. This group requires continuous protection and supervision. New Jersey has provided this kind of care for a long time.

The state program of residential care for the mentally retarded began over a century ago when twenty-seven children were accepted at what is now the Elwyn Training School in Pennsylvania. The State of New Jersey paid the bill. Currently there are about 6,000 mentally retarded persons of all ages cared for in the five institutions under the control of the state. Of this large number, about two-thirds are seriously handicapped, obviously incapable of caring for themselves in society. Thus a new trend arises.

Increase in the Severely Retarded. In New Jersey, as in the nation, mental deficiency has increased in severity among the cases in state institutions since the end of World War II. Although this should not be taken to indicate a serious increase in mental deficiency in the general population, the Department of Institutions and Agencies is increasingly concerned about the change.

The nature of this change is reflected in the large number of discharges among the mildly retarded cases. The effective treatment provided by modern psychiatric work enables these persons to work in a normal society, if they are closely supervised. This happy achievement is attended by two notable consequences. First, the institutions

*New Jersey State Commission on Mental Health, *Toward Better Mental Health in New Jersey,* 1961, p. 63.

are enabled to admit an equal number of cases from the long waiting lists. For example, new admissions rose from 238 in 1960 to 300 in 1961. Second, the pressure is so great for care that the more severely retarded are chosen for admission. This fact increases the demand for more nurses and staff to care for those who are less able to care for themselves. At the same time, the institutions are progressively handicapped by the loss of the slightly retarded patients, who spent most of their time in aiding their less fortunate fellows.

A related factor is the time that the new patients will probably stay in the institutions. The more retarded the individual is, the more care he needs, the longer he will remain in the institution, and the less he will be able to do for others during his period of preparation for re-entry into society.

One partial solution to this pressing problem may lie in increasing Field Service work in communities throughout the state. These units could aid the state institutions by providing more extended aid to the families of patients before the individual is accepted by the state for care, as well as more careful check-up attention after the individual has been returned to society. In the meantime, more and more families recognize the possibility of securing more adequate care from the state for their mentally retarded members than was heretofore available from any source.

Correction and Parole

New Jersey accepts its responsibility in the control of juvenile, as well as adult, delinquency through the work of the Division of Correction and Parole. The oldest of the division's institutions, the State Prison at Trenton, dates back to the 1790's, but, in contrast, much of the correctional work is rated among the finest in the nation. Highfields Treatment Center at Hopewell is a notable example.

The Division of Correction and Parole, which also includes the Bureau of State-Use Industries, co-ordinates the programs of the four major state penal institutions as well as those of the seven institutions devoted to correctional activities. The Bureau of Correction also carries out preventive work with juveniles by co-operating with local community organizations. Following commitment in a state institution, the individual involved encounters the Bureau of Parole. This bureau supervises parolees released from state and out-of-state institutions, and makes needed investigations into the backgrounds and future plans of the parolees, all the while maintaining approved parole practices, standards, and procedures. The Bureau of State-Use Industries maintains programs whereby inmates of penal and correctional institutions secure training in occupations acceptable in the open society to which they will eventually return.

Treatment of Juvenile Delinquents. Nearly a century ago, at the end of the Civil War, in 1865, New Jersey began its treatment of juveniles who were delinquent. In that year a Commission on Juvenile Delinquency recommended the establishment of a "State Reform Farm School" to deal with the problem of nonconforming youth. Legislative action quickly provided the needed land, with the finished building able to receive the first boys in 1867. The present name of "State Home for Boys at Jamesburg " was assigned to it in 1900.

This institution provides institutional care and training for over 500 boys between the ages of 7 and 18, all of whom have been committed by the juvenile courts of New Jersey. The other correctional institutions — Reformatory at Annandale, Reformatory for Women at Clinton, and the State Home for Girls at Trenton — all share related objectives. These involve the following elements of a balanced program: organized recreation, the development of effective work habits, encouragement of vocational and social interests, pursuance of formal schooling, and, finally, preparation for re-entry into a family life outside the institution.

Even more desirable than this carefully organized program is that of increasing the use of probation as an alternative to commitment in any institution. To make such weighty decisions the state is using (and demanding more) clinical facilities as well as residential group centers. These now consist of Highfields Treatment Center at Hopewell and the Warren and Turrel Group Centers, the latter located on the grounds of the Arthur Brisbane Child Treatment Center at Allaire.

Increasing study of juvenile delinquency, with the attendant use of new types of treatment, becomes more and more urgent as revealed by population trends in New Jersey. Between 1950 and 1960 New Jersey's population increased 25.5 per cent, but during the same time the 15- to 17-year-old age group increased 48.5 per cent! Even this huge jump was exceeded by the 12- to 14-year-old group, which rose from 39,000 to over 150,000 children, or 77 per cent. Added to these is the 64 per cent increase for the 7- to 11-year-old group. These impressive changes forecast a steady and substantial increase in the portion of the population from which come the individuals needing correctional care. State officials fear that the increase will continue for at least another decade, if not longer.

'New Jersey Children in a Changing World'

Intimately related to the topic of human welfare, but transcending in scope even the broad commitments of the Department of Institutions and Agencies, is the title quoted here. So many facets of state concern for children are involved in the 1960 Golden Anniversary White House Conference on Children and Youth that it seems appropriate to conclude this chapter with reference to the findings of that influential meeting.

The White House Conferences on Children and Youth. White House Conferences on Children and Youth began in 1909 with a call for such a meeting by President Theodore Roosevelt. At ten-year intervals since then, Presidents of the United States have issued similar calls. In 1959 President Eisenhower marked the fiftieth anniversary of the conference by calling together respresentative persons from all the fifty states to meet the following year under the direction of a National Committee. Each of the states appointed committees to hold conferences on the county level and then combine the findings in a state conference. By this method, carefully followed in New Jersey, the needs of each community in the nation would receive consideration. Past conferences have produced such lasting results that we may confidently expect equally significant changes in the coming decade. A brief summary is therefore enlightening:

Conference	Topic	Result
1909, President Roosevelt	The Dependent Child	Establishment of the U. S. Children's Bureau, 1912. Enactment of child labor laws.
1919, President Wilson	Standards of Child Welfare	Laws for protecting health of mothers and children.
1930, President Hoover	Child Health	Encyclopedic collection of health findings on children. Teaching of pediatrics in 1930's.
1940, President Roosevelt	Social and economic Problems of Children	Developed principles of maintaining services for children during wartime.

Conference	Topic	Result
1950, President Truman	Development of a Healthy Personality in Children	Evolved the "grass roots" technique of holding conferences at all levels, community to national.
1960, President Eisenhower	"To promote opportuities for children and youth to realize their full potential for a creative life in freedom and dignity"	

Recommendations for Action in New Jersey. If, as in the past, the national conference is followed by ten years of implementation of its recommendations in law and social change, New Jersey children will surely profit in the future. Leaders in social work, both private and public, look to the 670 recommendations adopted in Washington as something of a blueprint for significant social action. The New Jersey Committee on Children and Youth returned from the national convention assured that their findings were in accord with those of the other forty-nine delegations. Subsequently the committee reported to New Jersey sixteen statements of basic agreement on the need for action in the state. In view of the relations of these statements to New Jersey society as a whole, they serve as a guide to challenge every citizen whose concern is children in a democracy.

I. Creation of the New Jersey Citizen's Committee on Children and Youth was an immediate result of the Golden Anniversary White House Conference on Children and Youth. The conference in Washington took place during the final week in March, 1960, receiving and accepting 1,800 recommendations from the state delegations. These statements were consolidated into 670 recommendations, which make up the official report of the conference. Upon receipt of the final report by Governor Robert B. Meyner, the Board of Control, which directs the Department of Institutions and Agencies, took immediate action in creating the New Jersey Citizen's Committee on Children and Youth. This step put the voluntary committee, which had carried out the preliminary conferences in every part of the state, on a permanent basis. With the background provided by the decisions of more than one million qualified youth workers, who participated in the preconference meetings throughout the nation, it is to be expected that each year will see more of the specific recommendations enacted into law.

II. First of these steps to be taken should be the guarantee and protection of all basic human rights. The conference endorsed the United Nations Declaration of the Rights of Children, together with the "Pledge of Children," which latter document stemmed from the 1950 White House Conference. Noting the laudable progress New Jersey has made in its constitution and in the Division on Human Rights, the committee called for continuing support for agencies that are building better intergroup relations. There should be strengthening of programs and activities in fields of housing, recreation, religion, employment, and education, especially where integration is needed for minority groups.

III. The need for better planning and co-ordination of all agencies concerned with the growth and development of children also gained major attention. All levels of government, along with public and voluntary agencies, and management and labor organizations, engage in planning for social betterment, but New Jersey committee members emphasized that the duty of any state agency planning for the welfare of children was to aid the work of local communities, not displace them. This point of view would run counter to that of some state government agencies and bureaus.

IV. The role of the citizen of New Jersey in securing the best social conditions for children was found to need careful interpretation. In our democracy there is need for public awareness of, and active citizen participation in, public affairs relating to children. Services for children can be interpreted, sustained, stimulated, and improved by action of the citizenry of the state as a whole. Recognition of the opportunities to participate in the democratic process was, therefore, the goal of this portion of the New Jersey committee report. One warning was carefully noted, nevertheless. Even though citizen action through public, civic, and private organizations is essential, society suffers when advocates of a special interest use their power to force their will on the majority. To meet this danger the committee urged the state to carefully co-ordinate the efforts of all social planning bodies. Only by such co-operation will all the citizens be alerted to the damaging efforts of special-interest groups.

V. Shortages of trained personnel seems to be chronic in a state undergoing the growth as well as the urbanization seen in New Jersey. All the residents in the state should recognize that the quality of the services received by children depends upon the selection of proper personnel, their adequate education or training, the effective direction of their work, and the provision of adequate incentives. The report named thirteen fields of work needing immediate attention in

New Jersey. Among these professions were social workers, public health officers, nurses, dietitians, correctional personnel, teachers, vocational counsellors, and physicians.

VI. Social and economic problems of the family came in for a major share of committee concern. Granting excellent achievements in New Jersey in citizenship and parenthood education, the "hard-to-reach" families present the most serious problem. Counselling services, group care of pre-school children, working mothers, foster care, and public assistance for children are all areas in need of support as well as of continuing reappraisal. The committee recommended a thorough restudy of the problems of working mothers in areas of low incomes.

VII. Improved physical and mental health naturally received major attention. New Jersey was praised for its accomplishment in both these fields, but the committee stressed the fact that children could be protected directly through additional care for adults. In most cases ill health in an adult, either physical or mental, affects the well-being of some child. Stressing this connection will serve future generations well.

VIII. Educational problems are extremely well known and frequently aired, but some uncommon aspects of education occur in New Jersey as a result of the extreme mobility of the population, presence of older cities in which the schools are antiquated, and tension over the treatment of "normal," "gifted," or "disturbed" children. Despite the usual number of problems concerning education, the committee took no position on Federal aid to education in New Jersey.

IX. Problems of prevention and control of juvenile delinquency and the protection of children against abuse and neglect seem to be on the rise in the state. Chief among remedies suggested was the adoption of a "model" juvenile court law, with state co-ordination of all juvenile courts, and Federal aid to delinquency prevention and control.

X. The mass media were the subject of many recommendations, for they comprise radio, television, magazines, newspapers, movies, plays, and comic books. Since our culture is frequently judged by the quality or lack of quality in our mass media, this topic seemed most vital. Each organization in New Jersey dealing with children was urged to demand that mass media "produce materials in harmony with their objectives." This statement of faith in the democratic process of self-policing was accompanied by four recommendations of a much more specific nature. All avenues of mass media should, in the first place, avoid emphasis on horror, crime, and violence. Secondly, they should emphasize moral and ethical values. Thirdly, they should encourage respect for people by truthful portrayals and by avoiding occupational, national, or racial stereotypes. Lastly, they should offer a wide range of content to appeal to a greater variety of interests and needs.

XI. Cultural enrichment of community life can be found in the libraries, museums, theaters, and similar institutions. As this topic overlapped several others, the New Jersey committee gave it little special attention. Apparently more emphasis on community betterment may be coming in the near future.

XII. Population mobility, especially critical in New Jersey, drew concern over the need for special research in developing new forms of government organization, with new types of tax structure, to meet the new metropolitan movements of people. As central city populations are replaced with new peoples, frequently with previous experience more in rural areas, serious social stresses appear. Even the relatively small numbers of migrant workers in New Jersey's agricultural center and south invite attention to the provision of "mobile schools," to travel with the workers. The density of New Jersey's urban population of over 800 per square mile attests to the mobility that keeps the citizens on the move. A serious problem arises when industry moves outward from the center city to one community, but the population, including workers, concentrates in another area. Here again planning on a large scale seems to be essential.

XIII. Concern for costs of new and redirected services led the New Jersey committee to make a recommendation for a broadened tax base. Federal sources of additional funds tempted the committee, but two reservations also appeared: first, that Federal aid would reduce the feeling of personal responsibility for the welfare of children; and second, that it would develop into bureaucratic regulation without due care for variations existing in specific localities in New Jersey. Debate on this issue is expected in New Jersey for a long time.

XIV. The question of values and ideals in our democracy became a ticklish question in view of the dedication of our culture to religious freedom. Any prescription giving definite social values or ideals as a state-wide goal would seem to infringe upon the right of the individual New Jersey citizen to make up his own mind. In keeping with this goal of freedom, the conference could state that all should "reaffirm faith in the moral and spiritual foundations of our great democracy." To scholars, rather than to legislators, goes the task of determining the exact nature of our values and ideals.

XV. National and international recommendations regarding the

United Nations and the treatment of children in a world setting interested the New Jersey committee, but were outside the scope of state action.

XVI. In preparation for the 1970 White House Conference on Children and Youth, the committee identified two basic objectives: first, the establishment of a permanent state committee (already achieved); second, continued encouragement of social improvement in New Jersey through all levels of democratic procedures, in which the youth themselves should participate.

Summary

The responsible citizens of New Jersey slowly recognized their obligations to those with special need during the Colonial Period and the nineteenth century. Dorothea Dix gave a dramatic urgency to the needs of the mentally ill, with the result that legislation began to appear in support of state administration of aid programs.

In the twentieth century the state began to assemble a co-ordinated program of care for many types of needy persons. Thus, centralizing tendencies began to bring under state direction the twenty-one county organizations and the 375 municipal jurisdictions, to which number more are being added continually. Leaders in the field seem convinced that only the state can provide the needed planning, as well as the initiation of extensive projects in sociological, psychological, and biological research. Such projects are essential in keeping New Jersey up to date in fields related to mental and physical need. Only the state can license or establish professional educational institutions to train physicians, psychologists, psychiatric social workers, and occupational therapists — to mention but a few of the categories of professional workers needed.

Finally, the study of "New Jersey Children in a Changing World" serves as one example of the manner in which a democratic state may enlist the skills and knowledge of thousands of its citizens. In securing the aid of those best qualified to deal with children, New Jersey made definite recommendations for positive legislative and social action for the next decade.

DO/DISCUSS

1. Starting with "I Believe," write a Credo summarizing your principles or opinions concerning handicapped and impaired Americans in need of care. It should be designed as a plaque and artistically finished for wall or bulletin board display at a conspicuous location in the school or community.
2. Nine of the fifty states impose imprisonment for life instead of the death sentence (capital punishment) for first-degree murder. New Jersey, which has long debated the question, continues to permit a sentence of death by electrocution. Find out as much as you can about the merit of the policy and be prepared to debate it in class.
3. Endeavor to arrange to have a resource person from the Department of Institutions and Agencies talk to the class about some topic of interest. If possible, a small group may plan to visit one of the state's institutions for a special investigation and report.
4. Conduct a series of informal, small-group, round-table discussions on the causes and solutions of one or more of the following problems as they might relate to New Jersey:
   a. One of ten persons suffers from some form of mental health disorder.
   b. Upward trend in serious crime continues at a rate four times as rapid as the population; arrests of persons under 18 years of age have increased about 10 per cent.
   c. Welfare cases increase in complexity and number.
   d. Care for the aged is in need of attention.
   What responsibilities does the New Jersey citizen have in these troubled areas?

CHAPTER 12

Changing Metropolitan Patterns

In concluding this series of inquiries into the New Jersey that used to be, and the New Jersey that struggles with the varied problems of the present, it seems appropriate to consider the plans that New Jersey is making to ready itself for an exciting future.

Will the citizens of the future master the forces of progressive urbanization to preserve a healthy, self-determining way of life? Will the term "Garden State," used with affectionate pride for so long, have any meaning in 2000 A.D.? By that time, will farming have entirely disappeared from the state? Probably not, but the last Census revealed that only 3 per cent of the state's workers were engaged in agriculture, while the average for the nation was about 12 per cent. Differences of this significance indicate the need for a study of the plans New Jersey is making to adjust to the new metropolitan patterns so rapidly developing in the former "Garden State." But before discussing the nature of urban renewal or local, state, or regional planning, one should consider the new concentrations of population as they are being studied.

A New Vocabulary for New Patterns

The nature of the concentration of New Jersey's population in urban areas is of equal importance with the great increase in the state's total population (4,835,329 in 1950 — 6,066,782 in 1960). An expert body in such matters, the United States Bureau of the Census,

VITAL STATISTICS ON NEW JERSEY'S EMPLOYMENT (July 1960)

TOTAL MANUFACTURING EMPLOYMENT   770,200
TOTAL NON-MANUFACTURING INDUSTRY . . .   1,254,900

TOTAL NON-AGRICULTURAL   . . .   2,025,100
TOTAL AGRICULTURAL EMPLOYMENT   58,000

Total Work Force 2,551,450
Includes self-employed, domestic and unemployed

NON-MANUFACTURING INDUSTRY (1,254,900)

WHOLESALE & RETAIL TRADE   385,900
SERVICE AND MISC.   272,500
GOVERNMENT   239,700
TRANSPORTATION AND UTILITIES   149,600
CONSTRUCTION   109,900
FINANCE, INSURANCE AND REAL ESTATE . . .   93,700
MINING   3,600

MANUFACTURING (770,200)

Durable Goods (406,000) 52.7%

ELECTRICAL GOODS & MACHINES	116,100	15.1%
MACHINERY (EXCEPT ELECTRIC) .	55,700	7.2%
TRANSPORTATION EQUIPMENT .	40,500	5.3%
FABRICATED METAL PRODUCTS .	51,600	6.7%
PRIMARY METAL PRODUCTS . .	38,500	5.0%
STONE, CLAY, GLASS	32,800	4.3%
INSTRUMENTS, CLOCKS . . .	31,100	4.0%
FURNITURE & FIXTURES . . .	8,800	1.1%
LUMBER & WOOD	6,200	0.8%
MISCELLANEOUS	24,700	3.2%

Non-Durable Goods (364,200) 47.3%

CHEMICAL INDUSTRY . .	90,300	11.7%
APPAREL & NEEDLE . . .	78,100	10.1%
FOOD & KINDRED	63,400	8.2%
TEXTILE-MILL PRODUCTS .	28,600	3.7%
PRINTING, PUBLISHING .	32,500	4.2%
PAPER & PRODUCTS . . .	26,900	3.5%
RUBBER PRODUCTS . . .	22,000	2.9%
PETROLEUM & COAL . . .	10,900	1.4%
LEATHER INDUSTRY . . .	10,000	1.3%
TOBACCO MFG.	1,500	0.2%

has devised terms by which metropolitan and urban centers may be clearly defined. An understandable classification is essential in any state growing as rapidly as is New Jersey. The terms "city" and "country" have given way to a new vocabulary, including "urban places," "urbanized areas," "standard metropolitan statistical areas," and the "standard consolidated area." Informed students are learning to recognize the characteristics of each of these types of population concentration.

Urban Places. The first of these designations, urban places, includes all concentrations of population with at least 2,500 inhabitants, and reaching up to 10,000. Before the 1950 Census, such locations were considered urban only if they were incorporated, but in the 1960 Census all political units and all unincorporated places were considered to be urban as long as they met the required size. These rules apply to political divisions such as cities, boroughs, towns, villages, and townships; for example, Atlantic Highlands, Cape May, and Wrightstown.

Urbanized Areas. Somewhat larger and more extended is the urbanized area. Here the criteria for identification are more complex, but again both incorporated and unincorporated areas are included. The minimum population requirement is a city of 50,000 people, but the surrounding closely settled areas are likewise included if they meet certain further criteria. These conditions involve the fringe areas found around large concentrations of population; in addition, urbanized areas in unincorporated territory may be included if they have a population density of 1,000 per square mile. In short, the urbanized areas are thought of as central cities with their adjacent areas — technically called the "urban fringe." Of the five areas involving New Jersey, only Atlantic City and Trenton have the center city within the state boundaries.

Standard Metropolitan Statistical Areas.   The slightly formidable title of "standard metropolitan statistical area" (official abbreviation: SMSA) serves to identify the entire population of a city and those surrounding territories in which the activities of the city form an observable social and economic system. With emphasis on the nature of the activities, as well as on the size of the population, it becomes evident that some cities will be both urbanized areas and portions of the SMSA's. Each of the SMSA's contains a center city of at least 50,000 population with surrounding counties included if they can give evidence of being integrated socially and economically with the central city. To be integrated, the outlying county will be either a concentration of homes for nonagricultural workers or it will be the location of places of employment for nonagricultural workers. Three-fourths of those employed in the county must be in work other than farming if the county is to be included in the SMSA. Thirteen of New Jersey's twenty-one counties qualify under these criteria. Only Sussex, Hunterdon, Somerset, Middlesex, Monmouth, Ocean, Cumberland, and Cape May counties are presently considered rural areas. Of these, only the three ocean-front counties have less than two SMSA's on their borders. This rapid spread of metropolitan areas highlights the speed with which New Jersey is becoming completely urbanized.

Standard Consolidated Area.   One still more inclusive designation has come into use with the 1960 Census and needs to be understood. That term is the New York-Northeastern New Jersey Standard Consolidated Area. In view of the close relationships binding together the northeastern portion of New Jersey with the New York area, three SMSA's were included with the rural counties of Middlesex and Somerset to make New Jersey's share of one of the world's greatest population complexes. The total standard consolidated area involves portions of New York State, as well as New Jersey, with a combined population of 14,750,000. The United States Census of 1840 was the first one that reported a total for the entire nation as large as that of the current New York-Northeastern New Jersey Standard Consolidated Area.

After getting acquainted with these four terms identifying the different types of population concentration, it will be helpful to locate the specific cities and the counties included in each one. To place each area on a map will also emphasize the interrelationships with which New Jersey is bound to cities and counties outside its borders.

Urbanized Areas and Counties in Which They Are Located:

1. Atlantic City, N. J.:
        Parts of Atlantic and Cape May Counties

2. New York-Northeastern New Jersey
        Counties in New York
                Bronx
                Kings
                New York
                Queens
                Richmond
        Portions of
                Nassau
                Putnam
                Rockland
                Suffolk
                Westchester

        Counties in New Jersey
                Hudson
                Union
        Portions of
                Bergen
                Essex
                Middlesex

                    Morris
                    Passaic
                    Somerset

3. Philadelphia, Pa.-New Jersey
        Counties in Pennsylvania
            Philadelphia County
        Portions of
            Bucks
            Chester
            Delaware
            Montgomery
        Portions of Counties in New Jersey
            Burlington
            Camden
            Gloucester

4. Trenton, N. J.-Pennsylvania:
        Portions of Counties in New Jersey
            Burlington
            Mercer
        Portion of a County in Pennsylvania
            Bucks

5. Wilmington, Del.-New Jersey:
        Portion of a County in Delaware
            New Castle
        Portion of a County in New Jersey
            Salem

Standard Metropolitan Statistical Areas and Their Constituent Parts:

1. Allentown-Bethlehem-Easton, Pa.-New Jersey: Lehigh and Northhampton Counties, Pa.; Warren County, N. J.
2. Atlantic City, N. J.: Atlantic County, N. J.
3. Jersey City, N. J.: Hudson County, N. J.
4. Newark, N. J.: Essex, Morris, and Union Counties, N. J.
5. Paterson-Clifton-Passaic, N. J.: Bergen and Passaic Counties, N. J.
6. Philadelphia, Pa.-New Jersey: Bucks, Chester, Delaware, Montgomery, and Philadelphia Counties Pa.; Burlington, Camden, and Gloucester Counties, N. J.
7. Trenton, N. J.: Mercer County, N. J.
8. Wilmington, Del.-New Jersey: New Castle County, Del.; Salem County, N. J.

Urban Places: The United States Census for 1960 lists 153 urban places with populations of 10,000 or more, together with 165 urban places whose populations range from 2,500 to 10,000. Thus 318 places (and selected urban townships) meet the definition of urban places for New Jersey (281 in 1950).

The Standard Consolidated Area: New York-Northeastern New Jersey consists of four entire SMSA's and two New Jersey counties; New York, Newark, Jersey City, and Paterson-Clifton-Passaic, together with Middlesex and Somerset Counties.

'Megalopolis.' These terms have meaning to the extent that they serve to improve the precision with which one is able to think and plan for the future—a future in which, according to some predictions, labels for concentrations of population are as precise as modern methods of census-taking can make them. The categories are based on numbers of people or on areas involved; therefore, they are reasonably definite in size and location. By way of contrast, the term "megalopolis," rapidly becoming popular, deals with the relationships that bind large numbers of people or extensive geographical areas together.

Megalopolis, as a word describing an urban entity, indicates that various factors bind an area regardless of the exact number of people or the precise acreage involved. The great megalopolis extending down the Eastern seaboard of the United States from Portland, Maine, to Richmond, Virginia, finds New Jersey at its center. In the future, conditions that increase prosperity in one section of this vast area will reflect similar conditions in all the other sections. New Jersey cannot escape—it must play a new game according to new rules. No longer will cities develop with little reference to other types of urban areas: all must plan to co-operate or compete. It may be noted that some city officials are convinced that the world's great megalopoli—New York, Paris, Rome, London, and, largest of all, Tokyo—have more in common with each other than they have with smaller cities in their own countries. Nevertheless, the megalopolis is a great complex of relationships; and New Jersey is at the center of one.

Several cities once made up the area involved on the Eastern seaboard. As recently as 1900, each of these cities was separated from the others by broad bands of countryside. Now they are tied together with strips of urban or semiurban settlement. The city has chased away the country. Less compact than was the traditional city, the whole area is interrelated in problems of housing, water supply, pro-

MANUFACTURING
VALUE ADDED AND RANK OF NEW JERSEY COUNTIES 1954 C-MFG.

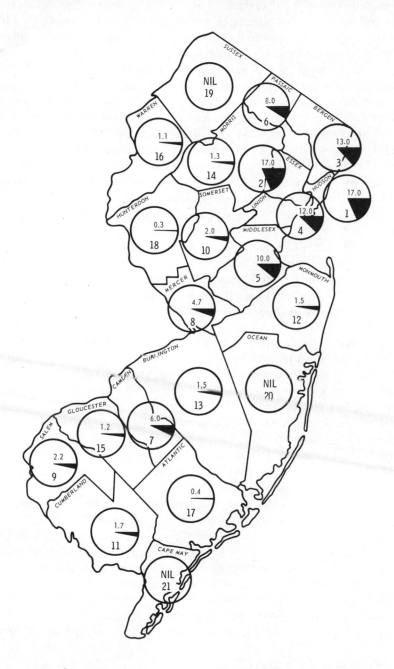

tection, industry, recreation, and, most dramatically, transportation. Although the cities and other areas in the megalopolis have many things in common, they lack political unity. As yet, government is carried on in each of the segments as it developed historically. Thus New Jersey is responsible for working out its own destiny despite its size in relation to the great super-city.

From Maine to central Virginia is an area where 20 per cent of the nation's total population lives on about 2 per cent of its total land. In the most strategic section of this concentration New Jersey lies between the two largest cities. New York, with 7,781,894 people in 1960 (the city alone), and Philadelphia, with 2,002,512 people in 1960, bracket New Jersey. It thus becomes evident that regardless of size, any state located between two giant cities, in the center of a "strip-city" nearly 500 miles long, will have unusual transportation problems, in addition to the difficulties of any urban state.

All these facts and figures have meaning in view of the fact that New Jersey has developed into the most urban of all fifty states, with the future dependent upon the reaction of enlightened citizens to their new urban and suburban status. Sociologists study the megalopolis to determine its effect on family life. These scientists are deeply concerned with the damaging effects on people who live in the suburbs, which naturally spread outward from the centers of cities in the SMSA's.

'Suburbia.' "Suburbia," as it is called, seems to exert a repressive force on the commuters who inhabit it. The residents appear to strive to achieve a uniformity in which each will attune to the average in his community. Competition to outdo all his fellows is restricted to increasing the conformity of his home, his car, his success in business, and his participation in the committee life of his community. Schools take on the largest portion of the upbringing of his children, so the citizen works hard to secure the best schools possible. But he is home so little that his wife accepts the responsibility for managing affairs in the home and the community.

The commuter-father, it is said, sees the authority of the "head of the family" pass to the committeewoman-mother. With the father out of the immediate community a large part of the time, the children assume more importance, with the result that fathers feel impelled to make a showing of overcomradeship whenever possible. Thus the children are urged to participate in numerous organizations, scouts, little leagues, and the like. In the former sandlot ball game the child took the initiative, but in the suburb the adult takes over by providing uniforms, paid coaches, and the paraphernalia of organized sport.

All is done for the good of the children, but sociologists note that the children are cast in adult molds earlier than in the past. They ask whether suburbia has seriously harmed the child by robbing him of the initiative to play his own games (or none at all, if he chooses); whether the mass of population in megalopolis has robbed adults, as well as children, of the freedom to develop as individuals.

Questions for Governments

Questions as disturbing as these confront officials in New Jersey at all levels—local, county, state, and national. Preserved in some respects from the damaging effects of city concentrations of population in the past, New Jersey now faces its new role as heart of megalopolis. Local officials receive requests from promoters for permission to build multistory apartment homes, zoning problems face all urban or suburban localities, rising costs of education bring calls for consolidation of school districts, and new freeways need land even in desirable residential areas. These and countless other related problems confront local city and town governments in all portions of the state, but they fall with extra pressure in the northeastern counties as well as in the Camden-Philadelphia section.

The megalopolis presents county governments with such questions as how much land in county park systems may be used for new housing, or for schools, or perhaps for new highways. Another long-range question has to do with political representation from the county divisions, which some political scientists consider completely outdated in the present urban state of New Jersey.

State government meets its most difficult questions related to population concentration in terms of the taxing of people who live in one state and work in another. New Jersey's attractiveness makes it the home of thousands who are willing to go to the business world of New York or Philadelphia to make a living. Will megalopolis someday create taxing procedures that may be applied to all its residents regardless of state boundaries? State officials in New Jersey, as well as in other states, fear the loss of prestige for their state if such a super-state develops.

State and national governments find the transportation situation of joint concern. National highway systems crossing the state supplement the 131-mile New Jersey Turnpike and the 173-mile Garden State Parkway. The site of a jetport raises questions of safety, sound, and surface routes, in addition to the real estate changes that such a new facility would create. Questions of such an inclusive nature involve all types of government authorities. More and more, such involved problems focus attention on the values of plans for the future, when land and space will be even less obtainable than at present.

Planning for Growth

In planning for the future, New Jersey can draw upon thirty years of experience with planning boards whose objectives were to "make room for the next million," to borrow the title of the 1961 State Planning Conference. With 2,500 persons added each week to the population, all levels of government realize the urgency of preparing land and resources for the future. Society has always built and then rebuilt its communities, but there were few master plans to serve as long-term guides. Most of the changes were privately inspired, with little thought for the welfare of large groups or areas.

At the end of the 1920's, several states established planning agencies to aid city or metropolitan slum clearance or the relocation of streets or parks. States also developed departments of conservation that included planning as part of their work. The beginnings of regional planning surveys in Los Angeles, New York, Philadelphia, Chicago, St. Louis, Washington, and Boston also came in the twenties.

State Planning Board's Early Days. On a still wider scale, the national Government put planning on a firm footing in the National Planning Board, established by the Roosevelt Administration in 1933-34. New Jersey kept pace when Governor A. Harry Moore set up a temporary state planning board in February, 1934. During the depression the work of such a board was largely related to the activities of the State Relief Administration. Why should new boards arise during a depression when money is so scarce? For the simple reason that the evidence of failure to plan shows most dramatically during times of economic and social difficulty. Then the slum areas become most noticeable; the poorly planned residential areas advertise their ugliness when depression withholds the money needed to paint and repair them. Thus one of the objectives of the Federal planning agency was to encourage the states to organize their own groups to prevent a repetition of the depression conditions.

The New Jersey State Planning Board was able to continue its work only through Federal assistance, to the extent of 80 per cent of the total budget of $225,000 between 1934 and 1939. This kind of Federal aid fell off as individual states took up the idea of conservation and development as a function of the entire state government. One drawback arose as the nineteenth-century concept of "development" overtook the twentieth-century idea of "planning." Development of the economic or agricultural resources of the state seemed to offer help in overcoming the effects of the depression. Planning, on the other hand, held hopes of managing the resources needed in the future by undreamed-of numbers of people. With the Federal Government more or less out of the picture, the State Planning Board in New Jersey struggled on into the 1940's. With small budgets and insufficient staff the work was necessarily limited to the making of studies, but these researches were done with care and foresight.

As war in Europe stimulated business in New Jersey few could give attention to charting the possible needs of coming generations. Yet the State Planning Board served as a source of information and advice on such problems as tax delinquency of rural lands, outdoor recreational facilities, parks to be developed along the eastern ocean front, and a proposed ship canal to be built from Raritan Bay to the Delaware River. At the same time an even more ambitious study was getting under way.

State Development Plan. The State Planning Board started work on a comprehensive study to result in a State Development Plan. Such a plan would involve careful conservation of resources needed in an urban state. Over two decades ago the Planning Board initiated studies on parks and public lands, water supply, sewage disposal, air and highway transportation, and electric and gas utilities, among other items. Involvement in World War II reduced the attention to planning, with the result that the planning functions were absorbed by the Department of Conservation and Economic Development during the 1944 revision of the state executive. Nevertheless, the "State Development Plan" was finally published in 1951. Included in the resulting action of the state were five significant developments.

The construction of both the New Jersey Turnpike and the Garden State Parkway gave the state national prominence in transportation. The latter is still noteworthy for its safety record for miles driven. In water conservation the acquisitions of the Round Valley Reservoir site, the Wharton Tract, and the Worthington Tract all looked to the day when urban New Jersey would be hard pressed for water supplies. In conclusion, the state followed the recommendation to purchase and then develop Island Beach, between Barnegat Bay and the ocean in Ocean County, as a state park.

Stature of Planning Is Raised. These varied activities highlight one of the serious questions in planning for the future: Should planning be a distinct function of a state government, or should it be an integral portion of the work of the department assigned to increase the state's economic or industrial welfare? Prior to changes in the Department of Conservation and Economic Development in 1955, the work of the Planning Board included aid to local municipal planners, aid to state economic development programs, administration of Federal programs, public works project direction, assistance to projects for industrial development, and, finally, state-wide planning. The question of correctly placing planning in the state government was answered in 1955 by the assignment of the Planning Board to the Department of Conservation and Economic Development, but its importance was recognized by the raising of its status to that of a "bureau."

This promotion in rank, and another similar elevation in 1961, reveal two significant aspects of New Jersey state government. A promotion in the rank of a bureau, agency, office, division, or the like gives the thoughtful observer a deep insight into the nature of the service the state officials feel should receive most attention at the time. Although political considerations are always exerting influence, the raising or lowering of the status of an important portion of the state's administrative machinery tends to reflect the way the officials are reading public opinion. In the second place, such a change indicates that the state is reacting to forces or pressures that may reach far beyond present considerations. Such indeed was the case when the realization of the spread of urban conditions raised planning to bureau status.

Even that title was soon to go. In 1961, a further promotion brought with it the title of "Division of State and Regional Planning." This honor was in part a recognition of the changing nature of the work necessary to meet changing urban living. As more and more urban places, as well as metropolitan areas, sought to plan or replan their futures, they found the Planning Bureau ready to help. Direct contact with local communities also gave the state officials additional experience with the construction of "master plans"—another of the terms that have come to mean so much to modern urban dwellers. At last New Jersey had committed itself to a serious attempt to plan for adequate use of land, buildings, parks, water, highways, and other physical aspects of cities, as well as for needed services.

A natural outgrowth of the work with local communities was the ability of state officials to produce co-ordinated plans that would encompass the entire state. Careful selection of urban places gave the bureau wide experience with all sections of New Jersey; it learned their need for new land as well as for revision of the manner in which present resources were used. Between 1956 and the elevation to a division in 1961, the Planning Bureau carried out programs with 151 municipalities. This assistance enabled the cities to qualify for funds from the Federal planning agencies, which demand that a master plan be formulated before money is advanced.

Local Planning and Urban Renewal. Traditionally, American government has its roots in the local community. Planning for future needs has kept the tradition with many types of local research, study, and planning boards or councils. The duty of the state is to serve as a co-ordinating agency to supply aid when needed, and to develop over-all plans. First in the community, however, is the local planning board for long-range planning, with urban renewal projects for the redevelopment of slum and blighted areas. This latter activity is considered an attempt to cure the results of insufficient planning in the past.

In its broadest sense, urban renewal is the total of all public and private actions taken to provide for the continuous, sound maintenance and development of an urban or metropolitan area. Urban renewal encompasses efforts to plan and program governmental services, to redevelop slum or blighted areas, to encourage the conservation and rehabilitation of neighborhoods, to develop sound and efficient commercial and industrial areas, to insure decent, safe, and sanitary housing for all groups, and to adequately provide basic community services and facilities.

No matter how much the local community wishes to carry out its own individual renewal program, all levels of government soon become involved. Basic community facilities, such as highways, water, sewage disposal, light, power, and so on, all involve other communities in ways that necessitate co-operation. Even county, state, and Federal agencies are affected when Newark, Paterson, Trenton, Camden, or any other city attempts to reclaim any of its blighted areas. The fact that most of New Jersey's cities are part of some one of the metropolitan statistical areas increases the need for co-ordinated plans, which require a thorough realization of the individual community's relation to the geography, economy, and society of the entire region. Obviously such problems as air pollution, superhighways, or any of the major public facilities are of concern to several, if not many, individual municipalities. The State Division of State and Regional Planning feels that it can provide the co-ordination needed.

Local communities do not have to work alone to cure their rapidly mounting problems. Since the passage of the Federal Housing Act of

1949, with its subsequent amendments, Federally financed programs have provided cash grants and other types of assistance for planning and urban renewal. As has been pointed out, in order to receive aid from Federal agencies, there must be a master plan. The master plan will include the local activity for which Federal aid is required. Such activities include clearance, assembling of ownership of land, and re-planning of blighted areas. The land may be used for private rede-velopment after the former slums have been cleared, or it may be used for co-operative housing projects, or even for municipally owned low-cost housing. Federal aid is also available for construction of colleges and other institutional housing, and even for making the pre-liminary surveys to determine the best procedures to use.

Planning and renewal are quite distinct in meaning, according to professional usage. Plans are more inclusive, for they are concerned with such solutions of physical problems as will achieve continuing improvement of the economic and social well-being of the community far into the future. Renewal is the rebuilding or alteration of a con-dition that exists at the present, probably due to the lack of previous planning, or to the changes brought about by intensification of urban population growth.

Both planning for the future and rectifying current deterioration require plans produced by local planning boards. The Municipal Planning Enabling Act of 1953 (with amendments) permits a munici-pality to create such a board, have a professional planning staff, pre-pare a master plan, and adopt it after public hearing. Finally, the act permits the municipality to take steps to implement the plan. Al-though New Jersey has over 450 planning boards, only half that num-ber have as yet developed their master plans. With each master plan there is developed an official community map, which shows both the results of all the surveys taken to analyze the nature of the com-munity and the areas involved in carrying out the objectives of the plan, whether it be new facilities, new streets, zoning changes, new public buildings, renewal projects, housing developments, or what-ever. These maps are helpful to all citizens in understanding their own communities in relation to all other communities.

In summarizing local planning and urban renewal it may be wise to note the comprehensive nature of this, one of the newest of func-tions of local government. Planning officials include each of the fol-lowing activities as a part of adequate preparation for modern urban government. First there must be a thorough analysis and determina-tion of the economic strengths and weaknesses of the community, with predictions for the future in services, retail and wholesale trade, industry, and other special factors. Then population studies will give a picture of the characteristics and probable geographical location of future concentrations. Land-use studies will give the size and function of each of the principal land usages. This will be followed by analysis of the several neighborhoods, which could lead to renewal programs for those areas that are blighted. Analytical studies of existing facilities for mass transportation would accompany the inevitable and continuous consideration given street and highway traffic. In traffic studies, the flow and congestion of travel has a large bearing on the nature of neighborhoods, existing or desired for the future. Business district parking relates traffic flow to the economic health of the commercial neighborhood. Careful recreational services studies will show the adequacy of existing recreation areas, both as to their size and as to their effective service to the neighborhood.

In addition to the above, adequate planning will be noted on the official maps to show sites for public buildings, all proposed changes in communities, highways, renewal projects, and so on. The map will also indicate present and future zoning provisions, including housing subdivisions. Last, but obviously not least, will be the preparation of a definitive capital budget for the coming year with estimates for both five and ten years in the future.

All of the fourteen activities enumerated here should be combined to produce a workable, comprehensive plan for community action; no part may be safely ignored. All should be well integrated and developed in four stages: survey, analysis, plan formation, and achievement.

State and Regional Planning. Faced with the probability of a full million people being added to New Jersey's population by 1970, state officials developed plans to meet the increase. All departments of the state government sought to adjust programs to meet the changing metropolitan patterns of life, but especially in the Division of State and Regional Planning were there new ideas introduced. With 90 per cent of the state's population now in urban places or metropolitan regions, co-ordination between the efforts of individual municipalities became essential to prevent an acceleration of the disturbing aspects of community life that exist at present. Somewhat parallel to the goals of any single community, but with state-wide scope, the division's aims were five in number. They were designed to meet the challenge of the rapid urbanization of most of the state, with its continuing technological advances and changing standards of living.

The first goal for state-wide planning involved the assembling and analyzing of facts pertinent to the current conditions or trends in the physical aspects of the state. The Green Acres Program is the prime fruit of this effort, for the voters approved a $60-million bond issue in November, 1961 to provide land for adequate recreation and open space in New Jersey.

The second goal included the preparing and maintaining of a comprehensive master plan for the future improvement and development of land and facilities throughout the entire state—similar to that of a municipality, but on the wider area.

In the third place the state undertook to secure fuller co-ordination between the several state departments, all of which have responsibilities in meeting the trends to more and more urbanization.

The fourth aim was similar in nature, but would co-ordinate, stimulate, and assist local, county, and regional planning activities.

The last of the five goals sought to initiate studies in developing and redeveloping the state's lands for those coming generations who will not have known New Jersey as a rural state.

In the carrying out of the state's planning functions, the regional aspects demand and receive major attention. The Meadowlands Regional Development Agency is a pioneer in the solution of problems that affect several municipalities. In the case of the Hackensack Meadows, thirteen distinct towns and cities own or control parts of the 14,500-acre tract, which lies in sight of the Empire State Building. Eleven of these communities participate in the Meadowlands Regional Development Agency, created by the State of New Jersey to aid in the reclamation and development of this poorly drained, largely open expanse of unused land. This area is probably the richest underdeveloped property in any metropolitan area in the world, yet little of a long-range nature could be accomplished until New Jersey pioneered in this venture in intermunicipal co-operation.

Another example of regional work, under state assistance, is that of the Lake Hopatcong Regional Planning Board, involving but four communities in Morris and Sussex counties. Thirty-two miles of shore frontage on Lake Hopatcong are to be managed by the board with the objective of preserving the rural nature of the lake for the enjoyment and benefit of the urbanites of the future.

The Pinelands Regional Planning Board involves the two largest counties in the state, Burlington and Ocean, in a vast project to make plans for utilizing an immense wooded area that has seen little development in a century and a half. Bog iron, charcoal burning, and glass making made the area a vital one during the Revolutionary War. How should it be treated as hamlets and towns become urban places?

Co-operation seems to be the key word as New Jersey seeks to answer this question for the future. No one agency, no one level of government, not even a department of the state government—can alone supply the answers. To preserve the freedom of action for all citizens, both in and out of government service, it seems that planning for the future points toward co-operation between many levels and agencies. This is true even between states, as evidenced by the Tri-State Transportation Committee and the Penn-Jersey Transportation Studies.

In the words of Governor Richard J. Hughes, "As the role of local government gains new significance through regional approaches— as the State provides an improved over-all framework for assistance— our total capability to meet new problems will be strengthened."

DO/DISCUSS

1. Create a balance sheet of the advantages and disadvantages that may result from a master regional plan to cope with a "megalopolis."
2. What are the relationships between automation, urbanization, and the Green Acres Program? Can you map out some recreational needs for New Jersey under this plan? Be specific in idea and location.
3. Envision the New Jersey of the future and make at least five predictions about developments and changes in the state for the year selected. Make two copies of your prognosis. One copy (along with those of other class members) should be placed in the school's safe or archive file and the other retained for your personal chronicles. It might be fun to revert to these documents at periodic class reunions.

Selected Bibliography

SECTION I

Boucher, B. P., et al, *A Guide to New Jersey Geography*, New Jersey Geographical Press, 1962.

Brush, John E., *The Population of New Jersey*, Rutgers University Press, 1956.

Climate and Man, Yearbook of Agriculture, 1941, U.S. Government Printing Office, 1941.

Cross, Dorothy, "The Indians of New Jersey," *Proceedings of the New Jersey Historical Society*, Vol. LXX, January, 1952, pp. 1-16.

Crowell, Victor L., *The Wonderful World of New Jersey*, Rutgers University Press, 1955.

Cunningham, John, *This Is New Jersey*, Rutgers University Press, 1954.

Flink, Salomon J., ed., *The Economy of New Jersey*, Rutgers University Press, 1958.

Jacobson, Daniel, "Origins of the Town of Newark," *Proceedings of the New Jersey Historical Society*, Vol. LXXV, July, 1957.

————, "The Pollution Problem of the Passaic River," *Proceedings of the New Jersey Historical Society*, Vol. LXXVI, July, 1958, pp. 186-198.

Klimm, Lester E., "Empty Areas of the Northeastern United States," *Geographical Review*, Vol. 44, No. 3, 1954, pp. 325-345.

Kummel, Henry B., *Geology of New Jersey*, Bull. 50, Geological Service, State Department of Conservation and Economic Development, 1940.

Lane, Wheaton, *From Indian Trail to Iron Horse*, Princeton University Press, 1939.

Milstead, Harley P., *New Jersey Geography and History*, Holt, Rinehart and Winston, 1955.

New Jersey — Land of Amazing Industrial Advantages, Public Service Electric and Gas Co., 3rd Edition, April, 1962.

Pierce, Arthur, *Iron in the Pines*, Rutgers University Press, 1957.

Putnam, Borden R., "The Chemical Industry in New Jersey," *Review of New Jersey Business,* Vol. 8, No. 4, January, 1953, pp. 3-6, 13.

Quakenbush, Granville A., *Our New Jersey Land,* Bull. 775, New Jersey Agricultural Experiment Station, Rutgers University, 1955.

Sister Mary Veronica, "Relative Relief of New Jersey," *New Jersey Geography Newsletter,* Vol. 7, No. 3, March, 1961, pp. 5-12.

U.S. Census of Population: 1960, General Population Characteristics, New Jersey, U.S. Government Printing Office, 1961.

Veit, Richard F., *The Old Canals of New Jersey,* New Jersey Geographical Press, 1963.

Vermeule, C. C., "Raritan Landing That Was: The History of a River Port from 1675 to 1875," *Proceedings of the New Jersey Historical Society,* Vol. LIV, April, 1936, pp. 85-115 and 197-205.

Wildes, Harry F., *The Delaware,* Farrar, Straus, 1940.

———, *Twin Rivers: The Raritan and the Passaic,* Farrar, Straus, 1943.

Wilkerson, Albert S., *Minerals of New Jersey,* Geological Society of New Jersey, 1959.

SECTION II

Cross, Dorothy, *The Indians of New Jersey,* Archeological Society of New Jersey, 1958.

Cunningham, John T., *Garden State,* Rutgers University Press, 1955.

———, *Made in New Jersey,* Rutgers University Press, 1954.

———, *The New Jersey Shore,* Rutgers University Press, 1958.

———, *This Is New Jersey,* Rutgers University Press, 1953.

Federal Writers Project, *New Jersey: A Guide to Its Present and Past,* Viking Press, 1939.

Jameson, J. F., ed., *Narratives of New Netherland 1609-1664,* Scribner, 1909.

Kemmerer, Donald L., *Path to Freedom,* Princeton University Press, 1940.

Leaming, Aaron, and Jacob Spicer, *The Grants, Concessions and Original Constitutions of the Province of New Jersey,* (n. p.), 1881.

Leiby, Adrian C., *The Revolutionary War in the Hackensack Valley,* Rutgers University Press, 1962.

Lundin, Leonard, *Cockpit of the Revolution,* Princeton University Press, 1940.

McCormick, Richard P., *Experiment in Independence: New Jersey in the Critical Period (1781-1789),* Rutgers University Press, 1950.

Myers, William S., *The Story of New Jersey,* five volumes, Lewis Historical Publishing Co., 1945.

New Jersey History Committee, *Outline History of New Jersey,* Rutgers University Press, 1950.

Noble, Ransome E., Jr., *New Jersey Progressivism Before Wilson,* Princeton University Press, 1946.

Philhower, Charles A., "Jersey Indian Lore," Newark *Sunday News Magazine,* The Evening News Publishing Co., 1949.

Pomfret, John E., *The Province of West New Jersey,* Princeton University Press, 1956.

The New Jersey Almanac, 1964-65, The New Jersey Almanac Co., 1963.

SECTION III

Brush, John E., *The Population of New Jersey,* Rutgers University Press, 1958.

Bureau of Government Research, *Handbook of New Jersey State Government,* Rutgers University Press, 1952.

Commission on State Tax Policy, *Tenth Report,* (n. p.), 1963.

Flink, Salomon J., ed., *The Economy of New Jersey,* Rutgers University Press, 1958.

Friedelbaum, Stanley, *Municipal Government in New Jersey,* Rutgers University Press, 1954.

Hackett, James P., *The New Jersey Citizen,* Rutgers University Press, 1957.

Manual of the Legislature of New Jersey, J. Joseph Gribbins, Editor and Publisher, (published annually).

New Jersey American History Committee, *The New Jersey Citizen: Rights and Responsibilities,* State Department of Education, 1954.

New Jersey Governor, *Budget Message,* (published annually).

New Jersey Taxation Committee, *Taxation in New Jersey,* State Department of Education, 1955.

Rich, Bennett, *The Government and Administration of New Jersey,* Crowell, 1957.

The New Jersey Almanac, 1964-65, The New Jersey Almanac Company, 1963.

Title 19: Elections, MacCrellish and Quigley Co., (published annually).

SECTION IV

Apgar, Ellis A., *History of Our School System,* 1879.

Barrett, John Franklin, "Growth of the Statutory Functions of the New Jersey State Board of Education, 1866-1946," Unpublished Ed.D. thesis, Rutgers University, 1946.

Brush, John E., *The Population of New Jersey,* Rutgers University Press, 1956.

Burr, Nelson R., *Education in New Jersey, 1630-1871,* Princeton University Press, 1942.

Bunce, Edgar F., "The Development of a Unified Program of Tax-Supported State-Controlled Teacher Education in New Jersey," Unpublished dissertation, New York University, 1939.

Compendium of Censuses, 1726-1905, State of New Jersey, Department of State, Census Bureau, 1906.

Fromm, Glenn E., "A History of the New Jersey State Teachers College at Trenton," Unpublished Ed.D. thesis, New York University, 1950.

Governors' Messages and Accompanying Documents of New Jersey (copies of the annual messages bound with the *Documents of the Legislature of the State of New Jersey*), 1830-1950.

Hackett, James P., *The New Jersey Citizen,* Rutgers University Press, 1957.

Hood, John, *Index to Laws, New Jersey 1663-1903,* 1905.

Leaming, Aaron, and Jacob Spicer, *The Grants, Concessions and Original Constitutions of the Province of New Jersey,* (n. p.), 1881.

Lee, Francis Bazley, *Genealogical and Memorial History of the State of New Jersey,* Lewis Historical Publishing Co., 1910.

————, *New Jersey, As a Colony and As a State,* four volumes, The Publishing Society of New Jersey, 1903.

Leech, Carl Graydon, *Constitutional and Legal Basis of Education in New Jersey,* University of Pennsylvania Press, 1932.

Lowther, William L., "Development of the Office of the State School Superintendent, and the Influence of the Men Who Served in This Office on Public Education in New Jersey," Unpublished dissertation, Temple University, 1964.

McCormick, Richard P., *Experiment in Independence,* Rutgers University Press, 1950.

Myers, William Starr, ed., *The Story of New Jersey,* Lewis Historical Publishing Co., 1945, Vol. II.

New Jersey Committee on Children and Youth, publications of:
  A Handbook for County Committees on Children and Youth, 1960.
  New Jersey Children in a Changing World, The New Jersey Committee Report prepared for the 1960 Golden Anniversary White House Conference on Children and Youth, 1960.
  A New Jersey Look at Recommendations of the 1960 Conference on Children and Youth, 1961.
  Recommendations: Composite Report of Forum Findings of the 1960 White House Conference on Children and Youth, 1960.
New Jersey Department of Institutions and Agencies, publications of:
  An Accounting Toward Better Care of New Jersey's Citizens, A report prepared by the public relations staff, 1957.
  Annual Reports, 1958, 1959, 1960, 1961.
  Design for the Future, Social Welfare in New Jersey, A condensed report of the Governor's Commission to Study the Department of Institutions and Agencies, 1959.
  Digest of a Study of Protective Services and The Problem of Neglect of Children in New Jersey, 1958.
  Gordon, Eleanor W., *The Child Welfare Worker and Adoption,* 1958.
  The Welfare Reporter, Monthly publication of the Department, 1958-1963.
New Jersey School Reports 1846 to date (annual volumes; reports of the State Superintendent and later the Commissioner of Education).
Population Trends in New Jersey, New Jersey Department of Conservation and Economic Development, Division of State and Regional Planning, Report No. 123, 1960.
Records of Governor and Council of East Jersey, 1682-1703, Published by the authority of the Legislature, 1872.
State Board of Education, Annual Report of, 1866 to 1956, (annual volumes)
Statutes Annotated, Title 18, Education, Soney and Sage, 1952 (with pocket parts for annual supplements).
U.S. Bureau of the Census, U.S. Census of Population: 1950: Vol. II, Characteristics of the Population, Part 30, New Jersey, Chapter B, U.S. Government Printing Office, 1952.
U.S. Bureau of the Census, U.S. Census of Population: 1960, General Population Characteristics, New Jersey, Final Report PC(1)-32B, U.S. Government Printing Office, 1962.
U.S. Bureau of the Census, U.S. Census of Population: 1960, General Social and Economic Characteristics, New Jersey, Final Report PC(1)-32C, U.S. Government Printing Office, 1962.
Woody, Thomas, *Quaker Education in the Colony and State of New Jersey,* University of Pennsylvania Press, 1923.

Appendix

CHRONOLOGICAL LIST OF GOVERNORS

Cornelius Jacobsen Mey (Director of New Netherland)	1624
William Verhulst (Director of New Netherland)	1625
Peter Minuit (Governor of New Netherland)	1626-1631
Bastiaen Janssen Krol (Director General of New Netherland)	1631-1633
Wouter Van Twiller (Governor of New Netherland)	1633-1637
William Kieft (Governor of New Netherland)	1637-1646
Colonel Johan Printz (Governor of New Sweden)	1642-1652
Peter Stuyvesant (Governor of New Netherland)	1646-1664
Philip Carteret (first English Governor)	1665-1676

East Jersey

Philip Carteret	1676-1682
Robert Barclay (Proprietary Governor in England)	1682-1690
Thomas Rudyard (Deputy Governor)	1682-1683
Gaven Lawrie (Deputy Governor)	1683-1686
Lord Neil Campbell (Deputy Governor)	1686-1687
Andrew Hamilton (Deputy Governor)	1687-1690
Sir Edmund Andros (Governor General of Dominion of New England)	1688-1689
John Tatham (Proprietary Governor—rejected by Province)	1690
Colonel Joseph Dudley (Proprietary Governor—rejected by Province)	1692-1697
Colonel Andrew Hamilton	1692-1697
Jeremiah Basse	1698-1699
Andrew Bowne (Deputy Governor)	1699
Colonel Andrew Hamilton	1699-1702

West Jersey

Board of Commissioners	1676-1680
Edward Byllinge (Governor)	1680-1687
Daniel Coxe	1687-1692
Sir Edmund Andros (Governor General of Dominion of New England)	1688-1689
Edward Hunloke (Deputy Governor)	1690
Colonel Andrew Hamilton	1692-1697
Jeremiah Basse	1698-1699
Colonel Andrew Hamilton	1699-1702

East and West Jersey United

Edward, Lord Cornbury	1703-1708
John, Lord Lovelace	1708
Richard Ingoldsby, Lieutenant Governor	1709-1710
General Robert Hunter	1710-1719
Lewis Morris (President of Council)	1719-1720
William Burnet	1720-1727
John Montgomerie	1728-1731
Lewis Morris (President of Council)	1731-1732
William Cosby	1732-1736
John Hamilton (President of Council)	1736-1738

(The foregoing were also Governors of New York at the same time.)

Separate from New York

Lewis Morris	1738-1746
John Hamilton (President of Council)	1746-1747
John Reading (President of Council)	1747
Jonathan Belcher	1747-1757
John Reading (President of Council)	1757-1758
Francis Bernard	1758-1760
Thomas Boone	1760-1761
Josiah Hardy	1761-1762
William Franklin	1763-1776

As a State

William Livingston (Federalist)	1776-1790
William Paterson (Federalist)	1790-1792
Richard Howell (Federalist)	1792-1801
Joseph Bloomfield (Jeffersonian Republican)	1801-1802
John Lambert, Vice-President of Council and Acting Governor (Jeffersonian Republican)	1802-1803
Joseph Bloomfield (Jeffersonian Republican)	1803-1812
Aaron Ogden (Federalist)	1812-1813
William S. Pennington (Jeffersonian Republican)	1813-1815
Mahlon Dickerson (Jeffersonian Republican	1815-1817
Isaac H. Williamson (Jeffersonian Republican)	1817-1829
Garret D. Wall (Democrat)	1829
Peter D. Vroom (Democrat)	1829-1832
Samuel L. Southard (Whig)	1832-1833
Elias P. Seeley (Whig)	1833
Peter D. Vroom (Democrat)	1833-1836
Philemon Dickerson (Democrat)	1836-1837
William Pennington (Whig)	1837-1843
Daniel Haines (Democrat)	1843-1844
Charles C. Stratton (Whig)	1845-1848
Daniel Haines (Democrat)	1848-1851
George F. Fort (Democrat)	1851-1854
Rodman M. Price (Democrat)	1854-1857
William A. Newell (Republican)	1857-1860
Charles S. Olden (Republican)	1860-1863
Joel Parker (Democrat)	1863-1866
Marcus L. Ward (Republican)	1866-1869
Theodore F. Randolph (Democrat)	1869-1872
Joel Parker (Democrat)	1872-1875
Joseph D. Bedle (Democrat)	1875-1878
George B. McClellan (Democrat)	1878-1881
George C. Ludlow (Democrat)	1881-1884
Leon Abbett (Democrat)	1884-1887
Robert S. Green (Democrat)	1887-1890
Leon Abbett (Democrat)	1890-1893
George T. Werts (Democrat)	1893-1896
John W. Griggs (Republican)	1896-1898
Foster M. Voorhees, Acting Governor (Republican)	1898
David O. Watkins, Acting Governor (Republican)	1898-1899
Foster M. Voorhees (Republican)	1899-1902

Franklin Murphy (Republican)	1902-1905
Edward C. Stokes (Republican)	1905-1908
John Franklin Fort (Republican)	1908-1911
Woodrow Wilson (Democrat)	1911-1913
James F. Fielder, Acting Governor (Democrat)	1913
Leon R. Taylor, Acting Governor (Democrat)	1913-1914
James F. Fielder (Democrat)	1914-1917
Walter E. Edge (Republican)	1917-1919
William N. Runyon, Acting Governor (Republican)	1919-1920
Edward I. Edwards (Democrat)	1920-1923
George S. Silzer (Democrat)	1923-1926
A. Harry Moore (Democrat)	1926-1929
Morgan F. Larson (Republican)	1929-1932
A. Harry Moore (Democrat)	1932-1935
Harold G. Hoffman (Republican)	1935-1938
A. Harry Moore (Democrat)	1938-1941
Charles Edison (Democrat)	1941-1944
Walter E. Edge (Republican)	1944-1947
Alfred E. Driscoll (Republican)	1947-1954
Robert B. Meyner (Democrat)	1954-1962
Richard J. Hughes (Democrat)	1962-1966

Index

258

261